European Studies of Population

Volume 24

The book series "European Studies of Population" (ESPO) aims at disseminating population research with special relevance for Europe. The series is multidisciplinary in character and includes both formal demographic analyses, as well as studies of the social, economic and other determinants and impacts of population trends. International comparison is of prime interest to ESPO, and both contemporary and historical perspectives may be applied. ESPO is open to methodological work and theoretical studies, as well as to studies that focus on the social and policy implications of demographic trends. The series includes monographs and edited volumes.

ESPO is published under the auspices of the European Association for Population Studies (EAPS).

More information about this series at http://www.springer.com/series/5940

Marie Digoix
Editor

Same-Sex Families and Legal Recognition in Europe

Springer Open

Editor
Marie Digoix
French Institute for Demographic Studies (INED)
Paris, France

ISSN 1381-3579
European Studies of Population
ISBN 978-3-030-37053-4 ISBN 978-3-030-37054-1 (eBook)
https://doi.org/10.1007/978-3-030-37054-1

This Springer imprint is published by the registered company Springer Nature Switzerland AG.
The registered company address is: Gewerbestrasse 11, 6330 Cham, Switzerland

Contents

Contributors

Clara Cortina Universitat Pompeu Fabra, Barcelona, Spain

Marie Digoix French Institute for Demographic Studies (INED), Paris, France

Patrick Festy French Institute for Demographic Studies (INED), Paris, France

Marina Franchi London School of Economics, London, UK

Wilfried Rault French Institute for Demographic Studies (INED), Paris, France

Giulia Selmi University of Verona, Verona, Italy

Matthias Thibeaud French Institute for Demographic Studies (INED), Paris, France

Kees Waaldijk Leiden University, Leiden, The Netherlands

Chapter 1
Introduction – LGBT Questions and the Family

Marie Digoix

Abstract The past decades have seen significant changes in the way non heterosexual sexualities are regulated in European countries. In a moment of ongoing transitions, the interdisciplinary research presented focuses on aspects related to homosexuals rights and the way LGBT individuals deal and perceive the impact that the presence (or absence) of laws has on their intimate lives.

The evolutions in family rights in European laws and the balance towards equal rights, whether you are homosexual or heterosexual, are first detailed with an analysis of typical sequences found in a legal survey.

Demographic analyses enrich these aspects in dealing with registration and parenting. Statistical analyses of same-sex partnerships and same-sex marriages show frequencies of registration together with a focus on parenting linked to the partnership status.

In the next chapters, same-sex families are specifically studied in their daily life in France, Iceland and Italy through qualitative data. It investigates from a legal point of view and from a social perspective, what is at stake in the changing life of homosexuals in the field of parenting, what brings to everyday life the support of the law and what its absence implies.

The Postface opens towards the future of LGBT research.

Keywords Same-sex couples · Comparative family law · Same-sex parenting · Family policies · Demographic behaviours

The author is grateful to Patrick Festy and Kees Waaldijk who kindly gave useful comments of the first draft of this introduction.

M. Digoix (✉)
French Institute for Demographic Studies (INED), Paris, France
e-mail: mad@ined.fr

M. Digoix (ed.), *Same-Sex Families and Legal Recognition in Europe*,
European Studies of Population 24, https://doi.org/10.1007/978-3-030-37054-1_1

Research on homosexuality in Europe has started to diversify. Until very recently, LGBT populations were mostly studied from a psychological or medical perspective, sometimes in feminist research. The homosexual couple began to interest social sciences researchers after the beginning of AIDS epidemics. The importance of lifestyles people lived in and died in the time of AIDS raised public awareness on the lack of rights. The first researches of Michael Pollak (1985) and Marie-Ange Schiltz (1998) focused on the gay couple giving a new definition of what the term could mean (differentiating sexuality from sociability). Jurists have also been interested in situations of injustice in which individuals were regarding citizenship. The interest for sexual minority rights began to rise in the academic world when recognition of same-sex unions' legalisation started to be a universal claim in gay and lesbian struggles.

In 1989, Denmark became the first country in the world to create a legal framework, based on marriage, to offer same-sex couples the possibility to register officially their union.

Thereafter, the opening up of marriage and other legal arrangements to same-sex couples in a growing number of countries changed the visibility of homosexuality. However, this acknowledgement of homosexuality through the legal recognition of homosexual couple, reveals more the acceptance of a compliance to normative behaviour via the heterosexual model than of the sexual orientation of the individual per se (Rydström 2011). If discrimination on sexual grounds is generally prohibited by law in most of Western European countries (Waaldijk and Bonini-Baraldi 2006), the homosexual, because of his sexuality, is still stigmatised in society (Baiocco et al. 2012; Digoix 2013a). Marrying/registering a partnership implies coming out and coming out still relates to the individual in a rational choice between what law can bring to a personal situation (social recognition or legal consequences, for example) compared to what it might deteriorate (visibility and the 'endless' repetition of coming out) (Fassin 2005; Andersen 2011; Harding 2011). With regards to the opening up of marriage and parental status to same-sex couples, European countries have not reached the same level of rights (Waaldijk 2005, 2013). Nordic countries have pioneered a common trend in adopting laws (Digoix 2013b) while the timing of legalisation varies among Southern European countries. Studies have rarely been conducted in a comparative perspective but in most cases, they have shown that equal citizenship has been put forward as a political means to reach equality (Albæk 1988; Bauer 2006; Calvo 2010; Paternotte 2011).

Up until recently, homosexual couples have diversified their types of unions, balancing differently sexual and social relations and living arrangements because they were not allowed to marry like heterosexual couples (Schiltz 1998). They are now faced with marriage which used to be inaccessible. Marriage brings a legal visibility and support they don't have in the other configurations they used to invent (Pichardo Galan 2011). Yet, marriage has become more symbolic since countries have allowed same-sex couples to register civil contracts or other legal forms of union with economic and practical rights previously attached to marriage alone. However, the fact that nearly all the countries that first adopted a different legal framework (registered partnership or contract) have opened up marriage to same-sex couples or are in the process of doing so (Digoix 2006; Pichardo Galan 2009, 2011; see Table 2.1) proves that marriage remains the target to reach equality.

In countries where the foundation of a family is not anymore mainly based on marriage, the legal focus on parenting is essential. Whereas the opening up of marriage has pulled same-sex couples towards the conjugal norm, same-sex parenting provides homosexuals with a means to assert their difference, which some perceived to have disappeared with the opening up of marriage, in compliance with heteronormativity.

In most countries, the laws about same-sex parenting have lagged behind behaviour, and homosexuals have found solutions to start families that are not covered by law, such as coparenting or surrogacy for example (SOU 2001; Traustadóttir and Kristinsson 2003; Descoutures 2010; Fine 2012).

This book aims to present researches that investigate the relationship between law and behaviours to see what is at stake in the changing life of homosexuals in the field of parenting, their perception of these changes, from a legal point of view, but also from a social perspective. The research was first undertaken in the FamiliesAndSocieties project and provided a wide covering of legal and social questions[1].

The book combines several disciplines, each of which can help to understand the importance of laws and how they evolve and are used by people. It begins with an analysis of the laws in force, and how they reached this state in a wide range of European countries and what can be understood from the different times rights have opened to same-sex couples. It continues with an analysis of demographic behaviour in a smaller number of countries. Finally, a sociological analysis of parenting behaviours is produced in three countries chosen for their different legal frameworks, for their geographical location determining diverse societal environments.

In Chap. 1, Kees Waaldijk uses the *LawsAndFamilies Database* (Waaldijk et al. 2017), which documents legal changes over a 50 year period, to draw a portrait of the legal consequences attached to different family formats (marriage, registered partnership, cohabitation) of same-sex partners and different-sex partners in 21 European countries. In each country, experts provided information on a survey of 60 different rights related to the family situation of couples. The rights gradually granted to same-sex couples are compared with those of different-sex couples who are taken as a reference. Then, the rights are compared internationally, providing information on the timescales of these changes in legislation and establishing country groups and trends towards more or less equalization of rights. In the last 50 years, there has been convergence towards a great improvement of the legal situation of same-sex couples in Western and Central Europe, while in Eastern Europe the landscape is more contrasted. The opening up of marriage comes most of the time after the introduction of registered partnerships in the legal system while rights come

[1]The research leading to this book has received funding from the European Union's Seventh Framework Programme (FP7/2007-2013) under grant agreement no. 320116 for the research project FamiliesAndSocieties (www.familiesandsocieties.eu).

before status. Public attitudes towards homosexuality seem as well correlated with the emergence of rights, whether it is prior to the legal dispositions or not. The study finds typical sequences in the changing of the laws that are discussed. Kees Waaldijk shows that the path to equal treatment is step by step, and is mostly due to social and political controversies that lead to grant more rights but rarely reaching full equality, and never in one step. One major finding about the timescale of laws' adoption is that "bad-times rights" typically come before "good–times rights" in the legal process, that is, countries are less reluctant to grant rights for "bad times" (such as sickness, death, or domestic violence) than extending them for better times in the lives of couples. A related finding is that responsibilities and duties often come before benefits.

Regarding the field of parenting which is discussed in the next chapters, Waaldijk shows that specific issues regarding lesbian couples (such as ART or second-parent adoption) are less advanced than others. Also rights regarding surrogacy and joint adoption, important for gay men, are still very controversial in Europe. This relative slowness of access to reproductive rights seems to corroborate the "bad times before good times" trend. All and all, a main conclusion of the chapter would be that attitudes come before rights and legal recognition before social legitimacy.

Kees Waaldijk's conclusion leads to further chapters of the book in opening the discussion to the social importance of the legal recognition. The laws shape the lives of individuals who are adopting strategies in everyday life according to the legal framework they live in. Laws are important to promote social changes and social acceptance.

Clara Cortina and Patrick Festy's chapter is at the junction of Kees Waaldijk's legal analysis and the sociological analyses presented in the three country specific chapters. It confronts the legal framework and people's behaviours. Laws are, in general, adopted to ensure the equality of citizens. In his chapter, Kees Waaldijk showed the gap between same-sex couples and different-sex couples, how this gap is narrowing, little by little, and the context for understanding the mechanisms of this trend. Beyond the principle of equality, Clara Cortina and Patrick Festy's demographical research focuses on how laws are used. As in the case of the previous legal analysis, the situation of same-sex couples is related to that of different-sex couples. Nine European countries are surveyed for the largest comparative analysis, while they focus on Spain as a case study for a more detailed analysis.

The analysis of the frequency of homosexual marriage or registered partnership is complicated by the fact that the number of same-sex couples, used as denominator in the calculation, is often overestimated in the available data (mostly survey data). Despite the data registration pitfalls, some interesting results can be found: For example, crude rates evidence that the decreasing nuptiality for different-sex couples is contrasted by the increasing level of nuptiality of same-sex couples.

On the field of parenting, one of the main objectives of Clara Cortina and Patrick Festy's study is also to associate the level of registration with the level of legal consequences attached to marriage or registration, using a "legal index" created from

25 legal questions of the *LawsAndFamilies Database*. When splitting the index in parenting and material consequences, the correlation shows that parenting items have an impact on lesbian marriage rates, while it is not the case for gay marriage rates.

In the Spanish case study, data from the Spanish Household survey has been used. Regarding the parenting field, the previous results are confirmed. It shows, in particular, that when the couple doesn't have children, heterosexuals marry more than homosexuals, while when they do have children, there is no difference between the two groups, and no difference either between gay and lesbian couples. Same-sex couples marry less because they have less children.

The study concludes that the law can have an influence and be an incentive on the marriage project, if it is the only way to establish kinship rights. As a result, the presence of children should be controlled for when analysing the partnership status. This finding is all the more interesting that as Kees Waaldijk showed in the previous chapter, parenting rights are often the last to be granted in the timeline of legal progresses while they are paramount to the life of individuals.

The child becomes a central point of the book in the following chapters, which are devoted to the study of parenting, in its practicalities. In the *FamiliesAndSocieties Project*, the aim of the research was to investigate individual and family practices as well as the symbolic meaning attached to them in different legal contexts. It specifically tackled the relationship to the laws. France, Iceland, and Italy were chosen according to their legal frameworks, which at the beginning of the research, were different. During the process of the qualitative survey (by semi-structured interviews), France originally chosen for the Pacs law, a private union contract, opened its marriage law to same-sex couples but with fewer rights concerning parenthood. It is only after the survey was conducted that Italy adopted a civil union contract. Iceland had already opened the marriage law. Parenting laws were also diverse in France and Iceland, absent in Italy.

In the three countries, all respondents were self-identified as LGBT and chosen to cover a similar diversity, by sex, age, couple status, parental status and geographical areas. The usual biases for this kind of surveys among voluntary samples and stigmatized populations apply (Schiltz 2005) but the project aimed to counterbalance it with a wide diversity of situation among the samples. The teams used a similar guideline for the interviews to allow a comparative perspective.

A comparative analysis (including Spain) yielded several results (Digoix et al. 2016) from the 120 interviews performed. The general conclusion was that laws were not a mere device of symbolic nature but a practical support needed in everyday life.

When the survey was conducted in 2014 and 2015, there was no legal provision regarding marriage, cohabitation, let alone parenting in Italy. The parenting question is so clearly out of context that even the minimum rights have been disregarded in the 2015 Cirinnà bill, which granted a legal status for same-sex couples. While in Iceland, the research focuses on how to organize parenthood in a legal context, France and Italy are confronted with situations where parenting is a challenge. In

Italy, however, the researchers found that at the regional level, mainly in the big cities, administrative actions were taken to diminish discrimination and grant some recognition to same-sex couples.

In this context, Marina Franchi and Giulia Selmi focus on the construction of the parental models and on the relation to heteronormativity. They show how informants relate to parenting by inhabiting norms differently, trying to redefine themselves without the traditional concepts of the family. This ranges from non-paternity relationships to the invention of words to define children or the "child-parent" relationship derived from existing terms.

Overall they found parenting choices are diverse. While some informants are in opposition to the norm, others are defining mothers' roles that reproduce the difference between the sexes. Similarly, an attachment to the biological link can be seen, when the same sperm donor is used in order to establish a blood connection between the children, or when two partners carry a child one after the other to create a relationship between the four people of a family. On the other hand, the absence of legal provisions for same-sex parenting can influence the choice of an anonymous sperm donor, so that the mothers are no likely to be exposed to a "paternity" claim, which takes precedence over social kinship in Italian law.

A final chapter is devoted to how informants give richness and meaning to their parenting by creating evidence of personal investment in child education that could be mobilized in the event of legal problem. In the Italian context, this model, which could be seen as a compliance to the heteronormative model, could rather be considered as a manipulation of norms and a challenge to heteronormativity.

One can see the different strategies, sometimes ambivalent from informants who evolve in an unfavourable environment.

In Chap. 5, Matthias Thibeaud chose a political sociological approach to study homosexual families in France and how they organize daily life in the existing legal system. Despite the opening up of marriage in 2013, the legal dispositions concerning same-sex couples parenting are few (joint adoption and adoption of partner's children). Matthias Thibeaud explores the families formed in this context, a set of social practices, norms and constraints. The laws are defining the familial order, which sets who and how a family can be recognized and controlled by the institutions (school, health care system, administration, etc.). All families are confronted to forms of legal and social control, since legal restrictions are supplemented by powerful social norms. Within this institutional framework, he describes how people are confronted to day-to-day structures and how they manage to bypass them since the dominant family model conveys a number of normative expectations that homosexuals do not meet. Having children in this context requires respondents to mobilize social and economic capital to succeed in their goal.

Investigating the daily lives of same-sex families, Matthias Thibeaud concludes that gender relations in parenting are reworked but not always innovative. Overall, among respondents, the distinction of parental roles is not part of a naturalized gendered norm and parents declare an equal investment towards children education, even if some recognize a bipolarity in the achievement of daily tasks, which tends to confirm that a difference in status within the homosexual couple substitutes for a gender difference.

This study of behaviours regarding the way homosexuals are "creating family" and are rearing children reveals the social regulation which frames the family and whose rainbow families stand out. The relation to the heteronorm is very present as repulsive or constraining. Facing the legal and social constraints, rainbow families question the heterosexual model of the family.

In Chap. 6, Marie Digoix is drawing from a complete change of legal framework as parenting laws were nearly a decade old when the survey was conducted in Iceland.

Iceland is a feminist and familialist country with strong family policies. With high births out of wedlock rates, heterosexual parenting had already bypassed marriage constraints when laws on same-sex partnerships were implemented. Marie Digoix has been conducting interviews with homosexual populations since 2004. In contrast to previous surveys where the mention of parenting was more distant from the concerns of respondents, especially men, in 2015, nearly all respondents declared a desire to become parent or are already parent.

The research explores the hypothesis of a familialist society pushing respondents to feel parenting prone like heterosexuals. However procreation is not so easy for homosexuals, even if the laws and the access to ART in particular, facilitate the achievement of the parental project. Research shows a diversity of situations which tends to prove that the personal choices of the various informants take precedence over an activist ideal that would see homosexual parenting stand out. Each parental project carries its peculiarities: some are totally innovative, especially when they are not covered by the laws as coparenting, but also bear their degree of compliance to heteronormativity. Even if lesbians' couples chose with ART to disregard the biological existence of a male donor, it still seems difficult for others to move away from a male/female constituent even when respondents reject it in theory.

Homosexual parenting shows a clear gender gap between lesbians who have access to ART and gays who declare first the desire of joint adoption, which is nearly impossible and coparenting, which is still out of the laws and difficult to organize, especially since lesbians now prefer to realise their parental project in a lesbian couple (through ART).

The survey took place at a moment when the law securing the position of homosexuals also offered parenting opportunities that people seized. It is probably safe to wait some time before one can conclude that this desire for parenthood is an assimilation to heteronormativity.

The postface of the book is opening towards a theoretical analysis of the findings explored in the previous chapters. Wilfried Rault, a French sociologist who did not participate in the FamiliesAndSocieties project, takes into account the various results presented to understand their meaning in a broader context but also to highlight what is still pending in the LGBT questions.

References

Albæk, E. (1988). Political ethics and public policy: Homosexuals between moral dilemmas and political considerations in Danish parliamentary debates. *Scandinavian Political Studies, 26*(3), 245–267.

Andersen, A. J. (2011). Sexual citizenship in Norway. *International Journal of Law, Policy and the Family, 25*(1), 120–134.

Baiocco, R., Argalia, M., & Laghi, F. (2012). The desire to marry and attitudes toward same-sex family legalization in a sample of Italian lesbians and gay men. *Journal of Family Issues* 2014, *35*(2), 181–200.

Bauer, D. (2006). Homosexuality within the context of social institutionalisation and moral sense. *Ethical Perspectives, 13*(1), 63–91.

Calvo, K. (2010). Movimientos Sociales y Reconocimiento de Derechos Civiles: La legalización del Matrimonio entre Personas del Mismo Sexo en España. *Revista de Estudios Políticos, 147*, 103–133.

Descoutures, V. (2010). *Les mères lesbiennes*. Paris: PUF.

Digoix, M. (2006). They should go all the way!. To register or not: Law and behaviour in France and Iceland: The symbolic and the social. In M. Digoix, E. Fassin, P. Festy, S. Kolbeinn, & K. Waaldijk (Eds.), *Les couples homosexuels et l'enregistrement de leur union* (pp. 95–132). Paris: Ined.

Digoix, M. (2013a). *Coming out et ordre normatif en Islande* (Documents de travail 198). Paris: Ined.

Digoix, M. (2013b). Mariage pour tous: Expériences scandinaves. *P@ges Europe, 28 janvier 2013, La Documentation française* © DILA.

Digoix, M., Franchi, M., Pichardo Galán, J. I., Selmi, G., de Stéfano Barbero, M., Thibeaud, M., & Vela, J. A. M. (2016). *Sexual orientation, family and kinship in France, Iceland, Italy and Spain* (Working papers series 54). Stockholm: FamiliesAndSocieties.

Fassin, E. (2005). *L'inversion de la question homosexuelle*. Paris: Ed. Amsterdam.

Fine, A. (2012). La question de l'adoption par les couples homosexuels. *Cahiers Français, 371*, 59–66.

Harding, R. (2011). *Regulating sexuality: Legal consciousness in lesbian and gay lives*. Oxford: Routledge.

Paternotte, D. (2011). *Revendiquer le « mariage gay ». Belgique, France, Espagne*. Bruxelles: Editions de l'Université de Bruxelles.

Pichardo Galan, J. I. (2009). *Entender la diversidad familiar*. Barcelona: Edicions bellaterra.

Pichardo Galan, J. I. (2011). We are family (or not). Social and legal recognition of same-sex relationships and lesbian and gay families in Spain. *Sexualities, 14*(5), 503–622.

Pollak, M. (1985). Male homosexuality- or happiness in the ghetto? In P. Aries & A. Bejin (Eds.), *Western sexuality. Practice and precept in past and present times* (pp. 40–60). Oxford: Basil Blackwell.

Rydström, J. (2011). *Odd couples: A history of gay marriage in Scandinavia*. Amsterdam: Aksant/Amsterdam University Press.

Schiltz, M.-A. (1998). Un ordinaire insolite: le couple homosexuel. *Actes de la recherche en sciences sociales, 125, "Homosexualités", 125*, 30–43.

Schiltz, M.-A. (2005). Faire et défaire des groupes: l'information chiffrée sur les « populations difficiles à atteindre ». *Bulletin de méthodologie sociologique, 86*, 30–54.

SOU 2001: 10. (2001). *Barn i homosexuella familjer, Betänkande från Kommittén om barn i homosexuella familjer*. Stockholm: Justitiedepartementet.

Traustadóttir, R., & Kristinsson, Þ. (2003). *Samkynhneigðir og fjölskyldulíf*. Reykjavík: Háskólaútgáfan.

Waaldijk, K. (2005). *More or less together: Levels of legal consequences of marriage, cohabitation and registered partnership for different-sex and same-sex partners. A comparative study of nine European countries* (in cooperation with John Asland et al.). (Documents de travail 125) Paris: Ined.

Waaldijk, K. (2013). The right to relate: On the importance of « orientation » in comparative sexual orientation law. *Duke Journal of Comparative & International Law, 24*, 161–199, http://scholarship.law.duke.edu/djcil/vol24/iss1/4/

Waaldijk, K., & Bonini-Baraldi, M. (2006). *Sexual orientation discrimination in the European Union: National laws and the employment equality directive*. The Hague: Asser Press.

Waaldijk, K., Digoix, M., Nikolina, N., Zago, G., Damonzé, D., Caporali, A., & Nait Abdellah, K. (Eds.) (2017). *The LawsAndFamilies database – Aspects of legal family formats for same-sex and different-sex couples*. Paris: INED. http://www.LawsAndFamilies.eu

Chapter 2
What First, What Later? Patterns in the Legal Recognition of Same-Sex Partners in European Countries

Kees Waaldijk

Abstract Among the 21 European countries surveyed for the *LawsAndFamilies Database*, there is a clear trend (fortified by European law) of offering same-sex couples the opportunity to formalise their relationship as marriage and/or as registered partnership, and of attaching more and more rights and responsibilities to the informal cohabitation, the registered partnership and/or the civil marriage of two people of the same sex. This chapter focusses on the timing of all these changes. In a *five periods* analysis, it establishes whether major partnership rights were extended to same-sex couples at the time of the introduction of registered partnership, or before, or at the time of the opening up of marriage, or between those two moments, or after the opening up of marriage. Thereby, and by calculating the *same-sex legal recognition consensus* among the countries surveyed for each of 26 selected rights,

Parts of this chapter were first published in the author's chapters in the report *More and more together* (Waaldijk 2017) and in a report the author wrote for the Council of Europe (Waaldijk 2018a). This chapter and these reports are based on the *LawsAndFamilies Database* (www.lawsandfamilies.eu, Waaldijk et al. 2017). The author is deeply grateful to all the legal experts across Europe who answered the detailed questions in the LawsAndFamilies questionnaire for their respective jurisdictions, and who reviewed answers given by their colleagues; to the people at INED in Paris (in particular Kamel Nait Abdellah, Arianna Caporali and Marie Digoix) who made the legal survey technically possible and who worked with dedication on the creation of the *LawsAndFamilies Database*; and to the researchers at Leiden Law School (José María Lorenzo Villaverde, Natalie Nikolina, Giuseppe Zago and Daniel Damonzé) who for different periods contributed with great commitment to the drafting and organisation of the legal questionnaire, the reviewing and editing of the answers, the creation of the legal database, and/or the comparative analysis. The research leading to these results has received funding from the European Union's Seventh Framework Programme (FP7/2007–2013) under grant agreement no. 320116 for the research project FamiliesAndSocieties (www.familiesandsocieties.eu). Additional funding was received from the Leiden University Fund (Betsy Brouwer Fonds) and from the Ministry of Foreign Affairs of Denmark.

K. Waaldijk (✉)
Leiden University, Leiden, The Netherlands
e-mail: c.waaldijk@law.leidenuniv.nl

M. Digoix (ed.), *Same-Sex Families and Legal Recognition in Europe*,
European Studies of Population 24, https://doi.org/10.1007/978-3-030-37054-1_2

it finds nine *typical sequences*: Attitudes before rights; Rights before status; Bad-times rights before good-times rights; Responsibilities before benefits; Individual partner rights before couple rights; Partnership before marriage; Immigration rights among the first to be gained; Parenting rights among the last to be gained; Legal recognition before social legitimacy.

Keywords Marriage · Registered partnership · Cohabitation · Same-sex couples · Comparative family law · European law

2.1 Detailed Picture of an Ongoing Process

Through the institute of marriage, the law of all European countries has been giving rights and responsibilities to different-sex couples. By excluding same-sex couples from marital status, it also excluded them from all those rights and responsibilities that – exclusively – came with being married.

Over the last few decades an emerging trend in Europe (and in some other parts of the world) has been to reduce this exclusion. On the one hand this is done by offering same-sex couples the opportunity to formalise their relationship as marriage or at least as registered partnership. And on the other hand more and more rights and responsibilities are being given to same-sex couples who live together in informal cohabitation and/or who formalise their relationship (by marrying each other or by registration of their partnership). These developments have taken place primarily at national level, but, as we will see, international human rights law and the law of the European Union (EU) have also played a role.

The *LawsAndFamilies Database* has documented major legal changes over a 50-year period. The legal survey of this project has traced how in 21 European countries, same-sex (and different-sex) partners started and continued to receive (some) legal recognition. It looked at marriage, registered partnership and cohabitation, and how these three legal family formats became available to same-sex couples (and/or to different-sex couples).

Of the 21 countries surveyed, 19 are members of the EU, and all (including Iceland and Norway) are part of the European Economic Area (EEA). Between them the 21 countries are a fairly representative sample for the 31 countries that are part of EEA, but less so for the 47 member states of the Council of Europe (Waaldijk 2017, p. 25). As regards the United Kingdom, the questions have been answered separately for its three component jurisdictions (England & Wales, Scotland, Northern Ireland). So in total 23 jurisdictions have been covered.

The legal survey focussed on 60 different rights and responsibilities that can be attached to these legal family formats. The methodology used for the creation of this database, including the introduction of the term "legal family format", the definition of the distinction between the concepts of cohabitation and registered partnership,[1] the selection of 60 closed and 9 open questions, their distribution over six main categories (Formalisation, Income and troubles, Parenting, Migration, Splitting up, and Death), the definition of the answer codes for the closed questions ("Yes", "Yes, but", "No, but", "No", "Doubt" etc.), the selection of two legal experts from all countries, and the organisation of the peer review of their answers to the questionnaire, are all described in the first chapter of the report *More and more together*.[2]

The result is an online interactive database (www.LawsAndFamilies.eu) with an enormous amount of legal information (about more than 60 legal topics, for two types of couples, in up to three legal family formats, in 23 jurisdictions, for the years 1965–2016). This offers a very detailed picture of major legal developments in European societies. It is not a snapshot, but a movie that is still running. This chapter aims to give a synopsis of the movie so far. The focus will be on the emerging European patterns, and specifically on the *typical sequences* that are characteristic for the legal developments captured in the database.

The process of legal recognition of same-sex couples in Europe is ongoing. During the 4 years of the project (2013–2017), among the sample of 23 jurisdictions in 21 countries, no less than four opened up marriage to same-sex couples (France, Scotland, England & Wales, Ireland), and three made registered partnership available to them (Malta, Greece, Italy). And soon after the project ended in January 2017, also Finland opened up marriage (Hiltunen 2017; Valleala 2017), and Slovenia strongly increased the range of rights and responsibilities attached to same-sex registered partnership (Kogovsek Salamon 2017). And since then also Germany, Malta and Austria opened up marriage, while various countries continued to attach more and more rights and responsibilities to the marriage, the registered partnership and/or the informal cohabitation of same-sex couples.

Since 2013 also more European countries outside the project have introduced registered partnership for same-sex couples (Croatia, Cyprus, Estonia, San Marino),[3] or have opened up marriage to them (Luxembourg). A full list of all European countries (and their dependencies in Europe) that now allow same-sex partners to formalise their relationship through marriage and/or registered partnership is given in Table 2.1.

The following sections will first compare the 21 countries, and then compare 26 selected substantive rights that have been extended to same-sex couples in those countries – or not.

---

[1] José María Lorenzo Villaverde (who as a researcher for this project at Leiden Law School played an important role in developing the questionnaire) contributed to the definition of this distinction, on the basis of his expertise on Spanish legislations, that he gained and developed for his PhD thesis: *The Legal Position of Same-Sex Couples in Spain and Denmark. A Comparative Study of Family Law* (Copenhagen: Faculty of Law of the University of Copenhagen 2015; defended April 2016). See also Waaldijk 2014.

[2] Waaldijk 2017, p. 7–24; for the text of the questionnaire, see Waaldijk et al. 2016.

[3] About the implementation problems regarding the still incomplete Estonian legislation on registered partnership, see Roudik 2016.

Table 2.1 Access for same-sex partners to marriage or registered partnership – since when

	Registered partnership	Marriage
Denmark	no longer (1989–2012)	2012
Norway	no longer (1993–2009)	2009
Sweden	no longer (1995–2009)	2009
Iceland	no longer (1996–2010)	2010
Greenland (DK)	no longer (1996–2016)	2016
Netherlands	1998	2001
France	1999	2013
Belgium	2000	2003
Germany	no longer (2001–2017)	2017
Finland	no longer (2002–2017)	2017
Luxembourg	2004	2015
Spain	no (regionally since 1998)	2005
England & Wales (UK)	2005	2014
Scotland (UK)	2005	2014
Northern Ireland (UK)	2005	2020
Slovenia	2006	no
Andorra	2006	no
Czech Republic	2006	no
Switzerland	2007 (regionally since 2001)	no
Hungary	2009	no
Portugal	no	2010
Austria	2010	2019
Ireland	no longer (2011–2015)	2015
Liechtenstein	2011	no
Jersey (UK)	2011	2018
Isle of Man (UK)	2011	2016
Malta	2014	2017
Gibraltar (UK)	2014	2016
Croatia	2014	no
Cyprus	2015	no
Greece	2016	no
Estonia	2016	no
Italy	2016	no
Faroe Islands (DK)	no	2017
Guernsey (UK)	no	2017
Alderney (UK)	no	2018
San Marino	2019	no

Source: Mendos (2019), ILGA Europe (2019), Waaldijk et al. (2017), and Wikipedia

2.2 Comparing Countries: Partnership Before Marriage – Rights Before Status – Attitudes Before Rights

In Western Europe now all countries surveyed allow same-sex couples to marry or to register as partners,[4] and in all those countries these legal family formats trigger a very broad range of legal consequences.

In Central and Eastern Europe, the picture is more mixed, with three of the surveyed countries allowing neither same-sex marriages nor partnership registrations (Poland, Bulgaria, Romania).[5] However, these three countries already provide some legal recognition to same-sex couples (see below), on a similarly limited scale as Greece, Italy and Malta did until very recently (see Table 2.2). And several countries in Central Europe offer same-sex couples registered partnership (Slovenia, Czech Republic, Croatia, Hungary), and for example Hungary attaches a wide range of rights and responsibilities to these partnerships (Polgari 2017; Dombos 2017). Of the countries surveyed the Czech Republic attaches a more limited range of legal consequences to its registered partnership (Otáhal 2017, Plesmid 2017), as did Slovenia until 2017 (Kogovsek Salamon 2017; Rajgelj 2017), and as do Belgium and France, but there same-sex couples also have access to a fuller range of rights and responsibilities by entering into marriage (Borghs 2017, Kouzmine 2017).

In short, there has been great convergence in the legal situation of same-sex couples in Western and Central Europe. At the same time, this has led to more divergence with countries in Eastern Europe (Waaldijk 2018a).

From Table 2.1 it can be concluded that in European countries the opening up of marriage to same-sex couples comes almost always after the introduction of same-sex registered partnership. The only independent European countries where there was no national registered partnership scheme in existence when marriage was opened up to same-sex couples, are Portugal and Spain. In Portugal extensive cohabitation recognition preceded same-sex marriage (Pamplona Côrte-Real 2017), while in Spain some form of partnership registration in several regions preceded same-sex marriage. In all other 14 independent countries that now allow same-sex marriages, the road had been paved by the nationwide introduction of registered partnership. This typical sequence is very strong. All 11 countries that introduced registered partnership before 2005, have now moved on to open up marriage. And of the 22 independent European countries that introduced registered partnership before 2015, 16 have already opened up marriage.

Yet, "partnership before marriage" is not the only typical sequence that characterises the developments in European countries. In most countries where same-sex couples gained access to formal family status (registered partnership or marriage), already before this happened some rights had been made available to informally

[4] In Western Europe the only member state of the Council of Europe without either possibility is Monaco.

[5] A total of 19 member states of the Council of Europe in Central or Eastern Europe (those not listed in Table *1.1*) do not yet offer at least one of these two options.

Table 2.2 Public attitudes and levels of substantive legal recognition

Ranking of countries according to surveys of public attitudes				Level of substantive legal recognition of same-sex couples	
2004–2012	2004–2008	2009–2013	Country	2006	2015/2016
–	6.02	7.37	Iceland	98%	98%
98%	5.84	6.67	Netherlands	96%	100%
94%	5.80	6.55	Sweden	100%	100%
91%	5.26	5.92	Norway	88%	100%
84%	5.24	5.92	Belgium	96%	100%
74%	5.05	5.74	France	63%	92%
68%	5.17	5.68	Ireland	26%	92%
73%	4.97	5.62	Germany	82%	94%
75% (GB)	5.01 (GB)	5.59 (GB)	UK	88%	100%
64%	4.76	5.26	Finland	83%	90%
42%	4.64	5.08	Malta	15%	95%
53%	4.46	4.77	Italy	10%	88%
42%	4.51	4.74	Portugal	46%	100%
45%	4.34	4.72	Czech	48%	64%
65%	4.35	4.55	Austria	38%	100%
51%	4.22	4.43	Slovenia	41%	75%
25%	4.09	4.26	Greece	16%	86%
29%	3.98	3.99	Poland	4%	19%
24%	3.91	3.90	Hungary	46%	85%
26%	3.78	3.79	Bulgaria	7%	11%
14%	3.52	3.25	Romania	9%	9%

Sources: Smith et al. (2014a, p. 9; 2014b) for the ranking of countries by public attitude based on surveys of public attitudes to homosexuality conducted in the period 2004–2012; Flores and Park (2018, p. 27–30) for the ranking of countries according to their LGBT Global Acceptance Index based on surveys of public attitudes to LGBT issues conducted in the periods 2004–2008 and 2009–2012; and Waaldijk (2017, p. 51–53) for the level of substantive legal recognition of same-sex couples in 2006 and in 2015/2016 (based on the *LawsAndFamilies Database*). In this table the order of countries is that of the figures in the third column

cohabiting same-sex couples. Among the 21 countries surveyed for the *LawsAndFamilies Database*, only five countries (Iceland, France, Germany, Slovenia, Greece) had hardly given any rights to same-sex cohabitants before the introduction of registered partnership (Waaldijk 2017, p. 43). All countries where by 2011 same-sex cohabitants were enjoying legal recognition as regards more than one or two legal issues, had by 2016 allowed same-sex couples to formalise their relationship through marriage and/or registered partnership (idem).

In the three countries surveyed where such formalisation is not yet available (Poland, Bulgaria, Romania), same-sex couples are already starting to enjoy some legal recognition as cohabitants (Waaldijk 2017, p. 51). In Romania there is for example some recognition for the right to leave to care for a same-sex partner or for a parent of that partner, and same-sex partners are possibly seen as next of kin and possibly protected by legislation on domestic violence (Cojocariu 2017). Since a recent judgment of the Court of Justice of the EU (CJEU), Romania also has to recognise foreign same-sex marriages for the purpose of free movement of persons.[6] In Poland there is for example recognition as next of kin and some as regards partner immigration (Pudzianowska 2017), and for a surviving same-sex partner as regards tenancy continuation, and possibly as regards compensation for wrongful death (Smiszek 2017). Also in Bulgaria there is for example recognition as regards compensation for wrongful death, and possibly as regards *simple* second-parent adoption or partner immigration (Furtunova 2017; Katchaunova 2017).

All this supports the conclusion that apart from "partnership before marriage" also "rights before status" is a typical sequence in the process of legal recognition of same-sex couples in European countries.

While rights typically precede status, it seems also possible that substantive rights are more important than formal status. Knowing which family formats have been made available to same-sex couples and when, is only part of the story. For practical legal purposes it is often less important to know by *which legal family format* a right or responsibility has become applicable to same-sex partners. More important to know is *which substantive rights and responsibilities* are now available to same-sex partners, and thereby no longer the exclusive privilege of different-sex couples.

The data in the *LawsAndFamilies Database* make it possible to track this development for many of the rights and responsibilities included in the questionnaire used to create this database. For tracking this development some of the 69 questions in the questionnaire seemed less useful. In fact, only 26 of the 69 questions have been used to assess the substantive legal recognition of same-sex couples.[7] These 26 questions all tell us something about the degree to which countries recognise same-sex partners by making substantive rights and responsibilities available to them. On the basis of the answers given by the legal experts to these 26 questions, a ranking of countries can be made according to what can be called their "level of substantive legal recognition of same-sex couples".[8] This is a measure that does not look at whether or not access has been given to marriage or registered partnership, but only at the amount of substantive rights to which same-sex couples have access, irrespective of these rights being made available through marriage, through registered partnership, or through recognition of informal cohabitation. The ranking of the 21 countries surveyed according to their "level of substantive legal recognition of same-sex couples" can be found in the last two columns of Table 2.2.

It is interesting to note that some recent rankings of countries according to public attitudes towards homosexuality, gay rights or LGBT issues (based on various pub-

[6] CJEU, 5 June 2018, *Coman and Others*, Case C-673/16. See also Ionescu 2017.

[7] The 26 questions are presented in Tables 2.3, 2.4 and 2.5 in Sect. 2.3 below. For the various reasons for excluding the other questions from this analysis, see Waaldijk 2017, p. 44–45.

[8] For an explanation of how this measure has been constructed, see Waaldijk 2017, p. 51–53.

lic attitude surveys conducted since 1981)[9] correlate quite well (though not perfectly) with this legal ranking, as is also shown in Table 2.2.

One possible explanation for correlation is that public attitudes towards homosexuality may well be an important factor contributing to the emergence of legal rights for same-sex partners. The *legal* process may typically start with rights, but it seems quite probable that *non-legal* phenomena (such as public attitudes) normally pave the way for extending such rights to same-sex couples.

Table 2.2 shows that higher rankings as regards public attitudes (for any of the three periods) correspond to higher rankings as regards legal recognition for 2015/2016, but less so as regards legal recognition by 2006. In fact, one conclusion that can be drawn from Table 2.2, is that the few countries where legal recognition in 2006 was still lagging far behind public attitudes (especially Ireland and Italy, but also Austria and Malta), have legally made up for that by 2015/2016. All this would suggest another typical sequence, that of "attitudes before rights". There also other possible explanations for the remarkable increase in legal recognition that can be seen in some countries. For example, case law of the European Court of Human Rights (ECtHR) and of the Court of Justice of the EU (CJEU) has had a direct impact on several countries where the legal recognition of same-sex couples fell behind the minimum norms that these European courts have been developing (Waaldijk 2014, 2018b), especially in Germany,[10] Greece,[11] France,[12] Croatia,[13] Italy,[14] Austria,[15] Poland,[16] and Romania.[17]

An additional explanation could be that the growing international trend of legal recognition of same-sex families in many countries (see Kollman 2007) can have a certain influence on national lawmaking in some other countries – even when national public attitudes there remain more hesitant on the topic.

Of course many more correlations – and outliers – between levels of legal recognition and public attitudes can be found and analysed. The dataset in the *LawsAndFamilies Database*, together with the various surveys on public attitudes towards homosexuality that have been done since the late 1980s, should make it possible to test various hypotheses about the relationship between law and public

---

[9] Smith et al. 2014a, p. 9; Flores and Park 2018, p. 27–30. The rankings by both teams of researchers are based on a range of major public attitude surveys (see also Smith et al. 2014b), and include more countries than listed here

[10] CJEU, 1 April 2008, *Maruko*, Case C-267/06.

[11] ECtHR, 7 November 2013, *Vallianatos v. Greece*, 29381/09 & 32684/09.

[12] CJEU, 12 December 2013, *Hay*, Case C-267/12.

[13] ECtHR, 23 February 2016, *Pajić v. Croatia*, 68453/13.

[14] ECtHR, 21 July 2015, *Oliari v. Italy*, 18766/11 & 36030/11; ECtHR, 30 June 2016, *Taddeucci & McCall v. Italy*, 51362/09.

[15] ECtHR, 24 July 2003, *Karner v. Austria*, 40016/98; ECtHR, 19 February 2013, *X and Others v. Austria,* 19010/07.

[16] ECtHR, 2 March 2010, *Kozak v. Poland*, 13102/02.

[17] CJEU, 5 June 2018, *Coman and Others*, Case C-673/16.

opinion. Similarly, the dataset should make it possible to analyse more closely the possible interactions between legal inclusion (of same-sex couples) and economic, political or other developments.[18]

2.3 Comparing Rights: Bad Times Before Good Times – Responsibilities Before Benefits – Partner Before Couple

For same-sex couples, rights and responsibilities, as argued above, have often come before status, and these rights and responsibilities say more about someone's actual legal situation than the (marital or other) status through which they have become available. The question then is, which rights and responsibilities typically come first. To this end a comparative analysis can be made between the main substantive rights and responsibilities that have been extended to same-sex partners in European countries.

Using the same selection of 26 questions as was used above to calculate the "level of substantive legal recognition of same-sex couples" for each country, here a ranking of the 26 rights and responsibilities will be made. The text of the 26 questions is presented in Tables 2.3, 2.4 and 2.5, where the questions are ranked according to what can be called the "same-sex legal recognition consensus" for 2015 or 2016 (that is: for the most recent year for which the questions have been answered for the country concerned). The "same-sex legal recognition" for each question has also been calculated for the year 2006.

The *same-sex legal recognition consensus* for a year is a percentage that indicates how many of the surveyed jurisdictions have started to recognise same-sex partners by giving them full or limited access to a specific substantive right or responsibility. This quantitative indicator is introduced to assess if there is common ground between European countries about what rights and responsibilities should at least be made available to same-sex couples.[19] So also in Tables 2.3, 2.4 and 2.5 it does not matter *how* a right or responsibility becomes available (through marriage, through registered partnership, through cohabitation, or through two or three of these legal family formats).

A first conclusions that can be drawn from Tables 2.3, 2.4 and 2.5 is that, among the 21 countries surveyed, the consensus on legal recognition for same-sex couples has increased considerably between 2006 and 2015/2016 for *each* of the 26 selected substantive rights and responsibilities (an increase of at least 20% points for each).

[18] On the relationship between legal LGB inclusion and economic development, see Badgett et al. 2019.

[19] For the exact methodology for calculating the "same-sex legal recognition consensus", and for the actual calculations for each of the 26 questions, see Waaldijk 2017, p. 44–46 and 57–66.

Table 2.3 Eleven rights and responsibilities (out of 26 selected substantive questions) with in 2015/2016 the highest "same-sex legal recognition consensus" among 21 countries

Question		Same-sex legal recognition consensus	
		2006	2015/16
2.2 – Loss of social benefit	When one partner (long-term unemployed or even never having been employed at all) would be entitled to a basic social benefit, will the income of the other partner then be taken into consideration and will it possibly result in loss or reduction of this entitlement?	71%	93%
6.1 – Tenancy continuation	When the partner who holds the rental contract dies, does the other partner then have a right to continue to rent the home?	63%	93%
2.6 – Next of kin	In case of accident or illness of one partner, is the other partner considered as next of kin for medical purposes (even without power of attorney)?	53%	89%
4.1 – Residence for partner of national citizen	When one partner is a residing national citizen, while the other is a foreigner from another continent, will the foreign partner then have a residence entitlement/eligibility? *(Please assume that they married/registered/cohabited in the country where they now want to reside […])*	57%	88%
6.5 – Survivor's pension	When one partner dies while being employed, is the surviving partner then normally entitled to a survivor's pension? *(For example on the basis of statutory law, and/or of a collective labour agreement or arrangements of the employer.)*	50%	88%
2.7 – Domestic violence protection	When one partner uses violence against the other partner, does specific statutory protection apply?	57%	86%
2.8 – No testifying in criminal case	In case of a criminal prosecution against one partner, can the other partner then refuse to testify against the partner who is being prosecuted?	57%	86%
6.6 – Wrongful death compensation	In case of wrongful death of one partner, is the other partner then entitled to compensation from the wrongdoer?	57%	86%
4.3 – Residence for partner of (non-EU) foreigner	When both partners are foreigners from another continent, and one of them is residing in the country, will the other partner then have a residence entitlement/eligibility? *(Please assume that they married/registered/cohabited in the country where they now want to reside.)*	50%	86%
5.10 – Alimony at dissolution	In case the partners split up, do statutory rules on alimony apply?	48%	86%
6.3 – Inheritance	When one partner dies without testament, is the other partner then an inheritor?	43%	86%

Source: Waaldijk 2017 (tables 2.21–2.29)

Table 2.4 Ten rights and responsibilities (out of 26 selected substantive questions) with in 2015/2016 the lowest "same-sex legal recognition consensus" among 21 countries

Question		Same-sex legal recognition consensus	
		2006	2015/16
4.7 – Citizenship	Does a relationship of this type make it easier for a foreign partner to obtain citizenship?	48%	81%
1.12 – Statutory contract	Are there specific statutory rules regarding such a contract? *(See question 1.11 about the possibility for the partners to make a contract to organise their relationship.)*	48%	81%
2.1 – Lower income tax	Can a relationship of this type result in lower income tax than for two individuals without a partner?	47%	80%
5.9 – Joint property at dissolution	In case the partners split up, do statutory rules consider as joint property any possessions acquired by either of them after they started this type of relationship?	50%	80%
6.2 – Joint property at death	When one partner dies, do statutory rules consider as joint property any possessions acquired by either of them after they started this type of relationship? *(In other words: would the surviving partner be deemed to own 50% of these possessions, while the other 50% are subject to relevant rules of inheritance law?)*	50%	80%
1.13 – Surname	Can (or must) one partner use or have the surname of the other partner?	48%	79%
3.9 – Second-parent adoption	When only one partner is the legal parent of a child, does the other partner then have the possibility of becoming the child's second parent by way of adoption?	33%	74%
3.1 – Assisted insemination	Is it legally possible in this type of relationship to become pregnant through medically assisted insemination using sperm of a donor?	43%	63%
3.10 – Joint adoption	Can partners jointly adopt a child?	21%	55%
3.4 – Legal parenthood presumption	When one partner gives birth, will (or can) the other partner then also become legal parent of the child, without having to go through adoption? *(For example automatically, or by way of recognition/acknowledgement.)*	7%	38%

Source: Waaldijk 2017 (tables 2.21–2.29)

Table 2.5 Five legal rights and responsibilities with a high "same-sex legal recognition consensus" in 2015/2016, but for which this is in part due to the low number of countries where these rights or responsibilities are applicable to married different-sex partners

Question		Same-sex legal recognition consensus	
		2006	2015/16
2.4 – Leave to care for partner	In case one partner is in need of care, does the other partner then have a statutory right to paid or unpaid leave to give that care?	61% *(11 of 18)*	83% *(15 of 18)*
3.7 – Parental leave for partner	When only one partner is the legal parent of a child, does each partner then have a statutory right to paid or unpaid parental leave?	54% *(7 of 13)*	92% *(12 of 13)*
3.5 – Joint parental authority	Is joint parental authority/responsibility possible for the couple, while only one of the partners is the legal parent of the child?	67% *(8 of 12)*	92% *(11 of 12)*
6.4 – Inheritance tax exemption	Is the surviving partner exempted from paying inheritance tax (or required to pay less than a mere friend would have to pay)?	50% *(9 of 18)*	88% *(14 of 16)*
2.5 – Leave to care for parent of partner	In case the parent of one partner is in need of care, does the other partner then have a statutory right to paid or unpaid leave to give that care?	50% *(8 of 16)*	88% *(14 of 16)*

Source: Waaldijk 2017 (tables 2.21–2.29)

Overall, the recognition consensus is increasing, which may inspire more countries to broaden their legal recognition of same-sex families. And this growing consensus could provide the European courts with extra arguments to require European countries to make a core minimum of specific rights and responsibilities available to same-sex families (see Sect. 2.7).

Cynically, but maybe not surprisingly, the issue with the highest *same-sex legal recognition consensus* (already in 2006) is the possibility of loss or reduction of social benefit because of the income of one's partner (question 2.2). Of all 26 rights and responsibilities selected, this is the only one that does not entail any benefit for either of the partners. It is as if legal systems did not need to think long before extending at least this burden of relationship recognition to same-sex couples.

Almost all of the rights and responsibilities in Table 2.3 with the highest recognition consensus, are about situations where one of the partners dies (tenancy continuation,[20] wrongful death compensation,[21] survivor's pension,[22] inheritance, inheritance tax exemption), or where the partners are hit by other seriously "bad times" (accident, illness, domestic violence,[23] criminal prosecution,[24] splitting up). It seems that lawmakers in a very large majority of countries now take the position that it would be unjust, unfair, non-compassionate to exclude same-sex partners from legal protections designed for such sad times.

The very high recognition consensus as regards residence entitlements for a foreign same-sex partner (questions 4.1 and 4.3), however, cannot be explained directly by the sadness factor. Probably here the common rationale is also one of compassion: without such a residence entitlement the two partners would not even be able to live together in the same country – let alone to have family life under the same roof.[25]

About issues where the "sadness" factor is absent or may seem less prominent, the consensus is more limited. The issues with the lowest "same-sex legal recognition consensus" (in Table 2.4) have all in common that they are about *sharing* live in "good times" – sharing each other's name or citizenship, sharing properties or tax advantages, sharing responsibility for children.

---

[20] ECtHR, 24 July 2003, *Karner v. Austria*, 40016/98; ECtHR, 2 March 2010, *Kozak v. Poland*, 13102/02.

[21] For a comparative analysis of the data regarding wrongful death compensation, see Damonzé 2017.

[22] CJEU, 1 April 2008, *Maruko*, Case C-267/06.

[23] For a comparative analysis of the data regarding domestic violence protection, see Damonzé 2017.

[24] For a comparative analysis of the data regarding testifying in criminal procedures, see Zago 2017.

[25] A good example of this is the case of *Taddeucci & McCall v. Italy*, where the ECtHR required Italy to provide a residence entitlement; see its judgment of 30 June 2016, 51362/09. See also ECtHR, 23 February 2016, *Pajić v. Croatia*, 68453/13; and CJEU, 5 June 2018, *Coman and Others*, Case C-673/16.

The right to use your partner's surname, for example, is a symbolic classic in traditional marriage law, but apparently too controversial for full inclusion in the registered partnership laws of Austria, Belgium, Czech Republic, Finland, France, Hungary and Slovenia. Maybe in some countries it is (or was until recently) still too difficult to think of such a right outside the context of marriage.

Medically assisted insemination (question 3.1) and the different ways for a child to have two legal parents of the same sex (questions 3.4, 3.9 and 3.10) are even more controversial. Nevertheless, also regarding these parenting issues, the same-sex legal recognition consensus has been growing considerably between 2006 and 2015/2016.[26] Interestingly, if you combine the information regarding the questions 3.5 (parental authority), 3.7 (parental leave) and 3.9 (second-parent adoption), there now seems to be a near-consensus that same-sex partners should at least be allowed to take *some* responsibility for each other's children. In only three of the 21 countries none of these three possibilities exists – precisely the three countries in this survey that still have not introduced any form of registered partnership (Bulgaria, Poland and Romania). More about developments in the recognition of parenting rights in Sect. 2.5.

It seems that the overall conclusion can be phrased with terms borrowed from classic wedding vows (such as "in good times and in bad, in sickness and in health" or "for better for worse, for richer for poorer, in sickness and in health"). As suggested in those vows, marriage (like other forms of relationship recognition) typically entails rights and responsibilities for good times, and rights and responsibilities for bad times. In gradually building up some legal recognition for same-sex couples, however, it seems that European countries have been much quicker and less reluctant in extending rights for *bad times* to them, than in extending rights for *good times*. This appears to be a fourth typical sequence (in addition to the three discussed in Sect. 2.2) that characterises the process of legal recognition of same-sex partners. The main exception to this "bad-times rights before good-times rights" pattern are the immigration rights of a foreign partner in a same-sex relationship, which are among the rights with the highest *same-sex legal recognition consensus*. It is therefore possible to point to another typical sequence: "immigration rights among the first to be gained".

Dividing the legal consequences of marriage, partnership or cohabitation in rights for bad times and rights for good times, however, is not the only possible categorisation. The 26 issues listed in Tables 2.3, 2.4 and 2.5 can be further categorised, for example by distinguishing between benefits and responsibilities, and between rights benefitting an individual partner and rights benefitting the couple as a whole. An attempt to do so, while acknowledging the special character of immigration and parenting rights, has been made in Table 2.6, where for each category the average "same-sex legal recognition consensus" has been calculated.

From Table 2.6 it appears there are two further typical sequences, both partly overlapping with the "bad-times rights before good-times rights" pattern, and with each other. European countries have been more ready to extend benefits to an indi-

[26] For a comparative analysis of the data regarding several parenting issues, see Nikolina 2017b.

Table 2.6 Possible categorisation of the 26 selected rights and responsibilities

Category	Rights and responsibilities	Average "same-sex legal recognition consensus" 2006	2015/16
Implied mutual responsibilities	*Loss of social benefit*	58%	88%
	Leave to care for partner		
	Leave to care for parent of partner		
	Next of kin		
	No testifying in criminal case		
Benefits for one partner, implying responsibility for the other	*Domestic violence protection*	53%	88%
	Alimony at dissolution		
	Tenancy continuation		
	Inheritance		
	Inheritance tax exemption		
	Survivor's pension		
	Wrongful death compensation		
Immigration rights	*Residence for partner of citizen*	54%	87%
	Residence for partner of foreigner		
Benefits recognising the couple as a unit	*Statutory contract*	49%	80%
	Surname		
	Lower income tax		
	Citizenship		
	Joint property		
Parenting rights	*Assisted insemination*	38%	69%
	Legal parenthood presumption		
	Joint parental authority		
	Parental leave for partner		
	Second-parent adoption		
	Joint adoption		

Source: Tables 2.3, 2.4 and 2.5

vidual partner than to extend benefits to a couple as a unit; so the sequence typically is "individual partner rights before couple rights". And European countries have been less reluctant and somewhat faster in extending (implied) responsibilities to same-sex partners, than in extending benefits to them; so "responsibilities before benefits".

It does not seem surprising that it has been easier for countries to recognise responsibilities for individual partners than to recognise benefits for couples, because individual responsibilities typically are only between the partners (think of domestic violence protection, or alimony), whereas couple benefits typically are between the couple and wider society (think of lower income tax, or citizenship).

Furthermore, recognition of individual responsibilities is typically relevant in sad situations where someone needs support (think of tenancy continuation after death, or survivor's pension), whereas recognising couples as units typically concerns happier times (think of sharing a surname, or responsibility for children), echoing the "bad-times rights before good-times rights" pattern. Recognising couples as units (think of joint property, or common citizenship) also comes closer to extending family status to them; therefore the "individual partner rights before couple rights" sequence echoes the "rights before status" pattern.

2.4 Five Periods of Legal Recognition

Apart from a tentative "attitudes before rights" pattern, so far five general typical sequences could be distinguished that characterise the ongoing process of legal recognition of same-sex partners in European countries:

- Rights before status
- Partnership before marriage
- Bad-times rights before good-times rights
- Individual partner rights before couple rights
- Responsibilities before benefits

While several other typical sequences will be highlighted in the remainder of this chapter, the first five typical sequences may now help in taking a closer look at the process of legal recognition in each of the countries surveyed. In these countries, the legal recognition of same-sex families did not only come when a form of registered partnership was introduced for same-sex couples, or when marriage was being opened up to them, but also in the period before all that, in the period between those two moments, and/or in the period after all that. So often rights and responsibilities for same-sex partners came during *five periods*. This incremental process has been visualised in Tables 2.7, 2.8, 2.9 and 2.10.

The first two of these tables focus on five specific rights that can be important when one of the partners dies or when one of the partners is a foreigner (each with a shorthand name for the right in question):[27]

- *Residence for partner of citizen* (Immigration)
- *Tenancy continuation after death* (Tenancy)
- *Wrongful death compensation* (Compensation)
- *Inheritance tax exemption* (InheriTax)
- *Inheritance without testament* (Inherit)

Tables 2.9 and 2.10 focus on six specific rights relating to parenting (also each with a shorthand name):[28]

[27] For the full text of the corresponding questions in the LawsAndFamilies questionnaire, see Tables 2.3 and 2.5 above.

[28] For the full text of the corresponding questions in the LawsAndFamilies questionnaire, see Tables 2.4 and 2.5 above.

Table 2.7 Five rights for foreign or surviving same-sex partner – recognition per period (in countries that opened up marriage before 2017)

	Before partnership registration	At introduction of partnership registration	←Between→	At opening up of marriage	After opening marriage	Not yet by 2016
Norway*		**1993**		**2009**		
	Tenancy	Compensation	–	–	–	–
	Immigration	Inherit				
Sweden*		**1995**		**2009**		
	Tenancy	Inherit	–	–	–	–
	Immigration					
	Compensation					
Iceland		**1996**		**2010**		
	–	All five rights	–	–	–	–
Netherlands		**1998**		**2001**		
	Tenancy	Inherit	–	–	–	–
	Immigration					
	Compensation					
	InheriTax					
France		**1999**		**2013**		
	–	Tenancy	–	Inherit	–	–
		Immigration				
		Compensation				
		InheriTax				
Belgium		**2000**		**2003**		
	Immigration	Compensation	InheriTax	Inherit	Tenancy	–
GrBritain**		**2005**		**2014**		
	Tenancy	Compensation	–	–	–	–
	Immigration	Inherit				
		InheriTax				
Portugal		**n/a**		**2010**		
	Tenancy	–	n/a	Inherit	–	–
	Immigration					
	Compensation					
	InheriTax					
Ireland		**2011**		**2015**		
	Immigration	Tenancy	–	–	–	–
		Compensation				
		Inherit				
		InheriTax				

Source: Waaldijk 2017 (Tables 2.27–2.29). * The inheritance tax exemption had been equal for same-sex and different-sex surviving partners in Sweden from 1988 until this tax was abolished in 2005 (Walleng 2017), and in Norway from 1993 until this tax was abolished in 2014 (Eeg 2017) There is also no inheritance tax in Austria (Graupner 2017) and Malta (Galea Borg 2017). ** No differences between Scotland on the one hand, and England & Wales on the other

Table 2.8 Five rights for foreign or surviving same-sex partner – recognition per period (in countries that before 2017 did not open up marriage)

	Before partnership registration	At introduction of partnership registration	After introduction of registration	Not yet by 2016
Germany		**2001**		
	Immigration	Tenancy & Inherit	InheriTax	–
		Compensation		
Finland		**2002**		
	Immigration	Tenancy	–	–
		Compensation		
		Inherit & InheriTax		
North. Ireland		**2005**		
	Tenancy	Compensation	–	–
	Immigration	Inherit & InheriTax		
Czech Rep.		**2006**		
	Compensation	Immigration	Tenancy	–
	InheriTax	Inherit		
Slovenia		**2006**		
	–	–	Immigration	Tenancy*
			Inherit & InheriTax	Compensation
Hungary		**2009**		
	Tenancy	Inherit	InheriTax	–
	Immigration			
	Compensation			
Austria		**2010**		
	Tenancy	Compensation	–	–
	Immigration	Inherit		
Malta		**2014**		
	Tenancy	Immigration	–	–
	Compensation	Inherit		
Greece		**2016**		
	–	All five rights	–	–
Italy		**2016**		
	Immigration	Tenancy	–	–
	Compensation	Inherit & InheriTax		
Poland		**n/a**		
	Tenancy	–	n/a	Immigration**
				Compensation
				Inherit & InheriTax
Bulgaria		**n/a**		
	Compensation	–	n/a	Tenancy
				Immigration
				Inherit & InheriTax
Romania		**n/a**		
	–	–	n/a	All five rights

Source: Waaldijk 2017 (tables 2.27–2.29). * Limited aspect of this right already available (Kogovsek Salamon 2017). ** Limited aspect already available (Pudzianowska 2017)

- *Parental leave for partner* (Leave)
- *Joint parental authority* (JointAuthority)
- *Medically assisted insemination* (Insemination)
- *Second-parent adoption* (2^{nd}P-Adoption)
- *Joint adoption* (JointAdoption)
- *Legal parenthood presumption* (Presumption)

The opening up of marriage in Finland, Malta and Germany (in 2017) and in Austria (in 2019), came after the *LawsAndFamilies Database* had been completed, so these and other recent developments have not been included in the four tables. Not always included in these tables, is the fact that limited aspects of some rights were already made available to same-sex couples before the period in which these rights were extended to a similar degree as to different-sex couples.[29] It should also be noted that in Austria, Malta, Norway and Sweden there is no inheritance tax. Therefore for those countries only four rights are listed in Tables 2.7 and 2.8. Furthermore, the questions about parental leave and about parental authority were only asked for the situation where only one of the two partners is the legal parent of a child. In such situations in several countries even a different-sex partner who is not a legal parent cannot have parental leave or parental authority. Therefore, in Tables 2.9 and 2.10 below, for some countries less than six parenting rights are listed.

Tables 2.7, 2.8, 2.9 and 2.10 illustrate the incremental build-up of the legal recognition of same-sex partners in European countries. The incremental character of this ongoing process is largely the result of the social and political controversies around the demand for equal treatment for same-sex families. The outcome of the resulting political and legal fights were almost always small legal steps in the direction of more equality, but hardly ever creating near-equality in one step, and rarely reaching full equality. This gradual character of legal recognition is further clarified in Table 2.11, which summarises the previous four tables.

In Table 2.11 it also becomes very clear that as regards the extension of substantive rights to same-sex partners, the opening up of marriage was mostly relatively unimportant: at the time of the opening up of marriage to same-sex partners only very few substantive rights were extended to them. Many more rights were extended at or even before the introduction of registered partnership, and in some countries some rights (especially rights that involve legal parental status) only were extended to same-sex couples after the opening up of marriage. So the opening up of marriage is rarely the beginning or the end – it typically is just one of the stages that countries go through on the road to full equality for same-sex families.

Interestingly, in the majority of countries surveyed, partner immigration became possible *before* the introduction of registered partnership. This confirms the pattern noted in Sect. 2.3: "immigration rights among the first to be gained". Therefore it is not surprising, that immigration rights for foreign partners have also been the sub-

[29] See the bracketed years in tables 2.21 to 2.29 in Waaldijk 2017.

Table 2.9 Six parenting rights for same-sex partners – recognition per period (in countries that opened up marriage before 2017)

	Before partnership registration	At introduction of partnership registration	←Between→	At opening up of marriage	After opening marriage	Not yet by 2016
Norway		**1993**		**2009**		
	Leave	–	2^{nd}P-Adoption	JointAdoption	–	–
				Insemination		
				Presumption		
Sweden		**1995**		**2009**		
	Insemination	Leave	Adoptions	–	–	–
		JointAuthority	Presumption			
Iceland		**1996**		**2010**		
	–	JointAuthority	Adoptions	–	–	–
			Insemination			
			Presumption			
Netherlands		**1998**		**2001**		
	Insemination	JointAuthority	–	Leave	Presumption	–
				Adoptions		
France		**1999**		**2013**		
	–	Leave	JointAuthority	Adoptions	–	Insemination
						Presumption
Belgium		**2000**		**2003**		
	Insemination	–	–	–	Leave	–
					Adoptions	
					Presumption	
Scotland		**2005**		**2014**		
	Leave	–	Adoptions	–	–	–
	JointAuthority		Presumption			
	Insemination					
England & Wales		**2005**		**2014**		
	Leave	Adoptions	Presumption	–	–	–
	JointAuthority					
	Insemination					
Portugal		**n/a**		**2010**		
	–	–	n/a	–	All five* rights	–
Ireland		**2011**		**2015**		
	Leave	–	–	JointAuthority	–	Presumption
	Insemination			Adoptions		

Source: Waaldijk 2017 (tables 2.25, 2.26). * Portugal is one of the countries where only *legal* parents can have parental leave (Freitas 2017)

Table 2.10 Six parenting rights for same-sex partners – recognition per period (in countries that before 2017 did not open up marriage)

	Before partnership registration	At introduction of partnership registration	After introduction of registration	Not yet by 2016
Germany		**2001**		
	JointAuthority	Leave	2^{nd}P-Adoption	JointAdoption*
		Insemination		Presumption
Finland		**2002**		
	JointAuthority	–	Leave	JointAdoption
	Insemination		2^{nd}P-Adoption	Presumption
Northern Ireland		**2005**		
	Leave	–	Adoptions	–
	JointAuthority		Presumption	
	Insemination			
Czech Republic		**2006**		
	–	JointAuthority	–	Adoptions
				Insemination
				Presumption
Slovenia		**2006**		
	–	–	Leave	JointAdoption
			2^{nd}P-Adoption	Insemination
				Presumption
Hungary		**2009**		
	–	Leave	JointAuthority	Adoptions
				Insemination
				Presumption
Austria		**2010**		
	Leave	–	Adoptions	–
			Insemination	
			Presumption	
Malta		**2014**		
	–	Adoptions	–	Insemination
				Presumption
Greece		**2016**		
	Insemination	–	–	Adoptions
				Presumption
Italy		**2016**		
	2^{nd}P-Adoption	–	–	JointAdoption
				Insemination
				Presumption
Bulgaria		**n/a**		
	–	–	n/a	All five** rights
Poland		**n/a**		
	–	–	n/a	All five*** rights
Romania		**n/a**		
	–	–	n/a	All six rights

Source: Waaldijk 2017 (tables 2.25, 2.26). * But *successive* adoption already possible (Markart 2017). ** But *simple* second-parent adoption may already be possible; Bulgaria is one of the countries where only *legal* parents can have parental authority (Furtunova 2017). *** Poland is one of the countries where only *legal* parents can have parental leave (Pudzianowska 2017)

Table 2.11 Number of countries that extended rights to same-sex partners – per period

	Before partnership registration	At introduction of partnership registration	After introduction partnership registration (and before marriage)	At opening up of marriage	After opening up of marriage	Not yet by 2016
Residence for partner of citizen	14	5	1	–	–	3
Tenancy continuation after death	11	7	1	–	1	3
Wrongful death compensation	8	12	–	–	–	3
Inheritance without testament	–	16	1	3	–	3
Inheritance tax exemption	3	9	4	–	–	3
Parental leave for partner	6	4	2	1	1	1
Joint parental authority	5	4	2	1	1	1
Medically assisted insemination	9	1	2	1	1	9
Second-parent adoption	1	2	9	3	2	6
Joint adoption	–	2	5	4	2	10
Legal parenthood presumption	–	–	6	1	3	13

Source: Tables 2.7, 2.8, 2.9 and 2.10. Highlighted are the most common periods for each right

ject matter in three of the cases on same-sex partnership that were successful in the European courts.[30]

Similarly, the right to continue to rent the home for which your deceased partner held the rental contract, is also a right mostly extended to same-sex partners *before* the introduction of a form of registered partnership. The very first successful case on same-sex partnership in the European Court of Human Rights was precisely about this issue: in 2003 this Court established the principle that rights such as this, when they have already been extended to unmarried different-sex partners, should also be extended to same-sex partners.[31]

[30] ECtHR, 30 June 2016, *Taddeucci & McCall v. Italy*, 51362/09; ECtHR, 23 February 2016, *Pajić v. Croatia*, 68453/13; CJEU, 5 June 2018, *Coman and Others*, Case C-673/16.

[31] ECtHR, 24 July 2003, *Karner v. Austria*, 40016/98.

The other three non-parenting rights that were highlighted in Tables 2.7 and 2.8 (wrongful death compensation, inheritance and inheritance tax) are typically made available to same-sex partners when registered partnership is introduced.

Also the parenting rights highlighted in Tables 2.9 and 2.10 are mostly extended to same-sex partners (if at all) before the opening up of marriage. And the three parenting rights that do not involve legal parental status (i.e. parental leave, parental authority and assisted insemination), are mostly among the very first parenting rights that become available to same-sex couples – even before the introduction of registered partnership. The situation in France, where same-sex marriage and same-sex adoptions are possible, but where medically assisted insemination is not yet lawful for women in a same-sex relationship (Ronzier 2017), is quite unique.

As can be seen in Tables 2.9 and 2.10, the first legal step towards parenting equality between same-sex and different-sex couples differs from country to country. In some countries (including Greece, Ireland, Netherlands and the United Kingdom) it started with not prohibiting medically assisted insemination of women in same-sex relationships. In a few other countries a first step was to allow the same-sex partner of a parent to take parental leave (as in Austria, Hungary and Norway), or to share in the parental authority over the child (as in Finland, France and Germany), or to apply for second-parent adoption (as in Italy and Slovenia). In a few countries (Portugal and Malta) a first step included both joint and second-parent adoption, while in at least one country (Portugal) almost all aspects of same-sex parenting became legal simultaneously.

In some countries, most recognition of same-sex parenting happened *before* same-sex marriages were allowed (as in Austria, Germany, Finland, Sweden, and the UK), while in other countries such recognition largely came *with* (as in France, Ireland, Malta, Netherlands, and Norway) or even *after* the opening up of marriage to same-sex couples (as in Belgium and Portugal).

2.5 Women and Children Last?

The relative slow, late and incomplete recognition of parenting rights begs questions about the gender-neutrality of the patterns in the legal recognition of same-sex partners. It seems that even in most countries where same-sex couples are widely recognised socially and legally, the law and its impact are (still) not fully gender-neutral. One indication for this is, that in most countries the crude female/female "marriage" rate is different from the crude male/male "marriage" rate (see Cortina and Festy 2014 and their chapter in this book).

In the legal survey of LawsAndFamilies only a few questions dealt specifically with issues that are not relevant to all same-sex couples, but only to *female* same-sex couples (and of course to different-sex couples): questions 3.1 (medically assisted insemination), 3.2 (IVF), and 3.4 (legal parenthood for the partner of the woman who gives birth).[32] The survey has shown that as regards same-sex couples, these three issues are very controversial: they are among the questions with the lowest *same-sex legal recognition consensus* in the countries surveyed (see Table 2.4 above). Assuming that in most countries it is still more common for a woman in a same-sex relationship to be a parent, than for a man in a same-sex relationship, several questions are relevant for rather more *lesbian couples* than gay couples. One of these (question 3.9, on second-parent adoption) is also among the questions with a low *same-sex legal recognition consensus*.

A few issues that in many countries have been historically gender-specific, including the right to use the surname of your spouse (question 1.13) and the right to acquire the citizenship of your spouse (question 4.7), are also among the questions with a low *same-sex legal recognition consensus* (see Table 2.4).

Finally, there are several questions about issues that in different-sex couples (because of economic and other disparities between men and women) have a greater impact on women than on men. It is telling that the issue with the highest *same-sex legal recognition consensus* (question 2.2, loss or reduction of social benefit because of the income of your partner) is one which (at least historically) has had a particularly negative impact on women (see Holtmaat 1996). However, also some key protections, that at least in traditional heterosexual relationships can be to the benefit of the female partner, are among the questions with a high *same-sex legal recognition consensus*: questions 2.7 (domestic violence protection), 6.1 (tenancy continuation), joint property (5.9 and 6.2), alimony (5.10) and 6.5 (survivor's pension). It is not clear if these (traditionally gendered) issues have the same importance in lesbian relationships as in gay relationships (but see also the other chapters in this book).

The legal survey did not look specifically at the impact of the legal rules on *bisexual, transgender, intersex* or *non-binary* individuals and their relationships. It seems likely that not only lesbians and gays, but also other sexual and gender minorities can benefit from increasingly gender-neutral rules of family law. It would be good if there would be research on the impact of the growing legal recognition of same-sex relationships on people from such other minorities.

Overall, it can be said that further research is needed to assess the gender-impact of the growing but still incomplete recognition of same-sex partners in European countries. However, there are already several indications that the pattern and impact of recognition have not been gender-neutral, especially in the field of parenting. Legal recognition of same-sex couples has advanced less – or slower – on some issues that are only or especially relevant to *lesbian* couples (questions 3.1, 3.2 and 3.4, see above).

This conclusion may be nuanced a little – but not contradicted – by pointing to the extra importance that rights to joint adoption and to surrogacy may have for gay men who wish to become parents.[33] Both rights are among the most controversial

[32] The outcomes for the IVF question are very similar to those for the question on medically assisted insemination.

[33] The *LawsAndFamilies Database* does include answers to a question about surrogacy (question 3.3), but this question implied so many different aspects (lawfulness of surrogacy contracts, of

issues covered in the survey, and joint adoption (question 3.10, see Table 2.4) is among the rights with the lowest *same-sex legal recognition consensus* among the countries surveyed.

Some legal protections during sickness (next of kin, leave to care for partner) and after death (tenancy continuation, survivor's pension, inheritance tax), which all have a high *same-sex legal recognition consensus* (see Tables 2.3, 2.4, 2.7 and 2.8), gained additional relevance for large numbers of gay men during the Aids crisis. The very first judgment of the European Court of Human Rights in a case about the rights of same-sex partners (*Karner v. Austria*) was of great symbolic and legal importance in this respect. In its judgment, before ruling that Austria must include same-sex partners in its tenancy continuation rules (which until then only applied to married and unmarried different-sex partners), the Court specifically pointed out that Mr. Karner (the applicant) from 1989:

> lived with Mr W., with whom he had a homosexual relationship, in a flat in Vienna, which the latter had rented a year earlier. They shared the expenses on the flat. […] In 1991 Mr W. discovered that he was infected with the Aids virus. His relationship with the applicant continued. In 1993, when Mr W. developed Aids, the applicant nursed him. In 1994 Mr W. died after designating the applicant as his heir.[34]

Also in other ways the Aids crisis seems to have speeded up the process of legal recognition of same-sex partners. A conclusion could be (again in terms derived from classic wedding vows) that sickness rights often have been extended to same-sex partners before reproductive health rights were. This sequence may be just a manifestation of the more general sequence of "bad-times rights before good-times rights". However, it also provides a further indication, but no conclusive evidence, that an additional pattern can be discerned in the process of legal recognition of same-sex partners in European countries: "men before women".

A stronger typical sequence that has emerged in this and the previous sections, is that of putting "parenting rights among the last to be gained". This may be a typical European phenomenon (Polikoff 2000). The *same-sex legal recognition consensus* among the countries surveyed is the lowest for parenting rights (Table 2.6), and recognition typically comes latest – if at all – for parenting rights that involve legal parental status: second-parent and joint adoption, and presumption of legal parenthood (Table 2.11). This can be seen as an illustration of the "rights before status" pattern, that was observed in Sect. 2.2.

In the gradual recognition of parenting rights, also some of the other typical sequences apply: The parenting rights that are about responsibilities for children that are already part of the household of same-sex partners (parental leave, parental authority, second-parent adoption) typically get recognised sooner or more often than the rights concerning "new" children (assisted insemination, joint adoption,

---

payments for the surrogate mother, of egg donations, etc. and of the possibility for two men to become both legal fathers of a child), that the – interesting – results do not lend themselves for inclusion in the quantitative analysis that is presented here. See Friðriksdóttir 2017 for upcoming legislation in Iceland.

[34] ECtHR, 24 July 2003, *Karner v. Austria*, 40016/98, par. 12.

presumption of legal parenthood). This illustrates both the "responsibilities before benefits" pattern and the "individual partner rights before couple rights" pattern. Legal systems seem to be more ready to give some parenting rights to the same-sex partner of a parent, than to give parental status to a whole same-sex couple.

In Sect. 2.3, we already noticed among European countries a near-consensus that same-sex partners should at least be allowed to take *some* responsibility for each other's children (through parental leave, or through joint parental authority, or even via second-parent adoption). In quite a few countries, same-sex couples can now take *full* responsibility for each other's children. This started around the turn of the century, when first Denmark in 1999, and later a large minority of European countries, extended the possibility of *second-parent adoption* – so that it is now possible there to adopt the child of your same-sex partner (Nikolina 2017a; Mendos 2019, p. 297–299; and Tables 2.9 and 2.10). And such adoptions of course trigger a whole range of legal rights and responsibilities between the child and the adoptive second parent.

A slightly smaller, but also growing group of European countries (starting with the Netherlands in 2001) has gone further by also allowing *joint* adoptions by same-sex couples (Nikolina 2017a, b; Mendos 2019, p. 291–292; and Tables 2.9 and 2.10). And in a similar group of European countries it is legally possible for a woman in a same-sex relationship to become pregnant through medically assisted insemination (Tables 2.9 and 2.10). The result is that in most of these countries same-sex couples now are allowed to create a family with children, *and* to formalise their relationship to these children.

However, in many countries this formalisation of parentage can only be done through adoption, typically involving time, money, a court procedure and an examination by the child welfare authorities. This is different in different-sex families, because there the relationship between child and father (even when he is not the biological father) is mostly created simply by the legal presumption of paternity (if the couple is married) or by recognition/acknowledgment of the child by the father (Nikolina 2017a). In some countries this major difference between heterosexual and lesbian families has started to disappear. In 2003 Sweden became the first European country where, when a woman gives birth to a child, her female partner can also become a legal parent of that child from the moment of birth (without having to go through an adoption procedure) (Ytterberg 2017). Although the conditions and procedures differ somewhat from country to country, such a possibility now exists already in a sizeable minority of European countries (Nikolina 2017a, p. 103; and Tables 2.9 and 2.10).

2.6 The Social Importance of Legal Recognition

Statistics show that there is real demand among same-sex couples to be able to formalise their relationships. The statistics collected by Cortina and Festy (2014, and their Chap. 3 in this book) indicate that each year tens of thousands of same-sex couples in European countries choose to marry or to register as partners. The initial peaks in the frequency of partnership registrations indicate that in the relevant countries there was already a pent-up demand for such legal formalisation of same-sex relationships. The *sustained* annual rates of male/male marriages and partnership registrations, and the *growing* annual rates in most countries for female/female marriages and partnership registrations, are evidence that the relevant legislation is not just symbolically important, but also practically important in the lives of the people concerned.

And such legislation shapes these lives (Digoix et al. 2016, p. 24; Neyer 2017, p. 21). Many of the laws that attach rights or responsibilities to different legal family formats, shape the relationships between partners, and between them and their parents, children, etc. See for example (in Tables 2.3 and 2.4) the questions from the legal survey on loss of social benefits, leave to care for partner, leave to care for parent of partner, next of kin provisions, parental authority, parental leave, alimony, inheritance and survivor's pension. A recent study showed how legislation (directly or indirectly) can mandate, block, generate or lighten intergenerational interdependence (Dykstra and Hagestad 2016, p. 57–58), "by defining rights and duties towards old and young in the family, and by reinforcing or lightening the reliance on older and younger family members" (idem, p. 59).

The social importance of laws for same-sex families is further evidenced in the interviews conducted in Italy, Iceland and France by other authors of this book. They emphasise that – apart from the actual practical use that couples make of the legal possibilities for marriage, partnership and parenting – the interviewees support these laws "because of the undebatable principle of equal citizenship" (Digoix et al. 2017, p. 147). And these authors point out that "the existence of laws also has a favourable effect on public perceptions of homosexuals" (idem), and that "the practical consequences of laws shape everyday life" (Digoix et al. 2016, p. 24). Interestingly, they illustrate the combination of these two aspects, with the practical effects that parenting by same-sex families can have on others and on society in general: "the visibility of parenting seems to facilitate an implied social insertion of homosexuals who are seen as parents and thus not simply reduced to their sexuality" (idem, p. 26). This is similar to what Takács et al. (2016, p. 1797) find: "In countries having legal institutions allowing for non-heteronormative family practices, people are more likely to directly encounter manifestations of same-gender family and partnership forms as ordinary facts of everyday life" and "in addition to the normative message of the state […] the introduction of these legal institutions can have longer-term socialization effects that can potentially contribute to increasing levels of acceptance toward non-heteronormative family forms."

Digoix et al. (2016, p. 26) also conclude from their research findings that the enactment of laws is extra important for promoting social change in this field, precisely because there are such strong "persisting heteronormative culture models across societies". Politically, the enactment of laws is often seen as the end of a process, but these sociological findings make us aware that laws are often just a "first step" in a social process; the interviewees apparently often see legal support "as essential for *initiating* social inclusion" (idem, p. 24, emphasis added).

It seems that the – practical and symbolic – social relevance of legal recognition of same-sex family life, is now also being acknowledged in European law. Various EU rules now refer to registered partnership, to non-marital partners, to persons living in a committed intimate relationship, etc., while both the Court of Justice of the EU and the European Court of Human Rights have recognised that distinctions between same-sex and different-sex partners amount to sexual orientation discrimination (Waaldijk 2014, 2018b). The latter Court has also ruled that non-marital partnerships are also covered by the right to respect for "family life",[35] and that this includes same-sex partnerships.[36] It has acknowledged that for a same-sex couple "an officially recognised alternative to marriage (would) have an intrinsic value", apart from its legal effects.[37] And that such recognition would further bring "a sense of legitimacy to same-sex couples".[38]

In Sect. 2.3 we found some evidence for the typical sequence of "attitudes before rights", although in some countries also the reverse sequence could be noticed. Presumably both these patterns are at play, with rights and attitudes regarding same-sex families reinforcing each other. In other words, attitudes facilitate rights, and in turn *legal recognition strengthens social legitimacy*.

2.7 Conclusion: From Core Rights to More Rights

There is a clear and rapid trend, among a large majority of the 21 countries surveyed for the *LawsAndFamilies Database*, of offering same-sex couples the opportunity to formalise their relationship as marriage and/or as registered partnership. The absence of any such opportunity in three of these 21 countries (and in 19 of the 47 Council of Europe countries) may well be against recent case law of the European Court of Human Rights.[39]

And there is a clear and rapid trend among the 21 countries surveyed of attaching more and more rights and responsibilities to the cohabitation, the registered partnership and/or the marriage of two people of the same sex. This trend, too, has been strengthened by case law of the European Court of Human Rights, by some EU legislation, and by case law of the Court of Justice of the EU (Crisafulli 2014; Orzan 2014; Waaldijk 2014, 2018b). And it has been encouraged by the recommendations and studies of other bodies of EU and Council of Europe.[40]

[35] ECtHR, 18 December 1986, *Johnston v Ireland*, 9697/82, par. 55–56.

[36] ECtHR, 24 June 2010, *Schalk & Kopf v Austria*, 30141/04, par. 94.

[37] ECtHR, 7 November 2013, *Vallianatos v. Greece*, 29381/09 & 32684/09, par. 81.

[38] ECtHR, 21 July 2015, *Oliari v. Italy*, 18766/11 & 36030/11, par. 174.

[39] ECtHR, 21 July 2015, *Oliari v. Italy*, 18766/11 & 36030/11.

[40] See for example the comprehensive reports by the Commissioner for Human Rights (2011) of the Council of Europe and by the EU Agency for Fundamental Rights (FRA 2015), and Resolution 2239 (2018) of the Parliamentary Assembly of the Council of Europe (PACE 2018).

Both these trends reflect the recognition – as articulated by the European Court of Human Rights – that same-sex couples are covered by the right to respect for family life.[41] And that they are "in a relevantly similar situation to a different-sex couple as regards their need for legal recognition and protection of their relationship",[42] and "have the same needs in terms of mutual support and assistance as different-sex couples".[43] Both trends show the growing awareness in European countries that there should be no discrimination based on anyone's sexual orientation – or on the sex of anyone's partner.

This chapter set out to find more specific patterns and typical sequences within this double trend of legal recognition of same-sex partners.

In Sects. 2.2 and 2.6 this chapter has signalled various indications for an interaction between the legal and the social. Positive social attitudes towards homosexuality seem to facilitate the legal recognition of same-sex partners, and this legal recognition in turn seems to strengthen the social legitimacy of same-sex families. In short, the following two *typical sequences* seem to be reinforcing each other:

- Attitudes before rights
- Legal recognition before social legitimacy

This chapter looked at the timing of the introduction of registered partnership and/or the opening up of marriage to same-sex couples (Sect. 2.2). In a *five periods* analysis, it established whether major partnership rights were extended to same-sex couples at the time of the introduction of registered partnership, or before, or at the time of the opening up of marriage, or between those two moments, or after the opening up of marriage (Sect. 2.4). Thereby, and by calculating the *same-sex legal recognition* consensus among the 21 European countries surveyed for each of 26 selected rights and responsibilities (Sect. 2.3), another seven *typical sequences* could be noticed. These typical sequences are characteristic for the process of legal recognition of same-sex partners in these countries. The following seven were found:

- Rights before status
- Partnership before marriage
- Bad-times rights before good-times rights
- Responsibilities before benefits
- Individual partner rights before couple rights
- Immigration rights among the first to be gained
- Parenting rights among the last to be gained

These typical sequences overlap and reinforce each other. And as discussed in Sect. 2.5, some may be making the process of legal recognition somewhat slower for female partners than for male partners. As noted in the previous sections, there are

[41] ECtHR, 24 June 2010, *Schalk & Kopf v. Austria*, 30141/04, par. 94.

[42] Idem, par. 99; see also ECtHR, 7 November 2013, *Vallianatos v. Greece*, 29381/09 & 32684/09, par. 78.

[43] ECtHR, 7 November 2013, *Vallianatos v. Greece*, 29381/09 & 32684/09, par. 81.

various exceptions to these typical sequences: in specific countries specific rights or responsibilities have been gained sooner or later than the general pattern suggests.

It is possible that the general pattern presented here, will already have some effect on countries that are only starting or considering to legally recognise same-sex couples and their children. Perhaps the typical sequences will inspire activists, lawmakers and judges in such countries – perhaps accelerating them or possibly slowing them down. At the very least the typical sequences can be read as advice on where to start (and what steps to take next) when political or legal actors in a country want to improve the legal situation of same-sex couples.

However, it seems likely that the mere example offered by the developments in 21 European countries here analysed, will not be enough to make changes happen in those countries (among and beyond this sample of 21) where legal recognition is still limited or even absent. Therefore political and judicial European institutions may have an important role to play (Waaldijk 2018a).

The European Court of Human Rights, for example, has spoken repeatedly about the "core rights relevant to a couple in a stable committed relationship".[44] And the Court has indicated many times that in considering whether or not a restriction, exclusion or distinction is justifiable under the European Convention of Human Rights, it would look at comparative studies of the situation in the member states of the Council of Europe.[45] This so-called "consensus analysis" of the Court, potentially gives extra importance to data as in the *LawsAndFamilies Database*.

The assessment of the *same-sex legal recognition consensus* for each of the 26 selected substantive rights and responsibilities (Tables 2.3, 2.4 and 2.5) suggests a core minimum of rights and responsibilities that should at least be made available to same-sex partners (be it through informal cohabitation, through registered partnership, or through civil marriage). The assessment in Sect. 2.3 suggests that a core minimum of rights would consist *at the very least* of those rights for which the *same-sex legal recognition consensus* is relatively high:

- legal protections for times of death (such as: tenancy continuation, wrongful death compensation, inheritance, inheritance tax exemption, survivor's pension);
- legal protections for times of other great sadness (such as: next of kin provisions, protection against domestic violence, leave from work in case your partner or your partner's parent is in need of care);
- the right to be able to live in the same country (residence permit for partner); and

[44] ECtHR, 21 July 2015, *Oliari v. Italy*, 18766/11 & 36030/11, par. 174 (see also par. 172, 185). In its later judgment in the case of *Taddeucci & McCall v. Italy*, the ECtHR spoke of "certain essential rights" (30 June 2016, 51362/09, par. 83, 95).

[45] See for example ECtHR, 19 February 2013, *X and Others v. Austria*, 19010/07, par. 54; and ECtHR, 30 June 2016, *Taddeucci & McCall v. Italy*, 51362/09, par. 88, 97. In the same-sex marriage case of *Schalk & Kopf v. Austria*, the ECtHR (24 June 2010, 30141/04, par. 31-34) based its description of the "state of relevant legislation in Council of Europe member States" implicitly on content of the report *More and more together* (Waaldijk 2005) that had introduced the methods and many of the questions later used for the *LawsAndFamilies Database*.

- the right to take at least *some* responsibility for each other's children (through parental leave, parental authority, or even second parent adoption).

If the European Court of Human Rights (and other European bodies) would adopt such a definition of mandatory *core rights*, it would mean that at the beginning only *some* equality will be required from countries. Of course this will fall short of *full* equality, but this is how other countries mostly have started. A large majority of the countries surveyed, before giving same-sex couples access to registered partnership or marriage, did actually begin with giving a few rights and responsibilities to such couples. And almost all have since then moved on from *core rights* to *more rights* or even to (almost) full equality. The legal recognition of same-sex partners is almost always a process. And that process has to start somewhere.

Before and at the start of this process, countries typically are reluctant to include same-sex couples in the rights and responsibilities that come with different-sex marriage. Given this reluctance or even hostility in such countries, it makes sense for activists, lawmakers and judges to first focus on specific rights (rather than on family status), on rights for bad times (rather than on rights for good times), on partner responsibilities (rather than on partner benefits), on rights for an individual partner (rather than on rights for the couple as a unit), on immigration rights (rather than on parental status), and on partnership registration (rather than on civil marriage). For many countries this will already take a lot of legal and political struggle. However, even small legal steps towards guaranteeing some *core rights* for same-sex couples, can pave the way for more. A beginning legal recognition can already have a positive effect on social attitudes, and on the social legitimacy of same-sex families. And all this in turn can pave the way for more European countries to give *more and more equal rights* to same-sex partners. If we look at the data, this is apparently how it works.

References[46]

Badgett, M. V. L., Waaldijk, K., & van der Meulen Rodgers, Y. (2019). The relationship between LGBT inclusion and economic development: Macro-level evidence. *World Development, 120*, 1–14.

Commissioner for Human Rights. (2011). *Discrimination on grounds of sexual orientation and gender identity in Europe – Background document*. Strasbourg: Council of Europe. www.coe.int/t/Commissioner/Source/LGBT/BackgroundDocument2011_en.pdf

Cortina, C., & Festy, P. (2014). *Comparative database on same-sex partnership in Europe: Contribution with marriage and partnership statistics* (paper for the FamiliesAndSocieties project). Paris/Madrid: Institut national d'études démographiques & Spanish National Research Council. www.LawsAndFamilies.eu

Crisafulli, F. (2014). Same-sex couples rights (Other than the right to Marry). In D. Gallo, L. Paladini, & P. Pustorino (Eds.), *Same-sex couples before national, supranational and international jurisdictions* (pp. 409–436). Heidelberg: Springer.

[46] See also below, for papers published in the LawsAndFamilies Database (Waaldijk et al. 2017).

Damonzé, D. (2017). Statutory protection against domestic violence in Europe; compensation for wrongful death in Europe. In K. Waaldijk (Ed.), *More and more together: Legal family formats for same-sex and different-sex couples in European countries* (Families And Societies working paper 75) (pp. 73–91, 123–135). Stockholm University. www.familiesandsocieties.eu

Digoix, M., Franchi, M., Pichardo Galán, J. I., Selmi, G., de Stéfano Barbero, M., Thibeaud, M., & Vela, J. A. M. (2016). *Sexual orientation, family and kinship in France, Iceland, Italy and Spain* (FamiliesAndSocieties working paper 54). Stockholm University. www.familiesandsocieties.eu

Digoix, M., Franchi, M., Pichardo Galán, J. I., Selmi, G., de Stéfano Barbero, M., Thibeaud, M., & Vela, J. A. M. (2017). Laws, sexual orientation and intimate lives in France, Iceland, Italy and Spain: A synthetic view from a sociological perspective. In K. Waaldijk (Ed.), *More and more together: Legal family formats for same-sex and different-sex couples in European countries* (Families And Societies working paper 75) (pp. 136–150). Stockholm University. www.familiesandsocieties.eu

Dykstra, P. A., & Hagestad, G. O. (2016). How demographic patterns and social policies shape interdependence among lives in the family realm. *Population Horizons, 13*(2), 54–62.

Flores, A. R., & Park, A. (2018). *Polarized progress – Social acceptance of LGBT people in 141 countries, 1981–2014*. Los Angeles: The Williams Institute at UCLA. https://williamsinstitute.law.ucla.edu

FRA. (2015). *Protection against discrimination on grounds of sexual orientation, gender identity and sex characteristics in the EU – Comparative legal analysis – Update 2015*. Vienna: European Union Agency for Fundamental Rights (FRA). http://fra.europa.eu/en/publication/2015/lgbti-comparative-legal-update-2015

Holtmaat, R. (1996). Economic Independence, Labour Law and Social Security. In Y. Kravaritou (Ed.), *The sex of labour law in Europe* (pp. 155–175). The Hague: Kluwer Law International.

ILGA Europe. (2019). *Annual review of the human rights situation of lesbian, gay, bisexual, trans and intersex people* (European region of the International Lesbian, Gay, Bisexual, Trans and Intersex Association). Brussels: ILGA Europe. www.ilga-europe.org/annualreview/2019

Kollman, K. (2007). Same-sex unions: The globalization of an idea. *International Studies Quarterly, 51*, 329–357.

Mendos, L. R. (2019). *State-sponsored homophobia* (International Lesbian, Gay, Bisexual, Trans and Intersex Association). Geneva: ILGA. www.ilga.org.

Neyer, G. (2017). *Summary of key findings from WP 9: Policies and diversity over the life course* (with contributions by Thévenon, O., Digoix, M., Cortina, C., Festy, P., Waaldijk, K., Duvander, A.-Z., Hobson, B., & Hellgren, Z., *FamiliesAndSocieties working paper* 72). Stockholm University. www.familiesandsocieties.eu

Nikolina, N. (2017a). Evolution of parenting rights in Europe. In K. Waaldijk (Ed.), *More and more together: Legal family formats for same-sex and different-sex couples in European countries* (Families And Societies working paper 75) (pp. 101–113). Stockholm University.. www.familiesandsocieties.eu

Orzan, M. F. (2014). Employment benefits for same-sex couples: The case-law of the CJEU. In D. Gallo, L. Paladini, & P. Pustorino (Eds.), *Same-sex couples before national, supranational and international jurisdictions* (pp. 493–509). Heidelberg: Springer.

PACE. (2018). Resolution 2239 (2018) on Private and family life: Achieving equality regardless of sexual orientation, adopted by the Parliamentary Assembly of the Council of Europe (based on the report Private and family life: Achieving equality regardless of sexual orientation, Doc. 14,620 (2018), of the Committee on Equality and Non-Discrimination).

Polikoff, N. D. (2000). Recognizing partners but not parents/recognizing parents but not partners: Gay and Lesbian family law in Europe and the United States, 17. *New York Law School Journal of Human Rights, 17*, 711–750.

Roudik, P. (2016). Estonia: Legalization of civil partnerships. *Global Legal Monitor*.

Smith, T. W., Son, J., & Kim, J. (2014a). *Public attitudes toward homosexuality and gay rights across time and countries*. Chicago/Los Angeles: NORC at the University of Chicago & The Williams Institute at UCLA. https://williamsinstitute.law.ucla.edu

Smith, T. W., Son, J., & Kim, J. (2014b). *A compilation of cross-national studies on attitudes toward homosexuality and gay rights*. Chicago/Los Angeles: NORC at the University of Chicago & The Williams Institute at UCLA. https://williamsinstitute.law.ucla.edu

Takács, J., Szalma, I., & Bartus, T. (2016). Social attitudes toward adoption by same-sex couples in Europe. *Archives of Sexual Behavior, 45*(7), 1787–1798.

Waaldijk, K. (Ed.). (2005). *More or less together: Levels of legal consequences of marriage, cohabitation and registered partnership for different-sex and same-sex partners. A comparative study of nine European countries*. Paris: INED. http://hdl.handle.net/1887/12585

Waaldijk, K. (2014). Great diversity and some equality: Non-marital legal family formats for same-sex couples in Europe. *GenIUS – Rivista di studi giuridici sull'orientamento sessuale e l'identità di genere, 1*(2), 42–56. http://hdl.handle.net/1887/39533

Waaldijk, K. (2017). Introduction to the legal survey and its method; Overview of the results from the legal survey; Conclusion. In K. Waaldijk (Ed.), *More and more together: Legal family formats for same-sex and different-sex couples in European countries – Comparative analysis of data in the LawsAndFamilies Database* (Families And Societies working paper 75) (pp. 7–24, 25–72, 151–181). Stockholm University. www.familiesandsocieties.eu

Waaldijk, K. (2018a). *Extending rights, responsibilities and status to same-sex families: Trends across Europe* (report for Council of Europe). Copenhagen: Ministry of Foreign Affairs of Denmark. http://hdl.handle.net/1887/70273

Waaldijk, K. (2018b). The gender-neutrality of the international right to marry: Same-sex couples may still be excluded from marriage, but their exclusion – and their foreign marriages – must be recognised (online draft chapter, forthcoming in Ziegler, A. R. (Ed.), *Handbook on International and Comparative SOGIESC Law*). https://ssrn.com/abstract=3218308

Waaldijk, K., Lorenzo Villaverde, J. M., Nikolina, N., & Zago, G. (2016). *The LawsAndFamilies questionnaire on legal family formats for same-sex and/or different-sex couples: Text of the questions and of the accompanying guidance document* (FamiliesAndSocieties working paper 64). Stockholm University. www.familiesandsocieties.eu

Zago, G. (2017). The right to refuse to testify against your partner in criminal procedures. In K. Waaldijk (Ed.), *More and more together: Legal family formats for same-sex and different-sex couples in European countries* (Families And Societies working paper 75) (pp. 92–100). Stockholm University. www.familiesandsocieties.eu

Waaldijk, K., Digoix, M., Nikolina, N., Zago, G., Damonzé, D., Caporali, A., & Nait Abdellah, K. (Eds.) (2017). *The LawsAndFamilies database – Aspects of legal family formats for same-sex and different-sex couples*. Paris: INED. www.LawsAndFamilies.eu. This interactive database also includes 138 legal source papers (six per jurisdiction) authored by: Adamietz, L., Attard, C., Blöndal, E. K., Gattuso, M., Frihagen, H., Hayward, A., Lima, D., Norrie, K., Papadopoulou, L., Ryan, F., Sloan, B., Sumner, I., Tobin, B., Willems, G., Winkler, M., and by the following people (who contributed several papers each, including the papers listed below that have been cited in this chapter):

Borghs, P. (2017). *Formalisation of legal family formats in Belgium*.

Cojocariu, C. (2017). *Income, troubles and legal family formats in Romania*.

Dombos, T. (2017. *Income, troubles and legal family formats in Hungary; Migration and legal family formats in Hungary*.

Eeg, T. (2017). *Death and legal family formats in Norway*.

Freitas, M. (2017). *Parenting and legal family formats in Portugal*.

Furtunova, D. (2017). *Parenting and legal family formats in Bulgaria*.

Friðriksdóttir, H. (2017). *Parenting and legal family formats in Iceland*.

Galea Borg, C. (2017). *Death and legal family formats in Malta*.

Graupner, H. (2017). *Death and legal family formats in Austria.*
Hiltunen, R. (2017). *Formalisation of legal family formats in Finland.*
Ionescu, I. (2017). *Migration and legal family formats in Romania.*
Katchaunova, A. (2017). *Migration and legal family formats in Bulgaria; Death and legal family formats in Bulgaria.*
Kogovsek Salamon, N. (2017). *Formalisation of legal family formats in Slovenia; Migration and legal family formats in Slovenia; Death and legal family formats in Slovenia.*
Kouzmine, J. (2017). *Formalisation of legal family formats in France.*
Markart, N. (2017). *Parenting and legal family formats in Germany.*
Nikolina, N. (2017b). *Parenting and legal family formats in the Netherlands.*
Otáhal, L. L. (2017). *Formalisation of legal family formats in the Czech Republic; Parenting and legal family formats in the Czech Republic; Splitting up and legal family formats in the Czech Republic.*
Pamplona Côrte-Real, C. (2017). *Formalisation of legal family formats in Portugal.*
Plesmid, O. (2017). *Income, troubles and legal family formats in the Czech Republic; Migration and legal family formats in the Czech Republic; Death and legal family formats in the Czech Republic.*
Polgari, E. (2017). *Formalisation of legal family formats in Hungary; Parenting and legal family formats in Hungary; Splitting up and legal family formats in Hungary; Death and legal family formats in Hungary.*
Pudzianowska, D. (2017). *Income, troubles and legal family formats in Poland; Parents Migration and legal family formats in Poland; Migration and legal family formats in Poland.*
Rajgelj, B. (2017). *Income, troubles and legal family formats in Slovenia; Parenting and legal family formats in Slovenia; Splitting up and legal family formats in Slovenia.*
Ronzier, E. (2017). *Parenting and legal family formats in France.*
Smiszek, K. (2017). *Death and legal family formats in Poland.*
Valleala, A. (2017). *Parenting and legal family formats in Finland.*
Walleng, K. (2017). *Death and legal family formats in Sweden.*
Ytterberg, H. (2017). *Parenting and legal family formats in Sweden.*

Chapter 3
Same-Sex Couples and Their Legalization in Europe: Laws and Numbers

Clara Cortina and Patrick Festy

Abstract We analyse same-sex partnership and family formation in Europe. We explore how the frequency of same-sex marriage or registered partnership can be associated to macro and micro factors and how parenting appears as a key determinant at both levels. We use the LawsAndFamilies Database, which includes both data on legal developments in family laws and statistical data on the legal recognition of same-sex couples, marriage and registered partnership for a large set of countries. We also use the French census and the Spanish household survey for specific purposes. We first determine crude rates of legal recognition for gay, lesbian and different-sex couples for nine European countries in the period 1980–2017. We second consider macro factors by measuring the impact of legal consequences attached to couples' recognition on the frequency of same-sex marriage or registered partnering. We expect that the opening of parenting to same-sex couples will affect lesbian more than gay couples and result in more positive trends in women's nuptiality. We finally explore micro factors related to the family structure expecting that the presence of children will work as an incentive to marry.

Keywords Marriage · Same-sex couples · Family law · Same-sex family

3.1 Introduction

There is an intimate and complex relationship between demography and law which has its roots in the very sources of population studies. Our discipline has indeed emerged from the act of compiling the two fundamental physiological events of

C. Cortina (✉)
Universitat Pompeu Fabra, Barcelona, Spain
e-mail: clara.cortina@upf.edu

P. Festy
French Institute for Demographic Studies (INED), Paris, France
e-mail: festy@ined.fr

M. Digoix (ed.), *Same-Sex Families and Legal Recognition in Europe*,
European Studies of Population 24, https://doi.org/10.1007/978-3-030-37054-1_3

birth and death in the civil or religious registers that attest to their legal and social recognition. We often even confuse the object of demography with what civil status allows us to study, thus including nuptiality, which is a purely social and legal phenomenon. Hence the recurrence of research on the relation between laws and numbers (or the evolution of laws and of numbers), which we briefly illustrate with elements borrowed from European social history.

Throughout the 1970s, a wave of divorce-law reform swept across Western Europe and was accompanied by an increase in the proportion of broken marriages, which was sometimes brutal from one year to the next and always more progressive over the wedding cohorts. These reforms "liberalized" access to divorce through a movement away from divorce-sanction, where marriage stability is an essential norm, in favour of a divorce-report, which only manages the consequences of the break decided by the spouses. The reduction in the ambition of the law makes it possible to keep the whole population in its reach. Statistical analysis showed that the increase in the number of divorces was the result of a complex process. A direct effect reflected distance, not between new and old laws, but between the practice of old laws and that of new laws. It was combined with a symbolic, indirect effect, where the change of reality reverberated with the change in representations of reality and could hardly distinguish broader cultural transformations related to the image of the couple and marriage (Commaille et al. 1983).

A quarter of a century later, the legal and statistical study of the forms of legalization offered to homosexual couples has confirmed both the complexity of the relationship between law and demography and the possibility of using it to reach the wellsprings of broad phenomena far beyond the behaviour of homosexuals alone with regard to marriage. In fact, the factors that encourage homosexual couples to legalize their union concern not only their own interests, measured by the extent of the rights opened by the new laws, but all forms of conjugality. More specifically, the factors that promote or discourage nuptiality, such as the respective weight given by the welfare state to the couple and the individual, or the legislator's desire to bring de facto situations closer to legal situations, are factors that affect all couples, whether homosexual or heterosexual (Festy 2006).

Both studies also showed the time needed to establish family institutions in the practice of populations. That is not new: according to Georges Duby, it took at least two centuries in the Middle Ages for the Catholic Church to impose marriage as a consecrated, clergy-controlled framework at the end of a long conflict in which the new order replaced an older one (Duby 1981).

In the Nordic countries, where the partnership laws offered an experience of several years in 2006, a gradual increase in the number of registered couples had begun to bring the behaviour of homosexual couples closer to that of heterosexuals. This increase was primarily the result of lesbians, whose registration frequency was lower in the first years of the law. With the passage of time, practices became established in the lives of couples without any change in the legislative framework (Festy 2006).

We resume the analysis of the marriage of same-sex couples in Europe, benefiting from 12 more years of statistical observation and an enriched analysis of the content of the laws. Over a prolonged period of time, we can now associate the evolution of the number of marriages with the dynamics of laws and not just a snapshot of them. The result is a deepening and questioning of the previous conclusions. The impressions we might have had initially will be submitted to a more systematic verification and measurement of the relationship between the consequences attached to same-sex legalization and the number of marriages or registered partnership.

However, the effect of the change in the legislative framework is only part of the explanation of marriage patterns of same-sex couples and the observed differences from opposite-sex couples. First, it is crucial to introduce a net measurement of nuptiality that relates the number of marriages to the actual number of couples in order to properly address the marriage propensity issue. We did it in 2006 for all the countries under study, but on the fragile basis of guessed estimates. We come back to the topic, focusing on a limited number of countries with sound, reliable data and we explore important elements that could explain marriage behaviour and the observed differences between same-sex and opposite sex-couples. On the one hand, there are the values that each couple attaches to the institution of marriage in a certain normative social framework. On the other hand, there are individual characteristics that are associated with a greater susceptibility to marriage. Finally, there are intermediate elements that could play on the first two and are, at the same time, variable throughout the life course. This is especially true of the relationship between the reproductive project and the project of the couple. The arrival of children, in relation to the existing kinship rights, can act as an encouragement for the marriage and consequently, couples without children would be less inclined to marriage. For this reason, we take into account the importance of the family dimension, and especially the presence of children, to better understand the different marriage rates between opposite-sex couples, gay couples and lesbian couples.

Therefore, the comparative analysis of the crude marriage patterns across Europe in a context of legal change is complemented in this chapter by tentative efforts to disentangle two important drivers of marriage propensity. The French data, based on the annual rounds of census (2005–2017), are introduced in the discussion of crude marriage rates; they exemplify how to switch from same-sex marriages to more meaningful and expressive nuptiality rates. In part IV, we introduce the presence of children as a driver of marriage to be controlled for when analysing partnership status. We then use the 2017 Spanish household survey data to explore the family determinants of marriage.

3.2 Trends in Marriage and Registered Partnership Frequency Throughout Europe

We use crude rates of marriage and/or registered partnership to compare levels and trends in union legalization in European countries that have opened possibilities of legal recognition to same-sex couples. We rely mostly on data collected and published by national statistical institutes.

3.2.1 *Marriage Rates: Data and Indices*

Traditionally, marriages are recorded administratively together with births and deaths and their statistics are generally published as "vital statistics". The extension to same-sex marriages hardly modifies the processing of statistical data, except for the details of tabulations, which are limited by small numbers (Festy 2007). It may take a couple of years before the process and publication of data on same-sex marriages become routine.

Our collection of data was problematic only in Sweden, where the 2009 law characterized marriage as gender-neutral, thus abolishing any distinction between female, male and heterosexual marriages. Consequently, marriage statistics include the three types of marriages but do not identify them. Special requests had to be made to Statistics Sweden through our colleague Gunnar Andersson (Stockholm University).

The situation of registered partnership is much more diverse in the different countries. A few contrasting examples follow. In the Nordic region and the Netherlands, registered partnership was considered from the beginning as a near equivalent to marriage and the statistics were processed and published apart from those of marriage but along similar lines. In France, the procedure of "pacs" is very different from that of marriage, and so is the process followed by the data; the statistics are published by the Ministry of Justice instead of Insee and they do not benefit from the long tradition of vital statistics. In Germany, the conditions of registration vary from region to region and no statistics have ever been published at national level.

Apart from extreme cases like Germany, published data include minimum details with a distinction between male and female partnerships, which is enough for our purpose. Note that this form of registration in countries like France and the Netherlands also concerns heterosexual partners.

In some countries where marriage is open to same-sex couples, registered partnership is also an option for them. Our objective being the measurement of the frequency of union legalization, whatever its form, we should simultaneously consider data on marriage and registered partnership, with the risk of double-counting essentially couples who first registered their partnership and then transformed it into marriage. It would be necessary to identify these cases and subtract them from the total.

It is possible in France, where "pacs" that are dissolved in order to marry are counted yearly. Similarly, Statistics Sweden identifies among the married those who were previously registered. We could not obtain the same information for Belgium or the Netherlands and we had to restrict our measurement of legalization to marriage frequency, which probably underestimates legal recognition slightly.

One of our main objectives is not only the analysis of the frequency of homosexual marriage or registered partnership, but also the association of this frequency with the importance of legal consequences attached to marriage or registration. We will perform the measurement of this association through correlations between yearly statistical and juridical information for a group of countries where data are available in both domains. In other words, we retain for our analysis of frequencies the countries that also provide juridical data. We will detail the latter type of information later.

The question is apparently simple: among same-sex couples, what is the proportion of those who choose to legitimize their union through marriage or registered partnership? The answer implies numbers of marriages or registered partnerships as a numerator and numbers of gay and lesbian couples as a denominator. The former has been considered above; they are readily available, at least globally, without refined breakdowns. The latter are much more problematic, so that very few reliable estimates exist and still fewer time-series that would be necessary for the production of trends.

In most censuses or very large surveys, the number of same-sex couples is grossly overestimated due to errors in the declaration or coding of sex among the different-sex couples. Let us take this oversimplified example: homosexual couples are few while heterosexual couples are many, say 1000 against 100,000; errors about sex are rare, say that one of the partners makes an error in 1 p. 100 of couples. Among same-sex couples, 10 appear wrongly as heterosexual, which impacts very little the number of different-sex couples; among heterosexual couples, 1000 are wrongly classified as homosexual, which implies an overestimate of same-sex couples by a factor of 2 (Cortina and Festy 2014).

Amendments to the questionnaires or cross-checking sex with first names may eliminate the overestimate of same-sex couples. That has been the case in France where a series of reliable estimates have been provided yearly since 2010. We will use them at a later stage. Another solution is to rely on population registers instead of censuses or very large surveys; people are characterized by their civil status, including sex or gender, rather than being questioned about it; but similarly, they are not questioned about their relation to other persons in the household and the sexual nature of the relation must be guessed. That was done for the Netherlands once; it was not repeated, so no time-series can be calculated (Steenhof and Harmsen 2004).

For the geographical coverage to be wide and for the time-series to be as long as possible, we had to rely on simpler indices: crude rates that report numbers of marriages and/or registered partnerships to total population instead of the population directly exposed to risk (i.e., same-sex couples). More precisely, gay marriages and/or registered partnerships are reported to total male population, and lesbian marriages and/or registered partnerships are reported to total female population.

The immediate meaning of crude rates is much more abstract than the meaning of refined rates, but we have good reasons to think that crude rates may provide a comparative view of levels and trends consistent with the comparative image that would be provided by refined rates. Countries we are dealing with are broadly similar in their demographic structure, for instance, in their degree of population aging, and we may suppose more generally that structural factors do not much affect comparisons based on crude rates. Nevertheless, we will develop the French case and will measure and compare trends in crude and refined rates for recent years below.

When the crude rates of a country are put on a graph for, say, 10 years, the first 2 or 3 years are generally much above any later trend. It is a classical "stock effect": couples who had been waiting for many years to legalize their union rush into the new law to get married or registered… at last! The overview of trends in Europe is much clearer when these early rates are omitted. This is the case with the graphs shown below.

3.2.2 Trends and Levels in Crude Marriage Rates

We have constructed graphs of yearly crude rates for male couples and for female couples; we have complemented our analysis by calculating sex ratios (crude rates for female couples/crude rates for male couples). Nine countries are considered; the Nordic countries are coloured in red (Finland, Norway, Sweden), the western countries in blue (Belgium, France, the Netherlands, the UK or rather England and Wales), the southern countries in green (Portugal, Slovenia). Note that the last group includes only two countries with short time-series; it will be difficult to draw firm conclusions.

Crude male rates are clearly lower in the north than in the west of Europe. Their increase—if any—is slow. Curves in the three countries are also remarkably intertwined, which points to regional homogeneity (Fig. 3.1).

Rates are clearly higher in western countries and they are also much more diverse. In Belgium and the UK they are twice as high as the Nordic rates, while the Netherlands is in an intermediate position, which is closer to the Nordic group; in all these countries rates are stable. By contrast, crude male rates have risen a lot in France, they have more than doubled in a dozen of years, they are now much higher than anywhere else. In the most recent years, they are four times higher than in Norway or Sweden.

In southern Europe, rates are low: as low as in the north for Portugal, much lower in Slovenia. Time-series are too short to speak about stability (Portugal) or rise (Slovenia).

The graph for crude female rates differs neatly from the previous one for crude male rates (Fig. 3.1).

In the Nordic countries, the rise is substantial and systematic. This is the case for the three countries, and the three curves are quite close: again, the region is homogeneous. The level is slightly lower than in Western Europe, but the distance between the two groups is much more limited for women than it is for men.

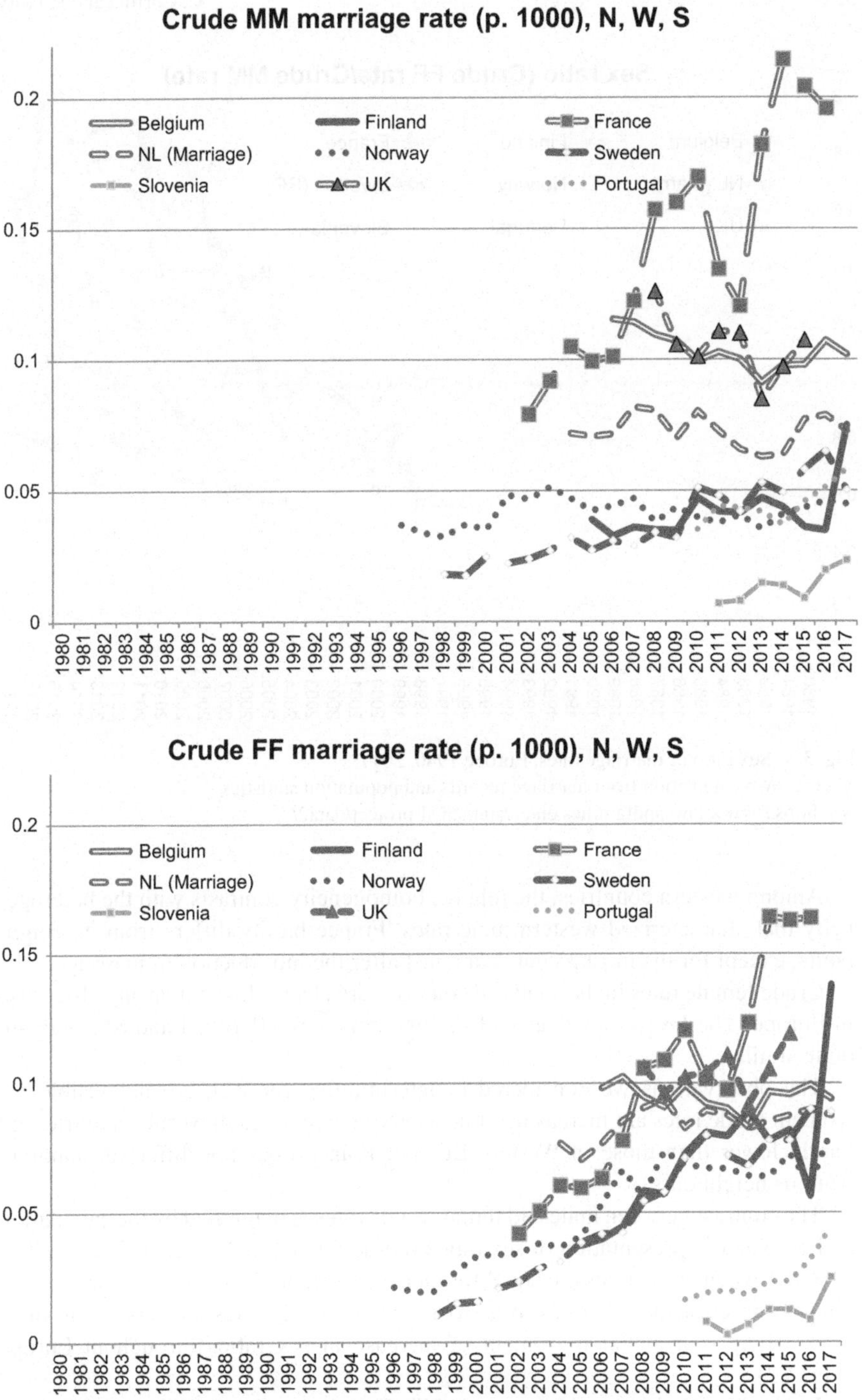

Fig. 3.1 Crude marriage rates by sex, Europe 1980–2017
Source: own calculation from marriage records and population statistics
See https://www.lawsandfamilies.eu/en/statistical-project/data2/

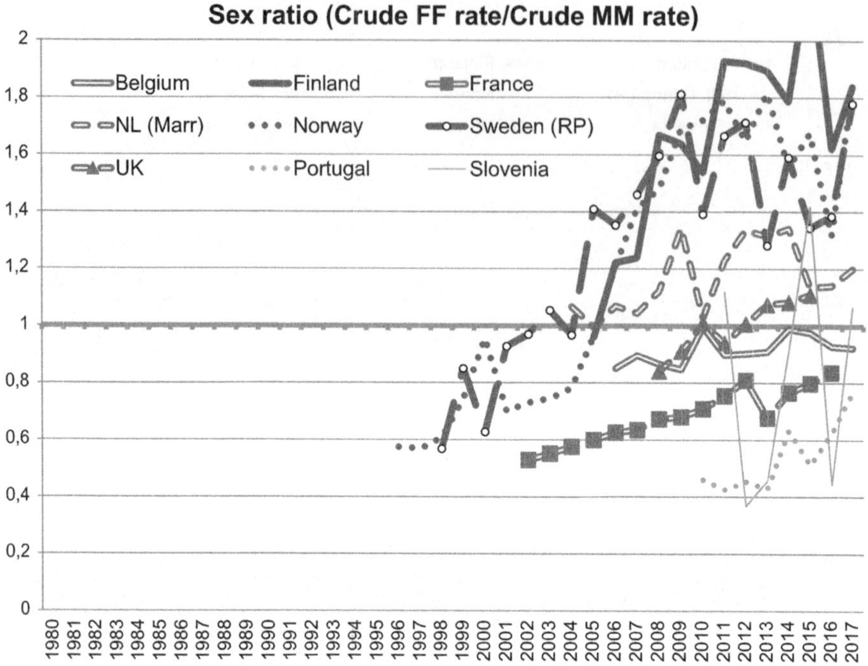

Fig. 3.2 Sex ratio of marriage rates, Europe 1980–2017
Source: own calculation from marriage records and population statistics
See https://www.lawsandfamilies.eu/en/statistical-project/data2/

Among western countries, the relative homogeneity contrasts with the heterogeneity that characterized western male rates. France hardly differs from its neighbours, except for the most recent years, just after the introduction of marriage.

Crude female rates in the southern countries are clearly lower than anywhere else in Europe. The levels and shapes of the two curves for Portugal and Slovenia are quite similar.

The observations we considered counterintuitive for men are not visible for women: crude rates are increasing almost everywhere; rates in Nordic countries are hardly lower than those in Western Europe; France does not differ substantially from its neighbours.

The contrast between male and female crude rates is magnified by the calculation and graphical representation of sex ratios (crude female rate/crude male rate). The ratio is 1 when crude rates are equal for men and women; it is below 1 when female rates are inferior to male rates; it is over 1 when female rates are superior to male rates. There is a global movement of increase in sex ratios throughout Europe (Fig. 3.2).

In Nordic countries, ratios move rapidly from below 1 (.6 in the late 1990s) to over 1 (more than 1.6 in the 2010s). The increase is spectacular: Finnish ratios are even occasionally over 2. The up rise may have come to an end, recent ratios oscillate around high stable values (1.6–1.8). The curves of the three countries are quite close to one another, thus confirming the homogeneity of the region. Ratios in any other European country are inferior.

In Western Europe, ratios have increased much more slowly; they are also more dispersed, over 1 in the Netherlands (1.2 in 2017), under 1 in France (.8 recently), around 1 in Belgium and the UK (in fact, England and Wales).

Ratios are still lower in Portugal, despite their increase. Numbers are so small in Slovenia for gays and lesbians that their ratios are erratic.

There are huge differentials through time in Nordic countries (multiplication by 3 in less than two decades) and large gaps between countries in north, west and south of Europe. Sex ratio is a factor associated to such a large heterogeneity in time and space.

3.2.3 Discussion

The progressive adoption of laws opening registration of partnership or marriage to same-sex couples in Nordic, and then western and southern countries (with a few exceptions like the early recognition of marriage in Spain) suggests similarities with the second demographic transition and the development of informal cohabitation as an alternative to marriage. The theory interprets the emergence of cohabitation as the consequence of a cultural reaction against traditional male breadwinner marriages (Lesthaeghe and van de Kaa 1986).

But instead of stability in a number of countries, one would have expected a gradual increase in the popularity of same-sex marriage or registered partnership everywhere, in conformity with processes of diffusion of social innovations, generally adopted first by a small minority of well-informed activists and then extended to larger circles by imitation (Nazio and Blossfeld 2003; Di Giulio and Rosina 2007). This process seems to have been, at best, unsystematic in terms of the adoption of marriage by gay and lesbian couples in each country.

More generally, it is somewhat paradoxical to compare trends and levels in same-sex marriage to those in cohabitation, an alternative to different-sex marriage. It might be more appropriate to refer same-sex to different-sex marriages. The latter offer a longer time perspective than the former for obvious reasons. Our graph starts in 1980 and evidences a global decline of heterosexual nuptiality. It is one of the main symptoms of the second demographic transition.

The decline in nuptiality together with the introduction of same-sex registered partnership has pushed a polemist to announce the end of marriage as a consequence of the legalization of gay and lesbian unions (Stanley Kurtz). But different-sex marriage rates had started decreasing well before the legal formalisation of homosexual couples, a movement initiated by Denmark in 1989. We cannot even discern an acceleration in nuptiality decline. On the contrary, crude rates in Nordic

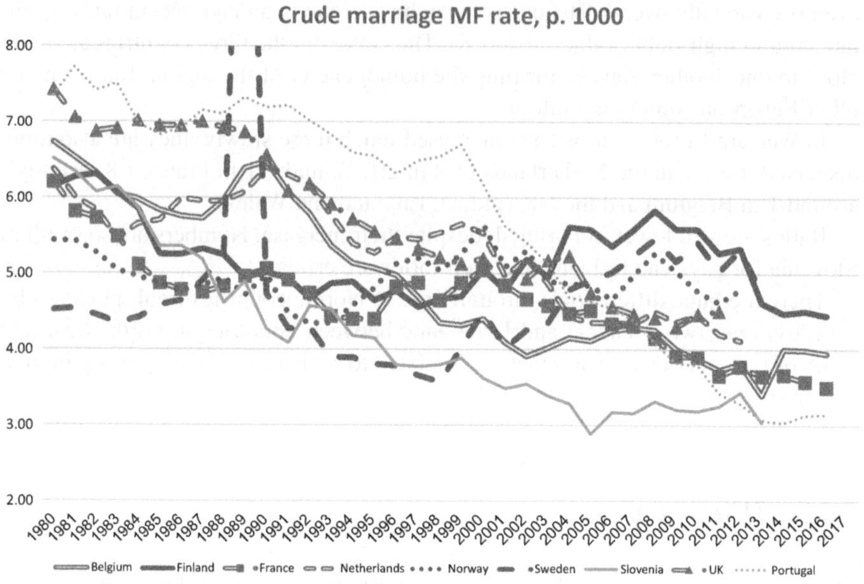

Fig. 3.3 Crude marriage rates, Europe 1980–2017
Source: own calculation from marriage records and population statistics

countries have gone through a remarkable reversal of trend at the end of the twentieth century, so that an unexpected rise in heterosexual nuptiality parallels the slow increase in gay marriage rates and the more rapid movement in lesbian marriages. Some analysts interpret it as a spiritual revival that temporarily contradicts the theory behind the second demographic transition.

But this is only an exception. In general, same-sex and different-sex marriage evolve in opposite directions (Fig. 3.3). The correlation with gay marriage rates is negative ($r = -0{,}36$); with lesbian marriage rates it is close to zero ($r = -0{,}12$). The absence of positive correlation between trends and levels in same-sex and different-sex marriage rates suggests that factors classically associated with the second demographic transition are not relevant for a contextual explanation of homosexual marriage rates in Europe. We will have a look at other contextual factors in the discussion of part 3.2.

France is the country with the largest increase in crude marriage rates for gays as well as lesbians. Male crude rates experience a rise from 0.1 p.1000 in 2005 to more than twice as much in 2017. Female rates follow the same pattern, but at lower levels, from 0.06 to 0.17. The gap between men and women is gradually reduced. The trend is steeper in France than anywhere else in Europe. Note a temporary decrease in 2011–2012, just before the extension of marriage to homosexuals in 2013. It may reflect a waiting behaviour of couples who preferred to run directly into marriage in 2013 rather than "pacsing" first in 2011–2012 and then switching to marriage. It may also result from a temporary deterioration of pacs registration when the procedure is partly transferred from courts to notaries.

Trends in crude rates can be due to changes in the number of gay and lesbian couples or to changes in the frequency of "marriage" among these couples. E.g., a rise in crude MM rates may result from an intensification in the formation of gay couples or an increase in the proportion of couples who legitimize their union. The disentangling of the two dimensions is only possible if reliable estimates of the numbers of gay and lesbian couples are available periodically, in the best case on a yearly basis. It is the case in France thanks to the annual rounds of census, despite classical pitfalls in this kind of data, mainly faulty declarations of sex by heterosexual couples. The number of "true" couples has been reconstituted since 2010 through the use of first names. The comparison of "true" couples and "apparent" couples in 2010–2011 has offered us the possibility of a backward estimate starting in 2005 and a complete time-series from 2005 to 2017 (Algava and Hallépée 2018).

Refined rates can be calculated and compared to crude rates. They tell a different story. From 2005 to 2017, there is hardly any rise in male rates, which went from .89 to .92, except for temporary ups and downs. The increase is slightly more important in female rates, which went from 0.89 to 1.10 and, more noticeably the frequency of lesbian marriages is continuously higher than that of gays and the gap increases between the two (Fig. 3.4).

In other words, the marked increase in French crude rates must be attributed to a rise in gay and lesbian couple formation, not to an intensification of nuptiality among these couples. Higher crude rates for men than women, sex ratios below 1, must be attributed to more numerous couples among gays than lesbians, not to the more intense nuptiality of gay couples. These conclusions, although limited to one country, will be on our mind when we interpret the association of trends and levels in crude rates with legal variables.

Referring marriages to couples opens the way to comparisons between same-sex and different-sex nuptiality. We concentrate on France in 2011, when a large survey was associated with the yearly census so as to give reliable information on couples, same-sex as well as different-sex; cohabiting and living apart partners are enumerated together (Buisson and Lapinte 2013).

A large majority of heterosexual couples were married or pacsed (77%), as compared with a minority of homosexual couples, only 47% of gay couples and 38% of lesbian couples were pacsed.

That may give the impression that different-sex couples legalize their union more frequently than same-sex. But this observation is misleading, essentially because heterosexuals have a longer history behind them, with more opportunities to marry or pacs than homosexuals.

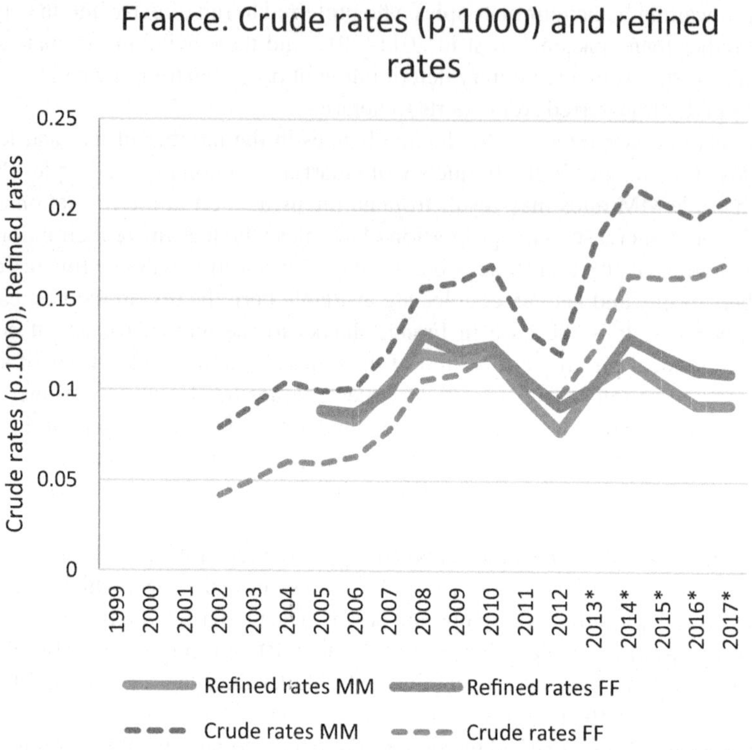

Fig. 3.4 Crude and refined marriage rates by sex. France 1999–2017
Source: own calculation from marriage records and population statistics

A fair view of the propensity to pacs or marry is obtained by relating pacs or marriages in a given year (2011) to the number of unmarried and unpacsed couples, different-sex and same-sex being equally "exposed to the risk of legalization". In these circumstances, specific rates are higher for homosexuals than heterosexuals, although the latter have the possibility to pacs OR marry while homosexuals are only entitled to pacs. Specific rates are almost similar for unpacsed gay and lesbian couples (respectively .133 and .131) and somewhat above specific rates for unpacsed and unmarried heterosexual couples (.098).

The French case brings two elements into the discussion: couples' nuptiality plays little role in the development of same-sex crude marriage rates and it is much higher than heterosexual nuptiality. These observations cannot be extended to other countries—France is also characterized by very high crude marriage rates, especially among gays—but they do confirm that trends and levels in same-sex and different-sex marriage depend on different determinants and react independently of one another. In particular, the factors associated with the second demographic transition, which are closely related to Ron Inglehart's concept of "post-materialism", are relevant for heterosexual marriage decline, but are probably useless to explain homosexual nuptiality.

3.3 Trends in Legal Consequences Attached to Marriage or Registered Partnership

Legal recognition of same-sex couples opens up legal consequences inferior or equal to consequences opened up by heterosexual marriage. Here we measure positive legal consequences and establish their levels and trends in the same 9 countries to which we referred in the first part. We then try to answer this question: Is the frequency of same-sex legal recognition correlated with the level of legal consequences attached to recognition?

3.3.1 On Legal Scores

In the LawsAndFamilies Database 60 questions have been addressed to legal experts in each European country about possible consequences attached to each conjugal form (marriage, registered partnership or cohabitation, same-sex or different-sex). E.g., "Can a relationship of this type result in lower income tax than for two individuals without a partner?" or "Does a relationship of this type make it easier for a foreign partner to obtain citizenship?" Here we use the 25 questions about positive legal consequences that were selected by Waaldijk (2017). In the Database, the answers given by the legal experts were coded by them as "Yes", "Yes but with restrictions", "No except in some cases" or "No" (Waaldijk et al. 2017). Here these answer codes are numbered respectively 3, 2, 1 and 0. Global scores for several questions result from additions. Global scores for same-sex forms are compared with global scores for different-sex marriages. The index is 1 if homosexual couples get as high a score as married heterosexuals; it is below 1 if legal consequences attached to same-sex registered partnership or marriage are inferior to those attached to different-sex marriage.

For each country, every year we retain the score obtained by the most positive same-sex status available at that moment. It implies switching from one status to the other when a new conjugal format is introduced, e.g., from registered partnership to marriage when same-sex marriage becomes possible and offers couples new advantages.

3.3.2 Trends and Levels of Legal Scores

In every country the global score increases over time: legal consequences attached to the best status offered to same-sex couples are gradually enlarged and look more and more like those attached to heterosexual marriage. For instance in Norway and Sweden, the early introduction of registered partnership offers homosexual couples

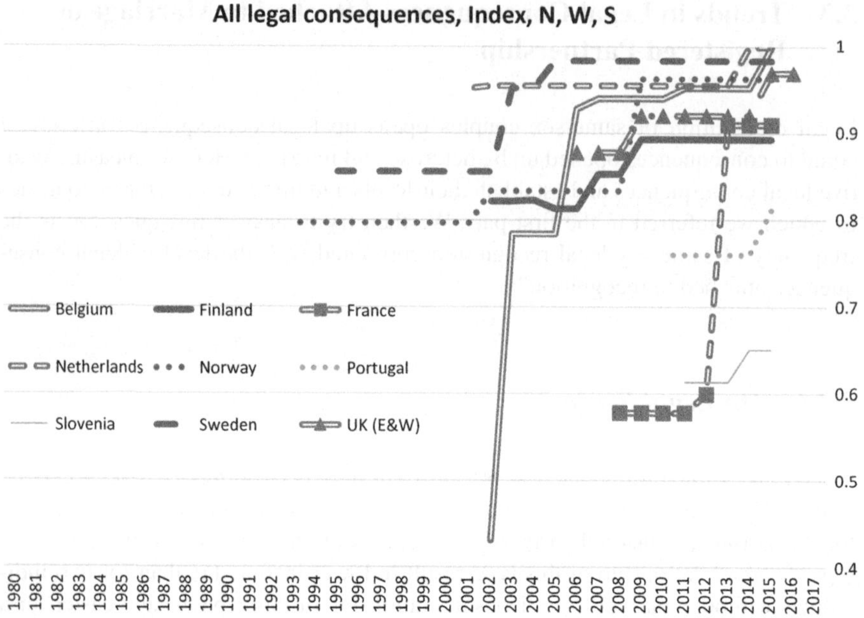

Fig. 3.5 Legal index (all consequences), Europe 1990–2017
Source: own calculation

at least 80% of rights associated with different-sex marriage; that score is later improved when the country moves to same-sex marriage (Norway 2009) or even before, through reform of registered partnership (Sweden). Very recently, the index culminates over 96% in Norway and over 98% in Sweden. Finland has experienced the same kind of trajectory but has reached "only" 89% (Fig. 3.5).

Western countries are more dispersed. In the Netherlands, registered partnership and then marriage have immediately offered same-sex couples 95% of the rights granted to married heterosexuals and the percentage has even risen to 100% since 2014. At the other extreme, pacs in France opened to same-sex couples less than 60% of legal consequences attached to heterosexual marriage; only the opening of marriage to homosexual couples in 2013 brought that percentage to 90%. Belgium and the UK are in intermediate positions but have recently reached percentages that are very close (UK) or even equal (Belgium) to 1.

Southern countries lag well behind: their short histories culminate at relatively low levels (Portugal 80%; Slovenia 65%).

In brief, Nordic countries like Norway or Sweden open the way to a continuous enlargement of rights offered to same-sex couples; some western countries like the Netherlands accompany the movement while others, like France, follow it with a delay; southern countries lag far behind.

Similarities between trends and levels in marriage rates on one hand and in legal indices on the other hand suggest the existence of a relationship between them. Dissimilarities point to no relationship.

Curves of male rates differ radically from those for legal consequences: stability in most curves instead of a systematic rise, a low level in Nordic countries compared to western countries instead of the reverse. By contrast, there are marked similarities between trends and levels in legal rights and sex ratios: all the curves increase, Nordic countries come first followed by western countries while southern Europe lags behind. There are also common traits for curves of lesbian rates, but these are less clear.

The calculation of coefficients of correlation through the ordinary least square (OLS) method confirms the visual impressions. Correlation is null with frequencies of gay marriage (.01), moderate with lesbian marriages (.34) and stronger with sex ratios (.49).

To better understand the meaning of any relationship between marriage rates and legal consequences attached to same-sex marriage, we have divided the latter into subgroups (material consequences, parenting, migration, other non-material consequences) and we have calculated scores following the same procedure as previously, with the consequences attached to heterosexual marriage as a reference. The first two subgroups offer the most illustrative results (Table 3.1).

The path followed by material consequences is very different from that previously described for all legal consequences. In all the Nordic countries but also in the Netherlands and Portugal, same-sex marriage or registered partnership offers the same material advantages as different-sex marriage as soon as union legalization becomes possible. Only Belgium, France, the UK and Slovenia evidence a progressive enlargement of material consequences opened to same-sex couples. For instance, in France, consequences attached to pacs were initially very restrictive; they were then enlarged and finally marriage put same-sex and different-sex couples on a par (Fig. 3.6).

This image of material consequences is also very different from those of rates and sex ratios. Coefficients of correlation are close to zero for women; they are negative for men (gay marriages are infrequent in the Nordic countries despite "generous" material rights); they are moderate for sex ratios.

On the contrary, parenting consequences have some similarities with all consequences. The major difference is the much lower initial level, even in pioneering countries like Norway or Sweden, but also in Belgium or France; it is followed by

Table 3.1 Correlation coefficients of legal scores and marriage indicators

All questions (25)			Parenting questions (6)			Material questions (9)		
MM rates	FF rates	Sex ratios	MM rates	FF rates	Sex ratios	MM rates	FF rates	Sex ratios
0,007	0,341	0,492	0,127	0,529	0,588	−0,322	−0,037	0,386

Source: Own calculation

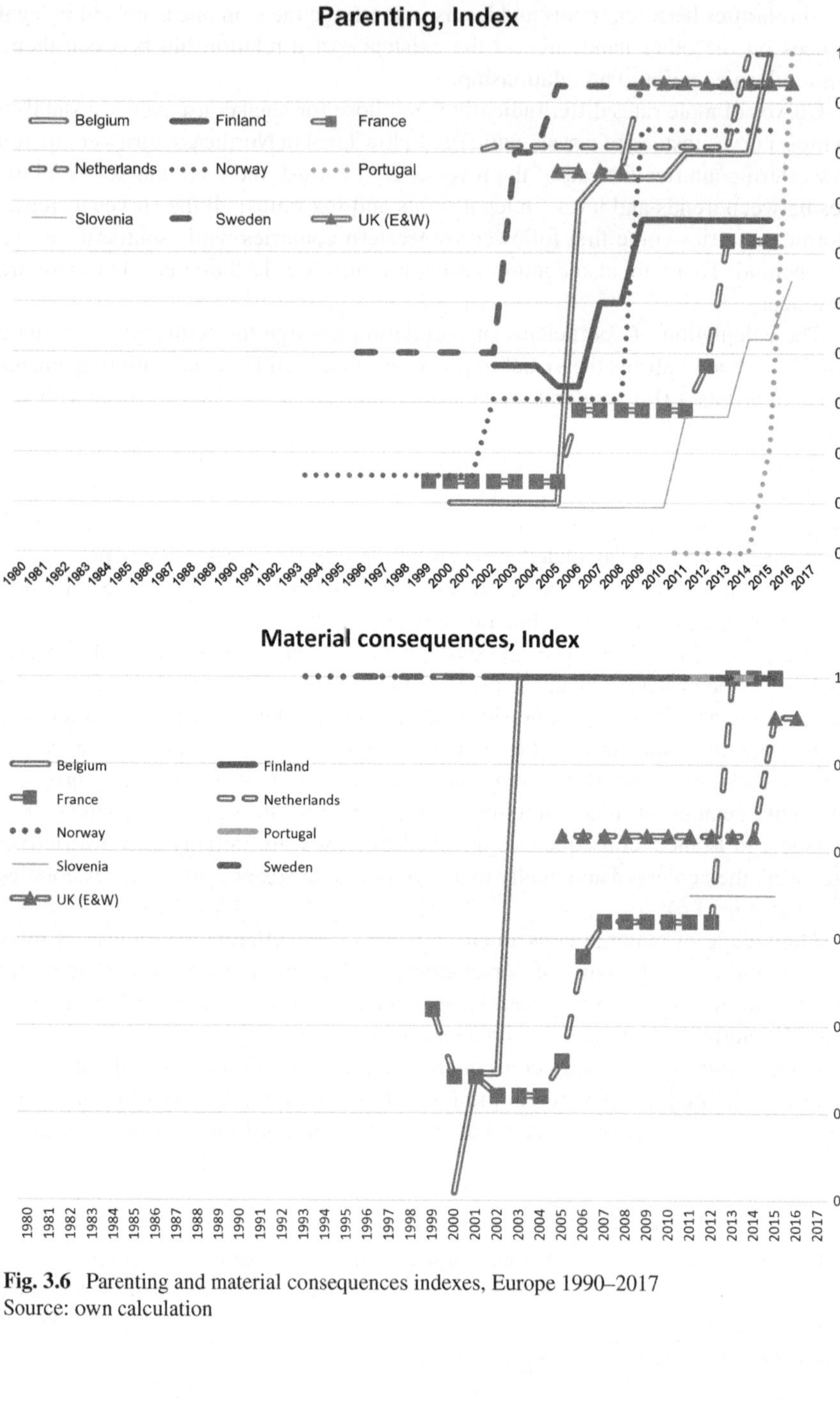

Fig. 3.6 Parenting and material consequences indexes, Europe 1990–2017
Source: own calculation

ample movements of aggiornamento that bring same-sex couples closer to heterosexual couples. Sweden's position in the forefront has been recently challenged by western countries like Belgium, the Netherlands and the UK, and, even more recently, by Portugal in the south.

Coefficients of correlation are clearly higher than those previously measured on all legal consequences. They remain weak for men (.13), but substantial for women (.53) and sex ratios (.59). The distance between gays and lesbians is important once again and is well summarized by the association of parenting consequences and sex ratios.

The coefficients measure the distance between bunches of curves characterized by trends and levels of national rates and scores. We emphasize comparisons of levels by focusing on a short period of time: 2011–2015. The correlation between parenting and sex ratios is slightly reduced (.53 instead of .59). The emphasis is put on time trends if we focus on specific groups of countries, e.g. northern or western. This time, the correlation is markedly increased: it is .71 or .81 respectively.

The distance between frequencies of gay and lesbian marriages is associated with parenting issues more than with other dimensions of the law. The enlargement of consequences attached to marriage in each country plays a more decisive role than differences between countries in the openness of national laws. In other words, the dynamics of laws in various countries on aspects of parenting is associated with the dynamics of lesbian marriages, not with those of gay marriages. This is reflected in a common movement towards increased sex ratios at various levels.

Let us first remind the reader that our analysis relies on country-level information on the content and consequences of laws and the number and rates of marriages, not on individual-level data. The second reminder is that both variables—legal scores and rates—are dated, so that a dynamic process is captured, not a static snapshot. The results must be read this way: lesbian marriage rates are higher, and their rise is steeper in countries where the legal consequences attached to marriage are broader and their development more rapid. There is no such association for gays. Among the different domains covered by marriage laws, those concerning parenting are essentially responsible for this divergence between women and men. The other domains are not relevant.

In a context of continuous enlargement of legal consequences attached to gay and lesbian marriages, the divergent trends among men and women result in an increase of sex ratios, which tend towards the dominance of female over male marriages. As homosexual and heterosexual marriages gradually open to similar consequences, in particular for parenting, sex ratios will tend to a limit; they appear to do so in the most advanced countries, the Nordic ones. It will be important to check whether lesbian couples are far more numerous than gay couples or if women in couples legalize their union more often than gay couples.

3.3.3 Discussion

The results presented so far confirm and add precision to those we had obtained previously. They confirm that the impact of legislation on marriage rates has its origin in parenting dimensions of the laws and essentially concerns women. They are more precise because they rely on longer time-series of marriage rates associated with an innovative analysis of the dynamics of law content, which makes possible a correlation between two processes rather than between two snapshots: levels and trends in marriage rates together with levels and trends in law variables.

It has been possible to show that the impact of changes in laws was reflected with no delay in changes in marriage rates. This is true even after the very first years after the introduction of registered partnership or marriage were eliminated, when couples who were expecting that the law would be passed rushed into it. Further legal changes create a similar, though less spectacular movement.

However, the French case, which is developed above, suggests a caveat: an increase in crude marriage rates may be due not only to more marriages among existing same-sex couples, but also to an acceleration in the formation of new couples. An extension of consequences attached to registered partnership or marriage may incentivize same-sex partners to come out and live together, in particular lesbian partners.

The association of levels and trends in crude marriage rates and legal content in a number of countries is a direct application of Durkheim's "sociological method", which is based on (international) comparisons and the analysis of "variations concomitantes": "*nous n'avons qu'un moyen de démontrer qu'un phénomène est cause d'un autre, c'est de comparer les cas où ils sont simultanément présents ou absents et de chercher si les variations qu'ils présentent dans ces différentes combinaisons de circonstances témoignent que l'un dépend de l'autre*." (Durkheim 1894).

Here we have established that female marriage rates are higher in countries that grant more parental facilities, which is a relationship between macro data. It raises two questions: Can we take it for granted that the content of the law influences the number of marriages or do we need to identify a third variable that simultaneously impacts the extent of the laws concerning parenting? And if we fail on the latter issue, can we switch from a macro to a micro formulation and evidence that parents marry more frequently?

For instance, we may assume and can check whether women's empowerment could have contributed to the adoption of laws favouring homoparenting and if it can be associated with the increase in the female marriage rate. Some researchers have assumed that the societies which are the most advanced in their movement towards gender equality benefited from an increase in fertility that contradicted the fertility decline dimension of the second demographic transition. This movement has some similarities with the recent increase in crude different-sex marriage rate in the Nordic countries described above (Myrskylä et al. 2009, 2011).

We measure gender equality through the Women's Political Empowerment Index (WPEI), which is based on yearly information concerning women's civil liberties, civil society participation and political participation, which offers long series of data for the 9 countries we examine. It was used recently to challenge Myrskylä's hypothesis (Kolk 2019; Sundström et al. 2017).

The coefficients of correlation do not confirm the assumption: WPEI is neither associated with the parenting index (r = −0,31) nor with female marriage crude rates (r = −19). We are left with the other assumption: in the next section, we will see whether higher rates in parent-friendly countries imply that same-sex parents do marry more frequently than non-parents.

3.4 Parenting and Same-Sex Nuptiality

The sociology of the family has done a good job of establishing the patterns and trends of non-marital cohabitation in Western societies (Kiernan 2001). The diffusion of unmarried couples and the normalization of having children outside marriage are related to the diversity of cohabitation typologies and to the complementarity of several profiles of cohabiters. These profiles range from young cohabiters who understand cohabitation as a trial period before marriage and exclude childbearing from their partnership project to older cohabiters who understand their partnership as a stable and committed relationship and whose fertility intentions do not differ significantly from those of married spouses (Hekel and Castro-Martín 2014). The differences in the stability and risk of union dissolution of marriages and cohabitations have also been explored (Axinn and Thornton 1992). Recent evidence has indicated that dissolution rates are higher for same-sex cohabitations than for different-sex cohabitations and marital unions but that the demographic determinants of union stability are rather similar among the different types of couples (Lau 2012; Manning et al. 2016).

Scholars have also more recently considered the reasons for getting married in contexts in which cohabitation is widespread and increasingly similar to marriage in terms of the rights accorded to the partners (Manning and Smock 1995). While some outline the importance of feelings (Billari and Liefbroer 2016), others refer to more material dimensions, such as class or socio-economic status (Manning and Smock 1995).

Interestingly enough, some researches based on qualitative evidence have tried to explore the specificities of the incentives for and barriers to same-sex marriage (Pichardo 2011). The list of potential factors operating as incentives includes: (i) considering marriage to be an act of activism; (ii) marriage as an asset protection; (iii) protection in case of the death of one of the members of the couple; (iv) adoption of children of one of the spouses by the other; (v) regularization of the immigrant spouse for social recognition for the couple relationship. In contrast, the barriers to marriage might be associated with (i) the social rejection that condemns discretion; (ii) the intent to adopt from abroad, where it is easier for a single person than for a homosexual couple; (iii) values that are antithetical to marriage, considering it a patriarchal and non-egalitarian institution with religious connotations.

The need to better understand the family-related attitudes and expectations of gays and lesbians emerges from this list of incentives and barriers. A recent study that uses German survey data shows that gays and lesbians expect fewer benefits and greater costs of being in a partnership than heterosexuals but at the same time they do not find differences in the expectations about parenthood according to sexual orientation. The authors think that same-sex parenthood attitudes might be affected by the fact that same-sex parenting is still not that common and that heteronormative values are more determinant than experience (Hank and Wetzel 2018).

Our main goal here is to do a nuptiality analysis and to explore the main individual and family determinants of marriage by comparing same-sex and opposite-sex couples. Building on the assumption that fertility levels and family structure differ considerably between these two types of couples, we are specifically interested in analysing whether the higher or lower presence of children in the household (either the progeny of the two partners or children from previous relationships) is associated with the partnership status of the different types of couples.

3.4.1 Same-Sex and Opposite-Sex Nuptiality in Spain

In order to carry out a comparative analysis of the nuptiality of same-sex and opposite-sex couples, we selected the Spanish case and we use data from 2017, which means 12 years after same-sex marriage was legal in Spain in 2005. We think that such a period is long enough to address the issue of the impact of rights expansion such as marriage and parenting on demographic behaviours. In addition to this wide period of observation with the marital option available, the choice of the Spanish case is also related to the dramatic transformation of family dynamics and attitudes towards family change. Specifically, union formation patterns have changed in Spain through the diffusion of non-marital cohabitation as a regular path to family formation (Domínguez-Folgueras and Castro-Martín 2013).

Spain offers statistical sources of exceptional value for studying same-sex families, namely the last two population censuses, those of 2001 and 2011. These make it possible to identify and recount same-sex couples who live in the same household and who are self-identified as spouses. These sources are now updated through a large Household Survey (*Encuesta Continua de Hogares*) which has been implemented annually since 2014 by the Spanish Statistical Institute (INE). For 2017, which is the last year available, the total sample size of the survey was 259.628 individuals, out of which 806 have a partner of the same sex. Unfortunately, Spain

Table 3.2 Distribution of partnered individuals by type of couple and partnership status, Spain 2017

	% Married	% Non-marital cohabitation	Total
Opposite-sex	86%	14%	11,135,140
Same-sex male	56%	44%	113,324
Same-sex female	55%	45%	60,907

Source: Spanish Household Survey, INE. Note: weighted data

Table 3.3 Distribution of partnered individuals by type of couple and family structure (presence of children), Spain 2017

	No children	Common children	Non-common children	Total
Opposite-sex	38%	59%	3%	11,135,139
Same-sex male	98%	2%	0.4%	113,324
Same-sex female	82%	11%	6%	60,908

Source: Spanish Household Survey, INE
Note: weighted data

does not have a unique and centralized register of partnerships, which implies that the analysis cannot be expanded to registered partnerships and has to be limited to unions formalized through marriage.

The primary variable of interest in our analysis is the type of couple based on the gender of the spouses: opposite sex, same sex male (two men), same sex female (two women); this information is obtained via reciprocal identification of the spouse or partner from the members of the household. This system is not free from problems, given that an incorrect declaration of the gender of the household members may affect the identification of the couples (O'Connell and Feliz 2011). The second relevant variable for the analysis is the partnership status: married or unmarried. An important characteristic of the household (family structure) is also considered: the presence of children. In our analysis, we also control for some individual demographic characteristics of the partners (age and educational level) and additional characteristics of the couples.

As shown in Table 3.2, the proportion of married couples clearly differs by type of union. In 2017 in Spain 14% of the total opposite-sex couples were cohabiting outside marriage while this proportion was around 45% for same-sex couples. These crude proportions are obviously affected by the socio-demographic composition and therefore we ran a logistic regression analysis to explore the probability of cohabiting outside marriage. One of the main reasons to do so is the remarkable difference in the family structures of each type of couple. As shown in Table 3.3, the large majority of opposite-sex couples of all ages have co-residing children (either common or not common, that is, coming from previous relationships and thus form-

Table 3.4 Logistic regression models on the partnership status (non-marital union vs. marriage) by type of couple, Spain 2017 (odds ratio)

	Bivariate	Multivariate
Type of couple		
Opposite sex (ref.)	1	1
Same-sex male	4.8**	2.1**
Same-sex female	5.0**	2.1**
Constant	−1.805	4.057
N	64,872	64,872
Log likelihood	14349119.3	18,374,986

Source: Spanish Household Survey, INE
Note: Sample not weighted
Note: the multivariate model includes the following variables: age, educational level, family structure (the presence of children), citizenship combination of the partners

ing step-families), around 62%. However, the presence of children is less common for same-sex couples, with a clear gender differential: 17% for lesbians and only 2.4% for gays, in line with what we observe in other Western countries (Andersson et al. 2006).

The results of the logistic regression indicate that the probability of cohabiting outside marriage is 5 times greater for same-sex couples as opposed to opposite sex couples (Table 3.4). When controlling for the characteristics of the couples which have been found to be positively associated with marriage (especially the presence of children in the household), the relationship of the probability is reduced by more than half: 2 times greater for both men and women. These results are in line with previous analysis conducted with the 2011 census (Cortina 2016), where the probabilities of cohabitation were higher (around 4 in the bivariate and around 3–4 in the multivariate), which is to be expected because marriage had been an option for a shorter period at that time.

If we analyse the individual and family determinants in detail (Table 3.5. and Fig. 3.7), we observe that the probability of being married increases with age and is higher for those partners holding a university degree, while it decreases when the two spouses have different citizenships (Table 3.5). Once these individual and couple characteristics are taken into account, the effect of family composition (having children or not) in interaction with the type of couple emerges as a key factor. As the margins plot clearly shows (Fig. 3.7), when the couple does not have children, the likelihood of being married is clearly higher for opposite-sex couples than for same-sex couples. However, when they have children there is no significant difference. The same predicted probabilities also indicate that there are no differences between gays and lesbians.

The analysis of the partnership status of the same-sex couples compared to the opposite-sex ones offers two major conclusions: (1) same-sex couples marry less due to a compositional issue: they have fewer children and couples without children are less likely to be married or more likely to cohabit; (2) when couples have chil-

Table 3.5 Logistic regression models on the partnership status (marriage vs. non-marital union) by type of couple, Spain 2017 (coefficients)

Type of couple	
Opposite sex (ref).	1.00
Same sex male	−1.11**
Same sex female	−1.08**
Age	0.13**
Age squared	0.00**
Educational level	
No university degree (ref)	1
University degree	0.04**
Family structure	
No children (ref)	1
Children	1.10**
Citizenship composition	
Both Spanish (ref)	1
Both foreign	0.62**
Intermarriage	−0.35**
No children (ref)	1
Children opposite-sex	1.00**
Children same-sex male	0.46**
Children same-sex female	0.60**
Constant	−4.08**
N	64,872
Log likelihood	−18588.246

Note: * $p < .05$, ** $p < .01$
Source: Spanish Household Survey, INE
Note: Sample not weighted

dren the probability of being married does not differ from same-sex and opposite-sex couples. Even if these results refer only to the Spanish case, we can infer without risk that family structure matters when it comes to formalizing partnerships and that the compositional effect of having lower fertility rates partially explains the lower marriage/registration rates of same-sex couples. For the same reason, it could explain the recent increase of lesbian crude marriage rates across Europe observed in the previous sections.

3.4.2 *Discussion*

Nuptiality and fertility patterns have always been connected. Traditionally, marriage was the earlier step and the necessary condition for childbearing. As we have discussed above, the relationship between these events has been substantially altered in recent decades. We could even argue that now parenthood often works as a deter-

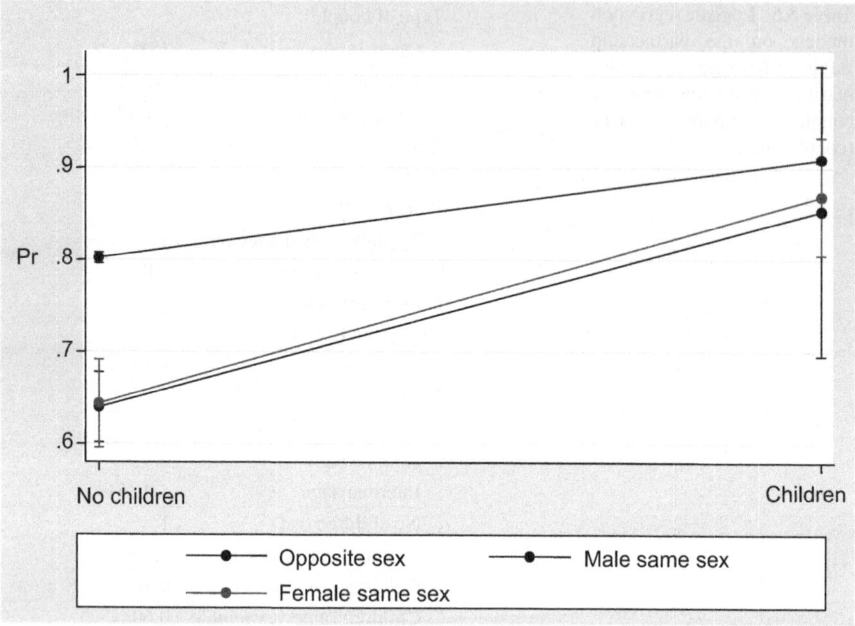

Fig. 3.7 Predicted probabilities of being in a married couple according to type of couple and family structure
Source: Spanish Household Survey, INE
Note: the multivariate model includes the following variables: age, educational level, citizenship combination of the partners

minant of marriage: children first, marriage second. This new reality of family sociology helps us to understand same-sex nuptiality. As long as the fertility patterns of same-sex couples are lower than those of opposite-sex couples, their nuptiality rates might also stay low.

The fact that the proportion of parents is lower for lesbians and especially for gays might also imply that their attitudes and expectations about marriage are different and less favourable to marriage. In this direction, Hank and Wetzel (2018) argue that "accounting for individuals' expectations might contribute to better explaining why, for example, marriage-like partnerships and cohabitation are less frequent in gay and lesbian couples than in heterosexual couples".

Considering the role of parenthood raises new questions for the future: if samesex family formation changes and its fertility rates increase, having more couples living with common children (and not for the most part children who were born to previous couples) might incline these parent couples towards marriage and at the same time might also modify the attitudes towards marriage of childless same-sex couples.

3.5 Conclusion

The frequency of same-sex marriage or registered partnership can be associated through statistical analysis with macro as well as micro factors. At both levels parenting appears as one of the key determinants.

At the societal level, we rely on international comparisons. In different countries, the content of the laws organizing access to marriage or registered partnership is associated with the frequency of union legalization, at least for women, not for men. In particular it is the case when countries enlarge the consequences attached to legal recognition in the domain of parenting. The result is an increase in the frequency of lesbian marriages while gay marriages tend to stagnate. The other consequences attached to legalization have no such impact.

At the micro level, we take advantage of the diversity of individual situations to compare nuptiality among homosexual and heterosexual couples, all other things being equal. We show that in Spain gay and lesbian couples marry less than different-sex couples but that this difference is substantially smaller when they have children. That confirms the importance of parenting in the decision of homosexuals to marry, but there are strict limits to the explanation given the low proportion of lesbian couples with children and the still lower proportion among gay couples.

For a more encompassing analytical framework it is tempting to treat the introduction of same-sex marriage as one of the various forms of union diversification that characterizes the second demographic transition, and to consider the factors associated with the latter as relevant for a global explanation of trends and levels in same-sex marriage. Our efforts in this direction have not been successful. That suggests to us that the second demographic transition does not constitute a comprehensive framework for the understanding of homosexual marriages.

Nevertheless, the comparison of attitudes, expectations and behaviours of same-sex and different-sex couples regarding marriage and parenthood is the most promising avenue to investigate. Homosexual nuptiality is a recent innovation and the evidence accumulated is still scanty: we need more data to explore its determinants.

References

Algava, E., & Hallépée, S. (2018). *Estimer les effectifs de couples de personnes de même sexe au recensement: expérimentation d'une solution de validation du sexe par le prénom*. Insee, Série des Documents de Travail de la Direction des Statistiques Démographiques Et Sociales, F1807.

Andersson, G., Noak, T., Seierstad, A., & Weedon-Fekjær, H. (2006). The demographics of same-sex marriage in Norway and Sweden. *Demography, 43*(1), 79–98.

Axinn, W., & Thornton, A. (1992). The relationship between cohabitation and divorce: Selectivity or causal influence? *Demography, 29*, 357–374.

Billari, F. C., & Liefbroer, A. C. (2016). Why still marry? The role of feelings in the persistence of marriage as an institution. *British Journal of Sociology, 67*(3), 516–540.

Buisson, G., & Lapinte, A. (2013). Le couple dans tous ses états. Non-cohabitaton, conjoints de même sexe, pacs.... *Insee Première* n°1432, 4 p.

Commaille, J., Festy, P., Guibentif, P., Kellerhals, J., Perrin, J.-F., & Roussel, L. (1983). *Le divorce en Europe occidentale. La loi et le nombre*. GIRD-CETEL (Genève)-INED, Paris: INED/PUF.
Cortina, C. (2016). Demographics of same-sex couples in Spain. *Revista Española de Investigaciones Sociológicas, 153*, 3–22.
Cortina C. & Festy P. (2014). Identification of same-sex couples and families in censuses, registers and surveys, Families and societies working paper series 8.
Di Giulio, P., & Rosina, A. (2007). Intergenerational family ties and the diffusion of cohabitation in Italy. *Demographic Research, 16*(14), 441–468.
Domínguez-Folgueras, M., & Castro-Martín, T. (2013). Cohabitation in Spain: No longer a marginal path to family formation. *Journal of Marriage and Family, 75*, 422–437.
Duby, G. (1981). *Le Chevalier, la Femme et le Prêtre: le mariage dans la France féodale*. Paris: Hachette.
Durkheim, E. (1894). Les règles de la méthode sociologique. *Revue Philosophique de la France et de L'étranger, 37*, 465–498.
Festy, P. (2006). La légalisation des couples homosexuels en Europe. *Population, 4*, 493–532.
Festy, P. (2007). Numbering same-sex couples in censuses and population registers. *Demographic Research, 17*(12), 339–368.
Hank, K., & Wetzel, M. (2018). Same-sex relationship experiences and expectations regarding partnership and parenthood. *Demographic Research, 39*(25), 701–718.
Hekel, N., & Castro-Martín, T. (2014). Grasping the diversity of cohabitation: Fertility intentions among cohabiters across Europe. *Journal of Marriage and Family, 76*(3), 489–505.
Kiernan, K. (2001). The rise of cohabitation and childbearing outside marriage in Western Europe. *International Journal of Law, Policy and the Family, 15*, 1–21.
Kolk, M. (2019). Weak support for a U-shaped pattern between societal gender equality and fertility when comparing societies across time. *Demographic Research, 40*(2), 27–48.
Lau, C. Q. (2012). The stability of same-sex cohabitation, different-sex cohabitation, and marriage. *Journal of Marriage and the Family, 74*(5), 973–988.
Lesthaeghe, R., & van de Kaa, D. (1986). Twee demografische transities? In *Groei en Krimp, Mens en Maatschappij* (pp. 9–24). Deventer: van Loghum Slaterus.
Manning, W., & Smock, P. (1995). Why marry? Race and the transition to marriage among cohabitors. *Demography, 32*, 509–520.
Manning, W., Brown, S. L., & Stykes, J. B. (2016). Same-sex and different-sex cohabiting couple relationship stability. *Demography, 53*(4), 937–953.
Myrskylä, M., Kohler, H.-P., & Billari, F. C. (2009). Advances in development reverse fertility declines. *Nature, 460*(7256), 741–743.
Myrskylä, M., Kohler, H.-P., & Billari, F. C. (2011). *High development and fertility: Fertility at older reproductive ages and gender equality explain the positive link* (MPIDR working paper WP-2011-017). Rostock: Max Planck Institute for Demographic Research.
Nazio, T., & Blossfeld, H.-P. (2003). The diffusion of cohabitation among young women in West Germany, East Germany and Italy. *European Journal of Population, 19*(1), 47–82.
O'Connell, M., & Feliz, S. (2011). Same-sex couple household statistics from the 2010 census.. US Bureau of the Census.
Pichardo, J. I. (2011). We are family (or not): Social and legal recognition of same-sex relationships and lesbian and gay families in Spain. *Sexualities, 14*(5), 544–561.
Steenhof, L., & Harmsen, C. (2004). Same-sex couples in the Netherlands. In M. Digoix & P. Festy (Eds.), *Same-sex couples, same-sex partnerships and homosexual marriages. A focus on cross-national differentials* (pp. 233–243). Ined: Document de travail 124.
Sundström, A., Paxton, P., Wang, Y.-T., & Lindberg, S. I. (2017). Women's political "empowerment": A new global index, 1900–2012. *World Development, 94*, 321–335.

Waaldijk, K. (2017). Introduction to the legal survey and its methods & Overview of the results from the legal survey & Conclusion. In K. Waaldijk (Ed.), *More and more together: Legal family formats for same-sex and different-sex couples in European countries – Comparative analysis of data in the LawsAndFamilies database*, (pp. 7–72, 151–181, FamiliesAndSocieties working paper 75(2017)).

Waaldijk, K., Digoix, M., Nikolina, N., Zago, G., Damonzé, D., Caporali, A., & Nait Abdellah, K. (Eds.). (2017). *The LawsAndFamilies database – Aspects of legal family formats for same-sex and different-sex couples*. Paris: INED. http://www.LawsAndFamilies.eu.

Chapter 4
Same-Sex Parents Negotiating the Law in Italy: Between Claims of Recognition and Practices of Exclusion

Marina Franchi and Giulia Selmi

Abstract Italy represents a particular case in the panorama of Southern Europe; it is going through a very crucial moment when issues of sexual politics are at the forefront of the political and societal debate. Against the backdrop of the plurality of ways in which individuals arrange their intimate lives, the increased visibility in the public and political sphere of LGBT issues, and the de-traditionalisation of gendered relations, we are witnessing a strong, at times violent heterosexist/conservative backlash. Against this background LGB individuals organise their intimate lives, make reproductive choices and develop strategies to protect themselves and their most vulnerable next of kin. Drawing on qualitative interviews with gay and lesbian couples in Italy this chapter aims to investigate the intersection between the context and the ways in which individuals in same-sex relationships organise their intimate lives. It highlights the impact of the law and the socio-cultural context on the intimate choices of individuals, but also contribute to the growing body of literature that complicates the assimilation/disruption dyad and caution against the translatability of notions of heteronormativity and homonormativity.

Keywords Intimate citizenship · Norms · Parenting · Heteronormativity · Familism

M. Franchi
London School of Economics, London, UK
e-mail: m.franchi@lse.ac.uk

G. Selmi (✉)
University of Verona, Verona, Italy
e-mail: giulia.selmi@univr.it

M. Digoix (ed.), *Same-Sex Families and Legal Recognition in Europe*, European Studies of Population 24, https://doi.org/10.1007/978-3-030-37054-1_4

4.1 Introduction

Familism and family matters are profoundly conservative cultural constructs that came to represent an internationally renowned trait of Italian culture. The centrality of the family has been incorporated into the Italian welfare regime where access to services and support, predicated on legally recognised kinship relationships, can be restricted to those who form care and support networks that are not legally recognized as family. Public and political discourses are occupied by a notion of the natural family fostered by Catholic Ideology and defended by political parties across the spectrum. Against this background, subsequent governments since the early 2000s routinely failed to approve laws that would provide legal recognition to same-sex unions. Only in February 2016, the Italian Senate approved the Cirinnà bill by an overwhelming majority. The law however excluded parents with no biological ties with their children from any recognition of parenting rights.

Such provision would have granted legal recognition to parents with no biological ties with their children. Within this scenario, LGBT individuals routinely negotiate the absence of legal recognition of their family, a task that becomes particularly costly in relation to parenting, since social parents are legally and socially invisible. Drawing on 29 in-depth interviews carried out with gay men and lesbian women aged between 20 and 60 years-old in five urban centres in Italy, this chapter analyses how respondents account for their experiences of parenting and analyses the practices enacted to be recognized as a family. In the context of the tensions that characterise contemporary Italy such practises carry a hefty symbolic and material costs. Does the absence of norms is conducive to opening a space for queering the family heteronormative ideal? Or, on the contrary, this void forces gay and lesbian couples to perform the heteronormative script in order to fully access citizenship rights?

4.2 The Long (and Incomplete) Road to Equality: LGBT Rights in the Italian Context

In order to make sense of the narratives that are analysed in the following sections, here we delineate the background against which the interviews have been collected, and sketch the social and legislative status quo that affected the interviewees' experiences. At the moment of conducting the interviews the Italian legislative system was still lacking any legal recognition for forms of unions other than heterosexual marriage and any law aimed at tackling homophobic violence, despite the continuous warnings of the European Union and the pressure of many groups and LGBT rights advocates. Approving a law has been, for subsequent governments since the years 2000s, a challenging political endeavour. During the Prodi II Government (2006–2008) two different bills reached the parliamentary vote in less than 6 months; the DICO bill (February 2007) and the CUS bill (July 2007). Both bills were supposed *to regulate* the relationship between two cohabiting adults.

Both bills have been fiercely opposed by conservative politicians and religious hierarchies that perceived the legal recognition of same-sex couples as a threat to the 'natural family'. LGBT advocates, on the other hand, criticised both bills for being a weak recognition of rights. Both texts, in fact, posed serious constraints to the legal effects of the partnership they aimed to regulate, in order to emphasise its status as different from marriage. Neither the DICO bill nor the CUS bill ever became laws. For a long time after the demise of the Prodi II Government, the issue of de facto unions was kept off the political agenda. In September 2008, Berlusconi's government drafted a bill entitled *Disciplina dei diritti e dei doveri di reciprocità dei conviventi* (DidoRe — 'Regulation of the rights and duties of reciprocity on the part of cohabitees'). The bill never passed the barrier of the Justice Commission of the Chambers of Deputies (Donà 2009: 343–344). Following the resignation of Berlusconi in 2011, the issue of the facto unions was again pushed out of the political agenda. Whilst it being a very contentious topic across parties, sexual citizenship rights were often framed as dangerous to the stability of governments as well as less of a priority in view of the ongoing economic crisis (Crowhurst and Bertone 2012: 416). The Renzi administration, supported by a very diverse coalition of parties, in power from February 2014 to December 2016, had been willing to reopen the discussion. Only in March 2015 the Justice Commission of the Senate reached a final agreement on a text on civil unions (the so-called *Cirinnà bill*, named after the first signer) aiming at legally recognising same-sex couples. The bill has been approved in May 2016 and finally became law.

The approval of the Cirinnà law has been defined by some as a milestone in the legal recognition of LGB couples in Italy. Others, however, define it as a watered-down recognition of rights (Mancina and Vassallo 2016), that emerged from a set of compromises within different groups of the Government majority. A central point of contention has been the legal recognition of parenting rights. In its original version the bill incorporated a provision that would allow social parents to be legally recognised. Right before the vote at the Senate, however, on February 26th following the *Five Star Movement's* withdrawal of support, the Prime Minister Renzi stripped the step-child adoption from the bill allegedly as a move to gain a solid majority and grant its full approval. The provision would have granted the right to adopt the children of one's partner to LG partners legally recognised under the new law. During the months that preceded the approval of the *Cirinnà Law* same-sex parenting rights became the forefront of the political and societal debate.

Public spaces were increasingly occupied by conservative Catholic Associations such as the *Sentinelle in Piedi* (Standing Sentinels) arguing that the recognition of same-sex couples and in particular their parenting rights was a threat against a 'natural order' (Garbagnoli 2014) that was particularly threatened by the 'marketisation of life' in relation to surrogacy. The debate was punctuated by references to biology, blood ties and the 'natural family' (Lasio and Serri 2017) hence reaffirming heterosexuality as the one and only prerequisite to (good) parenting. Societal anxiety around non-heterosexual parenting is not restricted to the Italian context (see also Butler 2002, Fassin 2001) and it is often evoked through the discursive trope of the wellbeing of the child that is constructed as impaired by the lack of complementary gender roles (Saraceno 2012).

At the core of these groups' protests was a fierce attack to what they termed *l'ideologia del gender* (the ideology of gender) and *la teoria del gender* (the theory of gender) an umbrella term defining any feminist and LGBTQ claim ranging from anti-bulling and anti-discrimination educational programs to gender equality and reproductive rights (Selmi 2015, Garbagnoli and Prearo 2018). Their argument is informed by a determinist understanding of gender, sexuality and family. Anti-discrimination policies are here understood as tools for undermining the primacy of heterosexuality as the premise for full citizenship rights.

Such a premise is also protected by a relentless opposition to any bill recognising homophobia as an aggravating circumstance in hate crimes. Conservative groups and part of the Catholic Church denounced any attempts to legislate against homophobic hate crimes as acts against free speech and frame them as attacks on the Catholic Church itself and on far right-wing groups and parties. Subsequent drafts have also been strongly criticised by representatives of LGBT groups, who questioned their efficacy in tackling institutional homophobia and the impunity of politicians and religious representatives. In particular, a draft presented in 2013 included an amendment proposed by Gregorio Gitti (PD-*Partito Democratico*) which stated that the definition of hate speech cannot be applied to opinions expressed within political parties or religious, cultural, and educational institutions de facto emptying the bill of its transformative power.

In opposition to the actions of a conservative part of the Italian society, local and regional governments have been at the forefront of implementing inclusive, non-discriminatory good practice, as well as creating a space for action and advocacy, especially at the time of collecting the interviews. For instance, local government created registries that granted some recognition to forms of unions in the form of cohabitation registries, way before the approval of the Cirinnà law in 2016. In over a hundred local governments in Italy, such registries were open to both heterosexual and same-sex couples and granted access to housing benefits and locally regulated services such as childcare and health care. While these provisions had no effect at the national level and outside the borders of the constituencies, municipalities and regional governments have been central to fostering cultural change that contributed to the creation of the conditions for the national law to be approved.

Following the approval of the Cirinnà law local authorities have been playing a particularly crucial role in the battle for the recognition of parental rights. The majors of many cities (i.e. Turin, Bologna, Milan, Palermo, Naples, etc.) are transcribing the birth certificates of the children born abroad by same sex parents; and since 2018 they are re-issuing the birth certificate of children born in Italy from same sex couples adding the name of the parent without biological bonds with the child in order to grant them full rights. Together with a series of rulings on *stepchild adoption* issued by several juvenile courts since 2014 (Farina 2017), local authorities are playing a key role in filling the equality gap between straight and same-sex parents and in fostering change toward the full recognition of sexual citizenship rights to LGBT couples and individuals.

Italy, then, appears to be characterised by an ambivalent attitude toward LGBT rights (Trappolin 2009): on one hand, public attitudes towards LGBT families and couples are changing (ISTAT 2012), on the other, the inclination towards denial of LGBT experiences (Bertone 2009a) is still persistent, and non-heterosexual life are routinely marginalised. In this context the legal recognition of sexual rights keeps being a difficult and tortuous path.

4.3 The Discrete Scent of 'Family': Changes and Resistance to a Social Model

The Italian public sphere is characterised by a peculiar resistance to "allowing discursive space even for a homonormative (Duggan 2003), familialised subject, despite the attempts made in this direction by LGBT movements" (Bertone and Gusmano 2013: 261–262). It is against this context that normativity and resistance become blurred concepts that need to be carefully unravelled. In a scenario were LGBT families are increasingly participating in public debates and claiming recognition from the State, marriage and the family appear to retain the high symbolic value that has characterised Italy's modernity (Rosina and Viazzo 2008; Ruspini 2005), and the hegemonic norm of the nuclear family remains incredibly strong (Ruspini 2009; Bertone 2009b).

In the context of Italy as elsewhere, claims for recognition of partnership, parenting and inclusion in the welfare state can be interpreted as having the power to produce and transform circulating meanings regarding family, sexuality, kinship and rights (Plummer 2003). The shift of discourses and practices from the political margins to the centre has often been defined as destabilising and potentially generative of new meanings. In particular in the West, the claims for recognition of the LGBT movements in the past decades has been interpreted as reconfiguring notion of belonging to the community of citizens (Weeks et al. 2001; Weeks 1998).

However, the claims for legally recognised relationships and parenting rights have also been interpreted as overlooking the normalising power of state recognition (Butler 2002). In the recognition of relationship and parental rights, it has been argued, lies the exclusion of forms of parenting and relationships that evade the monogamous, dyadic family form. The recognition of lesbian and gay rights has hence been interpreted as revealing how, while heterosexuality might in specific instances no longer be a *sine qua non* requirement for the recognition of rights, "heterosexuality has not yet been displaced as the reference point for "equality" and "normality"" but is maintained as the norm that polices the boundaries of belonging and exclusion (Richardson and Monro 2012: 65).

A similar tension with regard to the normalising power of individuals' context can also be traced in the sociological theories of late modernity. Within a sociological framework, theories of de-traditionalisation and transformations of intimacies such as Giddens' (1992), and Beck and Beck-Gernsheim's (1995), explored how interpersonal exchanges and kin formation develops in contemporary society once the functionalist traditional model declined and produced a "wholesale democratization of the interpersonal domain" (Giddens 1992: 3). Within this frame, great emphasis is placed on the way in which late modernity is characterised by a displacement of traditional ties and an emphasis on individual choice thus fundamentally reshaping the societal landscape (Beck and Beck-Gernsheim 1995; Giddens 1992).

This post – familial family (Beck-Gernsheim 1998: 70) is constructed around elective ties and it is understood as creative and self-determined both in terms of the constitution of kin networks and of emotional and relationship rules. Relationships therefore are imagined here free from societal and structural constraints and individuals are thought as able to negotiate their needs and desire free from power relationships. In this understanding, gay men and lesbian women have been defined as pioneers of 'pure relationships', which individuals enter on equal terms and which might end when those individuals' needs are no longer met (Giddens 1992).

These understandings have been met with scepticism by many scholars (Gabb 2008). In fact such theories appear to not take into due consideration how gendered politics of care continue to generate constraints (Skeggs 2004). Further, they do not account for the ways in which gender (Jamieson 1998) class (Skeggs 2004) sexuality and ethnicity (Hey 2005) place ongoing constraints on the possibilities of the self as a 'reflexive project'. At the level of the analysis of norms, it is also important not to overlook the hegemonic power of the ideal of the monogamous, generative couple sustained by the ideal notion of romantic love. Theories of detraditionalisation and individualisation also keep the couple (even if democratic, dialogic and equal) as the main reference for the development of an intimate life project. As Gross argues the couple is still a 'guiding cultural ideal' that permeates much of the Western societies. As such it invests also those LGBT communities that while in opposition with the heteronormative model still cannot escape it. As a normative ideal it remains a point of departure for any relationship narrative where the couple is the only suitable, desirable, thinkable project. In unveiling the hegemonic hold of the ideal of the couple in Contemporary America, Gross not only questions the potential of de-traditionalisation but also highlights the resilience of patriarchal beliefs and practices (Gross 2005: 297–301). As Gabb (2008) points out, families remain the norm of the structural framework of our private lives. The increasingly visible LGBT families "rather than destabilizing normative models testify the power of familial ideology in representing the family as the best ways to live our lives" (2008: 16). Families are therefore expected to conform to a two-parents model that remains the condition for recognition of same-sex parenting (Roseneil et al. 2013: 18).

It is however always necessary to take into consideration that normative power and destabilising forces are always dependent on the context. Roisin Ryan-Flood in her work on lesbian motherhood explores the reproductive choices among lesbian women in Sweden and in Ireland (2005). She argues that the "way in which lesbian parents in the two countries reinvent and reinscribe prevailing discourses of the family according to their own situatedness as social and cultural actors highlights the significance of context to understandings of lesbian parent experiences, possibilities, and constraints" (2005:190). In so doing Ryan-Flood warns about the crucial role structural constraints and societal values play in shaping the very definition of normative/hegemonic and disruptive power (2005).

4.4 Methodology and Sample

In this paper, we draw on 29 in-depth interviews focusing on the daily life experiences of gay and lesbian couples and parents. We conducted the interviews between October 2014 and 2015 before the Cirinnà law was approved with gay men and lesbian women that described themselves as in a long-term relationship. Twenty-two were individual interviews with one member of the couple, while seven were performed with both members.

Three cities in the Centre-North and three cities in the Centre-South were selected to carry out the research. Alongside the socio-cultural differences in terms of family values and ties between north and south, the six urban contexts where selected due to their different features in terms of local policies on LGBT families and individuals inclusion (i.e. city register of same-sex partnership, policies against discrimination, etc.) and the different degrees of relevance of the local LGBT movements (i.e. number of associations, advocacy programmes with the local government, etc.). The spectrum of policies represented in our sample, allowed to gather different life experiences in relation to the social context individuals live in. Within these six cities, participants were selected through a snowball sampling technique thanks both to personal contacts and the network of Italian LGBT associations that were asked for support to recruit participants.

On the whole we interviewed 13 men and 22 women. The youngest respondent in the group was 22 years old, while the oldest was 62. While we aimed to have an even distribution in term of age, in the sample those who are around or over 40 years old are overrepresented. This is a direct consequence of the focus of the research that aimed at collecting stories of people dealing with family issues (housing, planning parenthood, childcare, elderly care, etcetera) and hence conditioned the age of the participants. For instance, in Italy the average age when one becomes a parent is higher than the rest of Europe, and more so for people in a same-sex relationship.

At the time of the interviews, thirteen participants were parents or were expecting a child, while two were going through ART in order to conceive. Seven women had (or were having) children within a same-sex relationship (six through ART and one through self-insemination), while three women had children conceived while in a previous heterosexual relationship. Two men had children while in a previous heterosexual relationship, one gay couple had children through surrogacy and another one was fostering.

Interviews lasted on average between 1 hour and 1.5 hours and were transcribed verbatim. The interview script began with a generative question on the couple/family story in order to encourage the participants' storytelling (Riessman 2008). Then *ad hoc* questions were added to encourage further discussion about processes of visibility and identity negotiation in the circle of family and acquaintances as well as in the social context. We included also questions on the encounter with the public sphere (i.e. public services, institutions); and our informants' experiences of discrimination and homophobia. For the purpose of this chapter, we will draw particularly on the interviews collected with parents or prospective parents. The reason is twofold: first, the legal situation of same sex parents has not changed after the approval of the Cirinnà law, therefore the narratives we collected back then still mirror the actual challenges of gay and lesbian parents and their children; second, same-sex parenting epitomizes the tensions between the on-going change in family and kinship configurations and the endurance of heteronormative family models (Bertone 2015).

4.5 Navigating Heteronormativity in Contemporary Italy

One key feature of narratives is the uniqueness and the peculiarity of each story that refers to a specific subject in a situated context (Bruner 1996). However, even if every story is unique and peculiar, personal narratives are performed through and in relation to public narratives (Somers and Gibson 1994) or cultural repertoires. Social actors can embrace or challenge such tropes by contributing to their transformation and the construction of new stories (Plummer 1995). While heteronormativity is a "fundamental organizing principle throughout the social order" (Green [2002, 521], quoted in Gamson and Moon [2004, 48]), it is also the social and symbolic repertoire available to individuals to shape both their subjectivities and their public identities (Rosenfeld 2009). The analysis of the narratives collected therefore can open up a space for understanding how heteronormative discourses "are both subverted and reinscribed" (Ryan-Flood 2005: 201). We will explore the interviews collected first to grasp how and to what extent these narratives challenge or *queer* the notion of couple and family; second to explore the relationship between these narratives and the specific societal and legal Italian context.

4.5.1 Forcing the Boundaries of Heteronormative Kinship

As Ahmed points out on her notion of discomfort of queer families and couples, the point is "not about assimilation or resistance, but about inhabiting norms differently" (Ahmed 2004: 155). Some of our respondents' stories offer a space for redefining or, better, for forcing the boundaries of heteronormativity and for building new meanings able to account for their specific experiences. In doing so they challenge the notion of family trying to carve out space for their experiences (Franchi and Selmi 2018). In the accounts of some respondents the notions of coupledom, family and kinship are challenged through language. By trying to qualify their intimate relationships, interviewees creatively re-work the traditional *meanings* of the family to widen them and to make room for their experience (Gabb 2005). The family (and what follows in terms of heteronormativity, gender roles, etcetera) remains a cultural reference, but the narrative of the interviewees allows some shifts of meaning. For example, Gaia describes as *non-familial* the relationship they (her, her partner and the donor friend) want to create and as a 'non-paternity relationship' the one she and her partner envisage between their future child and the donor.

> G: Then we identify a donor, a friend that for various reasons was perfect and was willing to be part of the reproductive process but also was willing to gamble with us on the possibility of forms of non familial relationships, but sentimental relationships…i don't know how to explain it… he was, in principle at least, willing to create a relation of non-paternity with the newborn…
>
> R: What do you mean by non paternity?
>
> G: Not being a father from the legal point of view, hence not recognising (legally, the child), not taking on him the duties and honours of the role, and then being a male figure in the emotive universe of the boy or the girl that though does not imply being a father. Now like… I am going to say the nearest thing I can imagine in my stereotyped universe, like an uncle, but then he might not be an uncle and we might want to call thingumabob and it means whatever will grow out of (the interaction) between the two of them… (Gaia, 41)

A similar situation occurs in the story of Stefano and his partner, a gay foster couple.

> We do not feel the necessity to introduce ourselves… we arrive, that is what we are. Me and him, me, him and the boy […] My partner once said to a guy who lived next door and wanted to visit us: "Yes, I will be delighted (if you visit us), so you will meet my family, my (male) partner and our *affiglio*" we coined this term affiglio, that comes from *affido* (foster) and *figlio* (son). (Stefano, 49)

Stefano explicitly uses language to challenge their invisibility. By using the word '*affiglio*' Stefano challenges the trope of "as if we were a couple and parents like the others" (Cadoret 2008) and forces the boundaries of kinship to make room for their specific intimate relationships. A similar naming practices is narrated by Chiara while describing the way her two children call her and her partner:

> They call me mamma obviously. In a very spontaneous way, because I am always here…. I live here… and consequently… mamma… they also call me babba…. This is something I am really proud of… it happened because of a bad cold they caught last winter… They could not say mamma… it came out as babba. I loved it so much that I insisted on babba and now when they have to distinguish us they say mamma and babba… I think that babba really breaks every prejudice… (Chiara, 40)

'*Babbo*' is a regional variant of '*papà* (father)', here the word is re-gendered to accommodate Chiara as social mother. In a context that not only excludes parenting from legal recognition but also vociferously denies their very existence in the public sphere, the practices of naming and defining appear central in the narratives of some of the families and families-to-be. These narratives do not displace dyadic and differentiated form of parenting but do challenge the boundaries of kinship lexicon impacting a societal discourse that exclude them.

4.5.2 Love Is All You Need?

In other respondent's stories, mutual love and commitment emerge as key symbolic resources to account for their experience and define themselves as 'legitimate' families. Emblematic is the story of Enrica who at the time of the interview had been with her partner Roberta for 9 and a half years, got married in a North European Country 2 years before and had two children. As in many other narratives, the story of their couple and their family develops as a sequence of events that *naturally* arises from love, passes through cohabitation and finds their successful completion in the birth of their two children. The way Enrica narrates the couple's decision of becoming mothers is particularly interesting:

> E: After few time she expressed the wish to have children. For what concerns me.... Actually it wasn't an existential need, I never felt I would have been incomplete as a woman if I wouldn't have had children. Neither did she, however something resounded inside her. She always tells me that she thinks I am the person that made her feel capable to carry on such a life project. Honestly, I would have never had children with anyone else.
>
> R: Why you say that?
>
> E: I have many girlfriends that at some point felt the need to becoming mothers, and this is totally respectable. But for me it was a project... something that grew with her and even if I had many relationships before, this idea (of having children) never arose before. I like her as a mother, as a parent, how we are able to combine each other with our very different characteristics...and our children are the way in which we reaped the fruits of our love. (Enrica, 44)

Enrica's narrative of the decisions that lead to her and her partner's pregnancies resonates profoundly with the 'self-reflective' project ideal (Giddens 1992) that is envisaged as free of constraints and presents itself as rejecting any gendered expectations. She has a twofold trajectory in her story: on one side, she explicitly positions her parenting project out of the traditional and naturalizing narrative of procreative female roles and underlines twice that she doesn't feel that having children is what defines her identity as a woman. On the other, the ideal of the modern democratic monogamous couple defined by *love* is dominant in her narrative. The refusal of a normative gendered role is counterbalanced by the love that becomes generative of both the desire to have children and the act of having children. In doing so however, her narrative still maintains *procreation* as the ultimate goal of the monogamous couple. A couple that she narrates following the script of complementary roles.

> We are really interchangeable... but for reasons that have to do with our personalities. I am much more 'homely' and Roberta is much more 'outdoorsy'. She is always outdoor, on the bike, running... and eventually, we realised that the children ended up identifying a Mother Home and a Mother Play... I am more Mother Home and Roberta is more Mother Play... even though the girls stay home also with Roberta and play also with me the one they get really crazy with is Roberta... And with me... I don't know, we bake cakes together, biscuits for Christmas, we decorate the Christmas tree... but for instance, we both help Mirella with her homework... since I work from home more often, I am more... maybe I do the daily shopping. Also, I love cooking, so it is natural for me to take care of lunches and

dinners. However, on Sunday night is usually Roberta who cooks dinner… she cooks crêpes for everyone and… and that is the exception to the rule… we eat while watching a movie…. (Enrica, 44)

The 'mother-home' vs. 'mother-play' narrative resonates with a differentiation between a caring homely role and a more social outdoor role but in doing so disrupts its gendered assumptions. Enrica explains the division of roles within the parenting couple as the results of an organic encounter between hers and her partner's 'natural' inclinations and the children's desires. Gay and lesbian couples challenge *de facto* the assumptions that sexual complementarity mirrors sentimental complementarity and, above all, generative complementarity that guides traditional notions of couple and kinship (Cadoret 2008). Enrica's narrative, however, is tied to the heteronormative repertoire of a difference (between the partners) that is essentials to meet the children's need. As in Ryan-Flood's analysis, also in the case of our interviewees, we can see a tension whereby lesbian mothers seek to both repudiate and affirm heteronormative discourses that generate from their location and contexts and "are both constituted through and resisting of particular narratives of kinship" (2005: 201).

The tension between constitution and resistance is clear also in Enrica's discussion about both pregnancies, the role of the sperm donor and the subsequent negotiation of his parental roles. Enrica and his wife choose a friend as sperm donor, who was unwilling to play a parental role within the life of the newborns. While he pays yearly visits, he does not have any parent-like or relative-like relationship with their daughters.

We knew we did not want a project shared by four people. We always wanted to be the two mothers of our two children. [...] At one point we had this desire to… it became a really strong desire to not leave Mirella alone! We liked the idea of a brother or a sister for her [...] this time… I mean the second time I tried and I got pregnant really fast. (Enrica, 44)

He was the donor for both pregnancies as a way to create a biological connection between siblings. In this decision, it is possible to trace a tension between the desire to conform to a normative/biologically informed ideal of the family and the desire to disrupt the dominance of blood ties. Enrica's narrative does not contemplate alternatives to the dual parenting couple but, at the same time, acknowledges that there is the possibility of a 'natural' desires of their children to know their biological roots. Hence the decision for a known donor. The biological/natural trope became central in Enrica's narrative around the use of a single sperm donor for both pregnancies. Somehow the biological link, subverted in the case of the parenting relationship, is maintained to solidify the relationship between siblings. In Enrica's narration of the decisions that led to the second pregnancy, it is possible, once again, to see the dominance of the trope of love free of constraints. Enrica refers to the 'child interest'. In her narrative is central the desire not to leave their first child alone but there is no explicit reference to her position with regard to Roberta, the legally recognised parent of their first daughter. While this is acknowledged later, it is not expressed as the reason why a second pregnancy was planned. The dominance of a narrative organised around love does not leave space for acknowledging power dynamics in the dyadic couple- and in particular how the lack of legal recognition can impact the relationship. The *family* is narrated as a harmonious, conflict-free realm. By mobilising heteronormative narratives Enrica displays normativity as a desirable/comfortable place to be (Ahmed 2004: 147). Enrica's narrative is shared by other participants that equally construct the parenting project as connected to love and the fulfilment of the couple.

Unlike Enrica, Benedetta put forward a different narrative; while still relying on tropes of love and monogamous coupledom, her narrative underlines several times the problematic features of this process. A social mother-to-be, Benedetta is also thinking about getting pregnant herself, after her partner, but her narrative does not revolve around the desire to give birth as a woman nor around the desire to complete/complement the couple-project.

> Because I intend to... next summer maybe...or maybe next autumn.. to try but... but I really do not have this pregnancy thing... I'd do it only to create a familial bond on both sides. Between me and the child my partner is carrying and between her and a child I could potentially carry ... so that... I mean, I do not know... I fantasise that this will prevent a possible break-up... what I mean is [it will prevent that one of us is] stronger than the other. But I mean... unfortunately when you are 40... because I had relationships before her, really committed relationships that I never thought would ever end... even now that they are over I realise how I imagined them to last forever. (Benedetta, 38)

Central to Benedetta's narrative is the need to solidify the ties among her, her partner and their future child by complicating them, legally and emotionally. In Benedetta's narrative, the complexities of the parenting project and the lack of legal recognition to parenting are revealed and made explicit. A space is created to complicate the trope of *love until death do us part.* In so doing the power dynamics between the parent who is legally recognised and the one who isn't and their families of origin are also recognised. In the above, the impact of social and legal structures became apparent and difficult to escape, as it becomes evident how they might shape or have shaped the decisions of our respondents.

4.5.3 The Context-Dependent Challenge of Heteronormativity: The Role of Legal Constraints

The narratives analysed so far highlighted the tension between the comfort and discomfort with the heteronormative script and the ways families negotiate dominant meanings of family and coupledom. As discussed above, the Italian context is dominated not only by the trope of the 'natural family' in public discourses, but also by the absence of legal recognition. Besides the absence of recognition of the social parents, access to ART is denied to single women and lesbian couples, surrogacy is prohibited, and adoption is open to married heterosexual couples only. These legal constraints force LGB couples to travel abroad in order to conceive their children.

Lack of a legal framework for same-sex parents, therefore, influences the range of material options available to gay and lesbian couples as Silvia points out:

> I don't want to run the risk that, at some point, someone shows up and says "Since we are genetically tied, he is my son" … The Italian law allows this. (...) This means that even a (donor) friend is risky. If we had a legal recognition of parenting rights, I would not have had any problem (...) but as it is not so, it is way too risky, especially for the parent that is not legally recognised. (Silvia, 41)

The choice of recurring to ART abroad with an unknown donor and to retain the parental roles within the lesbian couple rather than an act of conforming to the dyadic heteronormative model of parenting and coupledom is here framed a 'bounded choice' resulting from the lack of sexual citizenship rights. In reading these narratives it is crucial to reflect on the constraints of the context in which they are produced and reflect on the role the heteronormative script plays in granting LG couples' cultural intelligibility (Butler 1990).

Cultural intelligibility is a disciplinary regime that strictly defines the symbolic resources available to individuals to perform their identity and a normative framework that defines the social field where identities can have a legitimate expression. Such a framework conditions who can be considered as a legitimate (and recognizable) subject. The necessity of being culturally intelligible becomes crucial when advancing claims for legal recognition of parenting rights to juvenile law courts. As discussed above, given the absence of a national law, Italian same-sex parents have appealed to law courts since 2015 to be granted parenting rights:

> The lawyer explained to me that (the result of the claim) really depends upon which Court (will examine your case), however, even in the case of a court willing to examine your case (of a step-child adoption) you have to demonstrate that your cohabitation dates back five, six years, that the child recognise you as… that he or she spent (with you) Christmas, the summer holidays (…) so, if in five, six years there still won't be a law, then we can try the step-child adoption, in the meantime we collect Christmas Cards, letters, home movies, as other couples told me (they are doing)… (Gaia, 41)

Christmas cards, home movies, and proof of a stable cohabitation materialise the couple's cultural intelligibility and become markers of a familial project worthy of recognition. The strategies of the Rainbow Families movement resonate in Gaia's narrative as the possibility to strategically adhere to normativity in order to pursue one's aim. As Benedetta discusses, this strategy is a response to the precariousness of the process of recognition. At the time of the interview, only one couple had been successfully through the process of step-child adoption; while at the time of writing several couples have been successfully through it, the process of scrutiny by Juvenile courts remains the same. Successful outcomes are framed as linked to the ability to demonstrate, during the trial, the couple stability, cohabitation and parenting long-term project as key prerequisite to be recognised as a 'good' (and worthy of recognition) family:

> Because the deal is this… there is no blueprint, they are making it up… the Rainbow Families association is helping us by saying that, statistically, it works to collect as many documents as possible [demonstrating] the existence of a shared familial project… from the pictures in the labour unit… in the clinic… both signatures [should appear] on every document. We both signed every document. When he will be born… for the nursery [the association suggests] that we ask to be both included in every documents. Because the only couple that managed… we are talking only about one sentence that might eventually be challenged… the couple followed this path… *the consolidamento familiare* (family stabilisation)... And they demonstrated the familial project, the family, the affective and economic ties… within the couple and between the non-biological mother and her daughter. (Benedetta, 38)

Requests for the legal recognition of same-sex couples, whether in the form of gay marriage or same-sex partnership, have been criticised as upholding values that replicate the discursive structures that reifies heterosexual family and kinship (Butler 2002: 21). The legal recognition of same-sex couples, as well as the debate on gay marriage, are framed as shifting the boundaries of acceptance to the stable monogamous couple, reaffirming the exclusion of queer sexualities (Butler 2002: 17; Bell and Binnie 2000). The forms of kinship that remain unnamed or do not respond to the possibility of legitimation, become in turn unintelligible (Butler 2000, 2002). The process of legitimation is in the State's own terms and to agree to it requires to abide by its lexicon and norms. However, cultural intelligibility has very material consequences in contemporary Italy. Not to participate in it comes at a cost of not being legally recognised in a context characterised by a strong familial welfare. Within this framework, gathering 'evidences' of being a 'proper family' rather than being defined as an homonormative move that solidify dominant discourses on family and kinship, could be interpreted as a 'contextual challenge to heteronormativity' (Ryan-flood 2005) that strategically manipulates the cultural and social resources available in order to claim citizenship rights.

4.6 Conclusion

LGB parents in Italy negotiate a societal context that, while more accepting of same-sex relationships (ISTAT 2012), keeps considering same sex parents unthinkable (Lingiardi 2013). The unthinkability of LGB parents, it has been argued, derives from a perceived misalignment of gender, generativity and parenting (Ferrari 2015) and is then reflected on and amplified by the lack of full access to citizenship rights. As discussed in the introduction, while a law has now recognised partnership rights, parenting rights are still denied to the parent who has no biological bond with the child(ren), a law on homophobia as aggravating circumstance in hate crimes is still missing, and access to ART is denied to lesbian couples and single women. Moreover, Italy is currently experiencing a strong backlash against minoritized groups. The frequent attacks on women and LGBT rights are exposing families that do not conform to the heteronorm, to homophobic violence in the public sphere

(Garbagnoli and Prearo 2018). Against the discursive violence of right wing politics and part of the Catholic Church, however, an increasing number of court cases have been recognising parenting rights to non-biological parents, de facto bypassing the Government's lack of action.

In this conflicting scenario, characterised by increasing institutional homophobia as well as support from the judicial power, gay men and lesbian women organise their intimate lives and manipulate the limits and resources of the Italian context. As the analysis conducted above has shown interviewees employ a set of different strategies to account for their familial and kinship relationships and to have those recognised by society.

These strategies sit often in an ambivalent space that both challenges and reifies the couple norm and the heteronormative model of kinship construction. Naming practices acknowledge roles that are not contemplated in public discourses such as that of a donor, a social mother, or a foster parent. On one side, gay and lesbian parents manipulate the lexicon of heteronormative kinship and in so doing they performatively create a new set of words that contribute to making a lesbian mother or a gay father as thinkable. On the other side, however, the lexicon of heterosexual kinship is hard to be displaced; even those experiences that aim to challenge the heterosexual family structure continue to use it as their reference point. Challenges to the dyadic couple still allude to a conventional family lexicon to define the affective and caring relationships that different adults might have with a child. Similarly, the trope of love and complementary care roles resound in our respondents' narratives. The dyadic parenting couple is rarely questioned as the starting point of parenting and love – conflict and power-free – is evoked as the generative device of the family.

At this stage, however, the tension between normativity and disruption appears to be an insufficient framework to account for the interviewees' experiences. From a certain perspective they seem to adhere to a homonormative ideal of coupledom and parenting that reproduces traditional kinship models and ideals. However, once we take into account the Italian context, these narratives reveal a strategic adherence to norms. They unravel how hegemonic norms govern cultural intelligibility of couple and kinship relationships. In a context of lack of basic parental rights and conservative beliefs around gender, sexuality and the family, adherence to the narrative of a 'proper' family appears to be strategic. In fact, it can be a way to gain access to social recognition and as in the case of court hearings, to legal recognition of one's parenting rights.

As some narratives showed, families seem to perform a strategic use of the heteronormative repertoire in order to challenge the material legal constraints and claim for sexual citizenship rights. In light of the collected narratives, we suggest thinking beyond the dichotomy of assimilation or resistance to heteronormativity and homonormativity and instead paying attention to the multiple and varied ways in which gay and lesbian parents' strategically manipulate the norms that are excluding them.

Appendixes

Appendix 1: Participants

	Pseudonym	Sex	Age	Couple Status	Parental Status	Geography
1	Carlo	Male	46	LAT	No children	North - City
2	Gaia	Female	41	Cohabitation	Going through ART at the time of the interview	North - City
3	Alessandra	Female	36	Cohabitation	No children	North - City
4	Silvia	Female	40	Cohabitation	No children	North - City
5	Lara	Female	36	Cohabitation	No children	North - City
6	Cristina	Female	51	Cohabitation	1 child, previous heterosexual relationship	North - City
7	Ernesto	Male	60	Cohabitation	2 children, through surrogacy	North - City
8	Marco	Male	40	Cohabitation	No children	North - City
9	Enrica	Female	44	Cohabitation	2 children, through self-insemination	North - City
10	Silvio	Male	62	Cohabitation	No children	North - City
11	Maurizio	Male	52	Cohabitation	2 children, previous heterosexual relationship	North - City
12	Daniele	Female	45	Cohabitation	No children	South - City
13	Andrea	Female	43			
14	Giorgia	Female	38	Cohabitation	1 child through ART	South - City
15	Tiziana	Female	36			
16	Flavia	Female	60	Cohabitation	2 children, previous hetero relation	South - City
17	Anna	Female	46	Cohabitation	No children	South - City
18	Irene	Female	22	LAT	No children	South - City
19	Francesco	Male	32	Cohabitation	No children	South - City
20	Domenico	Male	46	LAT	No children	South - City
21	Giorgio	Male	28	Cohabitation	No children	South - City
22	Benedetta	Female	38	LAT	Her partner was pregnant at the moment of interview	South - City
23	Maria	Female	34	Cohabitation	Going through ART at the time of the interview	North - City
24	Elisabetta	Female	34			
25	Amanda	Female	38	Cohabitation	1 child through ART	North - City
26	Isabella	Female	37			
27	Serena	Female	36	Cohabitation	Pregnant at the moment of interview	North - City
28	Donatella	Female	46	LAT	2 children, previous heterosexual relationship	North - City
29	Chiara	Female	40	Cohabitation	2 children through ART	North - City
30	Valeria	Female	40			

(continued)

	Pseudonym	Sex	Age	Couple Status	Parental Status	Geography
31	Tommaso	Male	45	Cohabitation	2 children, previous heterosexual relationship	South - City
32	Elia	Male	55			
33	Riccardo	Male	59	Cohabitation	No children	South - City
34	Luigi	Male	54			
35	Stefano	Male	49	Cohabitation	1 child in foster care	South - City
36	Fulvio	Male	56	Cohabitation	No children	North - City

Appendix 2: Interview Outline

After the first generative question, all others were asked only if the interviewee(s) didn't mention the theme autonomously.

Generative Question

Can you tell me the story of your current relationship?
(explore both genealogy and actual situation)

SECTION 1 – VISIBILITY

1. Are there contexts where you are not visible as partnered in a same sex relationship? (i.e. work, university, family of origin, friends, landlord, etcetera). If yes, can you tell me in which ones and why? Is it a joint choice with your partner or not? How do you manage it?
2. Concerning the family of origin:
   - Can you tell me about the last family celebration?
3. Concerning the workplace:
   - Do you take part in work events when partners are invited?
   - Do you usually tell colleagues about your holidays?
   - Do you have pictures of your partner and/ or your children on your desk/ at the workplace?
4. Have you ever been discriminated against for being in a same-sex relationship?
   - If yes, can you tell me what happened?

5. Do you think that being visible in a same-sex relationship exposes you differently to discrimination or homophobia?

SECTION 2 – COUPLE AND MARRIAGE

6. Have you symbolically celebrated your union? (i.e. a ritual, a party, etcetera)
    - If yes, can you tell me how it went? Were your families of origin invited and/or involved in the organization?
    - If no, do you think you will celebrate one day? How do you wish it will be?
7. Do you think that the legal recognition of your union will change your daily life?
    - If yes, how? If no, why? (investigate both the symbolic level – as the public recognition – and the material level – as the taxation, access to public services, etcetera.)
8. Which legal form should this recognition have? (i.e equal marriage, civil unions, registered partnership, etcetera). Why it should have this specific form of recognition?
9. Do you think that the legal recognition of same-sex unions would counteract homophobia and discrimination?
10. Do you think that a law against homophobia would change the quality and safety of your life? How?
    - Which rights should the law protect?
    - If no, why it wouldn't change it?

SECTION 3 – CHILDREN AND FAMILY LIFE.

11. How many children do you have? How old are they?
12. How and when did you decide to have children? *[for those interviewees who have (or are having) children within the couple]*
13. How did you decide to have children? (i.e. ART, self-insemination, surrogacy, adoption, co-parenting, etcetera).
    - Why did you choose this way over others?
    - Did you tell your family of origin about the decision of having children? Did it change your relationship with them? If yes, how?
14. What changed in your life when you became a parent? Explore the relationship with the families of origin, the workplace (parental leave, visibility, work-life balance) and within the couple (negotiation of care roles).

15. Did you feel supported beyond the couple? I.e. kinship networks, friends' networks.
16. Can you tell me about your experiences with public services as same sex parents
    - the first pediatrician appointment?
    - the enrolment to pre-school/school?
17. Has your child(ren) ever been discriminated for having same-sex parents?
    - If yes, can you tell me what happened? What did you do?
    - If not, are you worried it could happen in the future? What would you do in such a situation?
18. Did you decide how to deal with potential negative events as a break-up or death? (i.e. private agreements, will, etcetera).

References

Ahmed, S. (2004). *The cultural politics of emotion*. Edinburgh: Edinburgh University Press.

Beck-Gernsheim, E. (1998). On the way to a post-familial family: From a community of need to elective affinities. *Theory, Culture & Society, 15*(3–4), 53–70.

Beck, U., & Beck-Gernsheim, E. (1995). *The normal chaos of love*. Oxford: Polity Press.

Bell, D., & Binnie, J. (2000). *The sexual citizen: Queer politics and beyond*. Cambridge: Polity Press.

Bertone, C. (2009a). *Le omosessualità*. Roma: Carocci.

Bertone, C. (2009b). Una sfida a quale famiglia? Comprendere i mutamenti familiari attraverso le esperienze dei genitori non eterosessuali. In C. Cavina & D. Danna (Eds.), *Crescere in famiglie omogenitoriali*. Milano: Franco Angeli.

Bertone, C. (2015). Il fascino discreto delle famiglie omogenitoriali. Dilemmi e responsabilità della ricerca. *Cambio, 5*(9), 37–45.

Bertone, C., & Gusmano, B. (2013). Queerying the public administration in Italy: Local challenges to a national standstill. In Y. Taylor & M. Addison (Eds.), *Queer presences and absences* (pp. 260–278). London: Palgrave Macmillan.

Bruner, J. (1996). A narrative model of self construction. *Psyke & Logos, 17*(1), 154–170.

Butler, J. (1990). *Gender trouble: Feminism and the subversion of identity*. New York/London: Routledge.

Butler, J. (2000). *Antigone's claim: Kinship between life and death*. New York: Columbia University Press.

Butler, J. (2002). Is kinship always already heterosexual? *Differences, 13*(1), 14–34.

Cadoret, A. (2008). *Genitori come gli altri: omosessualità e genitorialità*. Milano: Feltrinelli.

Crowhurst, I., & Bertone, C. (2012). Introduction: The politics of sexuality in contemporary Italy. *Modern Italy, 17*(4), 1–6.

Donà, A. (2009). From *Pacs* to *Didore*: Why are civil partnership such a divisive issue in Italian politics? *Bulletin of Italian Politics, 1*(2), 333–346.

Duggan, L. (2003). *The twilight of equality? Neoliberalism, cultural politics, and the attack on democracy*. Boston, MA: Beacon Press.

Farina, M. (2017). Same-sex adoptions: The Italian case. *The Italian Law Journal, 3*, 207–220.

Fassin, E. (2001). Same sex, different politics: "Gay marriage" debates in France and the United States. *Public Culture, 13*(2), 215–232.

Ferrari, F. (2015). *La famiglia inattesa*. Milano: Mimesis.

Franchi, M., & Selmi, G. (2018). Challenging the unthinkable: Gay and lesbian parents between redefinition and exclusion in Italy. *AG About Gender-Rivista internazionale di studi di genere, 7*(14), 1–21.

Gabb, J. (2005). Lesbian M/otherhood. Strategies of familial-linguistic Management in Lesbian Parent Families. *Sociology, 39*(4), 585–603.

Gabb, J. (2008). *Researching intimacy in families*. Basingstoke: Palgrave Macmillan.

Gamson, J., & Moon, D. (2004). The sociology of sexualities: Queer and beyond. *Annual Review of Sociology, 20*, 47–64.

Garbagnoli, S. (2014). 'L'ideologia Del Genere': L'irresistibile Ascesa Di Un'invenzione Retorica Vaticana Contro La Denaturalizzazione Dell'ordine Sessuale. *AG About Gender, 3*(6), 250–263.

Garbagnoli, S., & Prearo, M. (2018). *La crociata "anti-gender". Dal Vaticano alle manif pour tous*. Torino: Kaplan.

Giddens, A. (1992). *The transformation of intimacy: Sexuality, love and eroticism in modern societies*. Oxford: Polity Press.

Gross, N. (2005). The detraditionalization of intimacy reconsidered. *Sociological Theory, 23*(3), 286–311.

Hey, V. (2005). The contrasting social logics of sociality and survival: Cultures of classed be/longing in late modernity. *Sociology, 39*(5), 855–872.

ISTAT. (2012). La popolazione omosessuale in Italia. In *Statistiche report*. Roma: ISTAT.

Jamieson, L. (1998). *Intimacy: Personal relationships in modern societies*. Cambridge: Polity Press.

Lasio, D., & Serri, F. (2017). The Italian public debate on same-sex civil unions and gay and lesbian parenting, *Sexualities*, online version.

Lingiardi, V. (2013). La famiglia inconcepibile. *Infanzia e adolescenza, 12*(2), 74–85.

Mancina, C., & Vassallo, N. (2016). Unioni civili? Un dialogo sulla legge approvata dal Parlamento italiano. *Iride, 29*(79), 551–564.

Plummer, K. (1995). *Telling sexual stories: Power, change, and social worlds*. London/New York: Routledge.

Plummer, K. (2003). *Intimate citizenship: Private decisions and public dialogues*. Montréal: McGill-Queen's University Press.

Richardson, D., & Monro, S. (2012). *Sexuality, equality and diversity*. Basingstoke: Palgrave Macmillan.

Riessman, C. K. (2008). *Narrative methods for the human sciences*. London: Sage.

Roseneil, S., Crowhurst, I., Santos, C., & Stoilova, M. (2013). Reproduction and citizenship/reproducing citizens: Editorial introduction. *Citizenship Studies, 17*(8), 901–911.

Rosenfeld, D. (2009). Heteronormativity and homonormativity as practical and moral resources: The case of lesbian and gay elders. *Gender & Society, 23*(5), 617–638.

Rosina, A., & Viazzo, P. (2008). *Oltre le mura domestiche: famiglia e legami intergenerazionali dall'unità d'Italia ad oggi*. Udine: Forum.

Ruspini, E. (2005). Il silenzio e la parola. In E. Ruspini (Ed.), *Donne e uomini che cambiano* (pp. 11–36). Milano: Guerini.

Ruspini, E. (2009). "Italian forms of masculinity between Familism and social change." in. *Culture, Society & Masculinities, 1*(2), 121–136.

Ryan-Flood, R. (2005). Contested Heteronormativities: Discourses of fatherhood among lesbian parents in Sweden and Ireland. *Sexualities, 8*(2), 189–204.

Saraceno, C. (2012). *Coppie e famiglie. Non è questione di natura*. Milano: Feltrinelli.

Selmi, G. (2015). Chi ha paura della libertà? La così detta ideologia del gender sui banchi di scuola. *AG About Gender-Rivista internazionale di studi di genere, 4*(7), 263–268.
Skeggs, B. (2004). *Class, self, culture*. London: Routledge.
Somers, M. R., & Gibson, G. D. (1994). Reclaiming the epistemological "other": Narrative and the social constitution of identity. In C. Calhoun (Ed.), *Social theory and the politics of identity* (pp. 35–99). Oxford: Blackwell.
Trappolin, L. (2009). Lotte Per Il Riconoscimento E Ruolo Dei Mass-Media. I Significati Del "Gay Pride". *Partecipazione e conflitto, 1*, 123–145.
Weeks, J. (1998). The sexual citizen. *Theory Culture and Society, 15*(3), 35–52.
Weeks, J., Heaphy, B., & Donovan, C. (2001). *Same sex intimacies: Families of choice and other life experiments*. London: Routledge.

Chapter 5
Same-Sex Families Challenging Norms and the Law in France

Matthias Thibeaud

Abstract Legal context has become more inclusive for same-sex couples in French society over the recent decade. It was not until 2013 that the marriage law was amended to allow same-sex couples to marry and adopt children. However, the law still lacks collateral parenting rights: access to ART and surrogacy are still illegal in France for same sex couples, and they must turn to foreign countries to access these rights. Consequently, same-sex parenting is a bit of a "makeshift job", i.e., a legal and social grey area. This chapter analyses how lesbian and gay individuals deal with the law to "make" family, based on a series of in-depth interviews. The retelling of the procreation process they adopt and the story of their daily life as parents provide revealing examples of the different way they negotiate the legal and social obstacles they face. With many roads leading to parenthood, one key aspect of same-sex parenting is the legal recognition of the status and obligations to parent(s), whatever their gender, sexual orientation or number. The different same-sex families configurations challenge the certainties about the "right way to be parent" supported by the law, questioning the dominant and legitimate definition of the "normal" family.

Keywords Same-sex parenting · France · Family policies · Assisted reproductive technology · Surrogacy

5.1 Introduction

A bill permitting female couples and single women to access assisted reproductive technology (ART) in France will be presented to the National Assembly in 2019 as part of the revision of the French Bioethics Law. If the bill is voted, ART will no longer be reserved to heterosexual couples, becoming legal for all women regardless of their conjugal status or sexual orientation. The bill is a further example of the progress achieved on the rights of sexual minorities in France in the last few decades,

M. Thibeaud (✉)
French Institute for Demographic Studies (INED), Paris, France

M. Digoix (ed.), *Same-Sex Families and Legal Recognition in Europe*,
European Studies of Population 24, https://doi.org/10.1007/978-3-030-37054-1_5

other key breakthroughs including the legalization of the civil partnership (PACS) in 1999 and same-sex marriage in 2013. The political and social debates preceding the legalization of same-sex marriage focused on the issue of filiation and same-sex parenting. While the law of 2013 made it possible for same-sex couples to adopt, it failed to respond to the full set of issues raised by the plurality of existing same-sex families. These legal advances have been accompanied by the increasing social acceptance of homosexuality in French society, as reflected in the latest major survey on sexuality in France (Bajos and Beltzer 2008). But that acceptance remains socially differentiated and is more prevalent among young people, women and the most educated. Reticence over same-sex parenting remains more persistent, even if French society is no longer as divided as the media hype around the "Manif pour tous" demonstrations may have suggested. The survey shows that 53% of women and 46% of men accept the idea of two women raising a child together and 46% and 34%, respectively, of two men doing so. The underlying social logics appear to be similar to those at play in the acceptance of homosexuality but are heightened by the strength of gender-specific perceptions of maternity.

Despite the legal obstacles and constraints in terms of social acceptance, a number of same-sex parent families now exist in France, though they are difficult to identify (Rault 2009). Demographer Patrick Festy estimated that the number of children living with a same-sex couple in 2005 was between 24,000 and 40,000, the large majority with a female couple (Festy 2006). More recently, the French National Institute for Statistical and Economic Studies, INSEE, estimated the number of same-sex couples at around 200,000, 10% of them living at times with at least one child. A variety of family arrangements are involved, with most children being born from a previous union and some living part of the time with the other parent. The study confirms that women represent the majority, at roughly eight couples out of ten (Buisson and Lapinte 2013).

Supplementing a quantitative approach, this chapter looks at the way in which lesbians and gays manage their visibility, couple and family, as well as the difficulties they are confronted with owing to their homosexuality as regards the existing legal system in France. The chapter draws on the results of the French part of a comparative survey made in a number of European countries in 2014 and 2015 as part of the European research project, FamiliesAndSocieties[1]. On the basis of semi-structured interviews, and with a sociological approach inspired by Max Weber's comprehensive sociology[2], the idea was to explore how lesbian and gay sexual minorities "construct families". The research work was informed by a number of questions. What legal and social obstacles do these individuals face in their efforts to become parents? What kinds of access to parenting are open to them? What are the different types of same-sex parenting configurations? How do they address the normative expectations weighing on families? To what kinds of domestic arrange-

[1]This research project led to a range of publications: (Digoix et al. 2016, 2017, 2018), and a university dissertation: (Thibeaud 2015)

[2]Max Weber's comprehensive sociology seeks to understand the meaning of social activities on the basis of the meaning given to them by individuals.

ments does this give rise? How are parental roles negotiated among the various family configurations? What kind of visibility is given to same-sex-parent households at child care institutions? What types of difficulties do they encounter?

From a qualitative standpoint, the survey population was constituted so as to comprise the broadest range of profiles relative to the social phenomenon addressed, the idea being to obtain in-depth information on the experiences of the most diverse population possible. Fourteen semi-structured interviews were administered, seven of them with the two members of a couple and seven with individuals, for a total of 21 people interviewed, self-identified as lesbian or gay[3]. The survey population thus included a diverse range of family configurations – including single parents, two parents and multiple parents – and parenting access methods, such as adoption, artificial insemination with a donor (AID) or in vitro fertilization (IVF), gestational surrogacy, and children born from a previous heterosexual union. The interviewees comprise ten women and eleven men, aged from 26 to 57 with a median age of 43, living in Paris or the suburbs of Paris (six interviewees), in another large French city (four interviewees) or in rural areas (four interviewees). However, the population is relatively similar in socio-cultural terms, most of the interviewees belonging to a high socio-occupational category and with at least a Bachelor's degree or equivalent. While the distortion may largely stem from the way in which the sample was recruited[4], it also clearly reveals the characteristics of the studied population, as the declaration of homosexual or bisexual practices is more common among people with university degrees, all generations combined (Bajos and Beltzer 2008), and people in a same-sex couple have a higher education level than the population as a whole (Rault 2017). All of which suggests that same-sex parenting underscores the importance of socio-cultural status, with same-sex parenting, because it remains subject to considerable social constraints, calling for substantial resources in economic, cultural and activist terms.

Before presenting the results of the survey, the concept of same-sex parenting will be reviewed, along with previous work on the subject in France. In 1997, the *Association des Parents et futurs parents Gays et Lesbiens* (association of parents and future gay and lesbian parents, APGL) referred to same-sex parenting as "any family situation in which at least one adult who is the parent of at least one child self-identifies as homosexual." The concept of same-sex parenting was forged as part of an activist viewpoint to lend visibility to families whose social reality was hitherto hidden and was gradually adopted in everyday speech. The term covers a range of configurations, distinguished by the number of "day-to-day parents" and the reproduction method used, be it AID, insemination from a heterosexual relationship, adoption or gestational surrogacy. In other words, same-sex parenting may involve a single parent self-identified as gay or lesbian, a parental couple of the same sex, or a coparenting arrangement between different parents – in a couple or otherwise and at least one of whom self-identifying as homosexual – who agree to

[3] See the information on the interviewees in the appendix.

[4] Recruited through organizations and the personal network of friends or family.

bring into the world and raise one or several children. As such, same-sex parenting involves a number of distinct situations, each one raising specific issues.

The growing visibility of same-sex parenting in activist, media and political milieus has generated considerable scientific interest in the question. Extensive work was produced on the subject in the 2000s in France, following on from queer studies in the United States. Anthropologist Anne Cadoret (2002) paved the way with the first ethnological approach to same-sex parenting. From a clinical sociology perspective, Emmanuel Gratton (2008) has explored the desire of men to have a child and a new form of paternity through interviews with gay men who are or aspire to become fathers. Virginie Descoutures (2010) has focused on lesbian mothers, and in particular on the norms weighing on the relationship between maternity and homosexuality. Also of note is the work of Martine Gross (2012), who has addressed the paternity of gay men by looking at how they access parenthood. She has also demonstrated the difficulty of the social sciences to produce research on same-sex parenting, a research topic that apparently still carries little legitimacy in France at the start of the twenty-first century (Gross 2007).

The present research work aims to contribute to these studies through an approach based on institutional political sociology[5], until now relatively unexplored. This theoretical framework is particularly conducive to explorations of same-sex parenting as it breaks with preconceptions relating to the dominant norm of the two-parent homosexual family. With this approach, families can be seen as a set of practices, norms, constraints and conventions that are formalized, stabilized and interiorized to a varying degree and whose apparent self-evidence makes them harder to read. From this viewpoint, access to parenting is conditioned by a set of rules that structure what may be referred to as the "family order". The latter defines which agents are authorized to legitimately form a family (any adult old enough to procreate), the composition of the "teams" that these agents may form (a two-parent couple, with the exception constituted today by the possibility of adopting as a single person), the way in which the conception of child is to proceed (heterosexual sex, together with the possibility of ART for heterosexual couples unable to procreate, as well as adoption) and the official registration to which the resulting configurations are subject (and notably declaration in the civil status records). These rules governing the establishment of filiation and access to parenting are controlled by the state, which has the power to institute the various configurations that may legitimately claim to constitute a "family" in our society. The family order refers not just to the framing of parentage but also to the way families work on a daily basis, through numerous more or less formalized prescriptions on the "right way to be a parent". In this respect, a number of "institutional guardians"[6] exist that convey normative perceptions of what a family should be, issuing calls to order that are more or less binding as regards school, administration, medicine and religion, as well as the close rela-

[5] For a summary of existing work, the reader may notably refer to (Dulong 2012) and (Lagroye and Offerlé 2011)

[6] The expression is relatively similar to what Virgine Descoutures (2010) refers to as "normative agents".

tional environment through friends, family, work colleagues, and so on. All families are thus confronted by a form of control that is as legal as it is social. Given their atypical character relative to the dominant model, same-sex-parent families serve to highlight these forms of regulation, together with the possibilities of micro-resistance that they offer. The theoretical framework enables thinking on the room for negotiation held by individuals relative to norms. They have a certain room for manoeuvre with these norms, which do not completely limit their practices and perceptions.

This chapter begins by examining the normative guidelines on the conception of a child, looking at how lesbian and gay parents access parenting within the legal and social confines facing them. It also reviews the specific issues relating to different same-sex parenting configurations. It then goes on to investigate the daily life of same-sex-parent families, addressing the ways in which lesbians and gays approach their roles as parents through arrangements with the gendered hierarchical model dictating the division of domestic tasks. The chapter also analyses the relationship of these individuals with infant care institutions.

5.2 Becoming a Parent: Conceiving a Child in the Face of Legal and Social Norms

To become parents, lesbians and gays are required to deal with the legal and social constraints governing the access to parentage in France. The legalization of same-sex marriage in 2013 enshrined this possibility in the law, but it remains extremely complicated to accomplish in practice.

In France, ART remains limited to heterosexual couples, pending the presentation of a bill that would make this possible for female couples and single women, to be examined by the French National Assembly in 2019. Gestational surrogacy is also illegal in France, but, like ART, can be accessed outside France. ART can thus lead to the recognition of the rights of the biological mother's partner relative to their child, subject to an adoption as part of a marriage, which is not without obstacles. Gestational surrogacy poses problems as regards the change in the child's civil status. Meanwhile, though adoption[7] has been authorized as part of a marriage, demand in France is substantially greater than the number of children available for adoption. Outside France, practically none of the countries traditionally open to international adoption authorizes people known or declared as homosexual to adopt children, according to the French adoption agency. The legal restrictions on access to parentage are supplemented by powerful social norms. The dominant family model conveys a number of normative expectations, chief among which are the difference of the sexes (the idea that a child needs a father and a mother) and having

[7] For more information on adoption, the reader may notably refer to the work of Bruno Perreau (2003, 2012)

two parents (raised in a household by two people), which are often said to be necessary conditions for the child's psycho-social development. Perceptions equating filiation with "blood ties" also remain highly pervasive. In addition, a differential perception of parenting skills appears to exist according to gender, as reflected in the greater social acceptance of female single parents and same-sex parents than of their male counterparts (Bajos and Beltzer 2008).

To become parents, lesbians and gays are obliged to deal with these legal and social constraints, drawing on their resources and social situations and in accordance with their own value systems and perceptions. They may place more or less importance on the presence of a paternal or maternal figure in the family, on couple parenting, on the establishment of a biological connection with the child, or on the question of "origins". Each same-sex parenting configuration is built case by case on the basis of the prevailing legal and social norms. The issues stemming from these norms are analyzed on the basis of the accounts given by the interviewees of how they chose to conceive the child and become parents.

5.2.1 Coparenting

Coparenting is a family configuration in which a woman or two women forming a couple join forces with a man or two men forming a couple to conceive and raise a child together. The survey population included three such situations, involving two, three or four parents. Philippe (interview 10), 43, single, is the father of two girls aged six and eight with Caroline, a heterosexual friend. Laurent (interview 5), 36, is the father of a 1-year-old boy with Vincent, his partner, and Marine and Sophie, a couple of friends. Alexandre (interview 4), 26, single, is the father of a 3-year-old boy with a couple of female friends.

The interviewees' explanations of their choice of family configuration shed light on the way in which they address current social norms and their own system of perceptions of the family. Some of the coparents interviewed said that they were not particularly concerned about establishing a biological link with the child. They stressed the importance of investing on a daily basis in the child, which they see as the best definition of what parenting means. According to Alexandre:

> I wasn't obsessed about it 'having to be my blood'. This is really important for some people and I respect that. But for me, parenting isn't about blood... Even parentage in itself is just about being there for the child and passing on values. Quite simply, we are there for him, and he is there for us.

For Alexandre, being a parent is not "about blood" but a commitment to the child ("being there for the child and passing on values"). In this respect, Virginie Descoutures' analysis (2010) is particularly enlightening. She inverts the terms of the kinship/parenting couple. The second is often perceived as a sub-set of the first, with the establishment of filiation instituting the parent as such, which conditions their investment in the child. Inversely, she encourages the idea of "parenting as a set, of which filiation is a component among others", thus making a conceptual distinction whereby parenting can be thought of as a combination of reproduction, filiation, parental work[8] and parental authority – aspects that do not always overlap. The importance placed by the interviewees in the commitment to the child can, in the light of this analysis, be seen as a challenge to the basis of parental legitimacy, based less on establishing parentage through the transmission of a genetic link via reproduction and more on the recognition of the commitment and day-to-day parental work.

The choice of this configuration can also be motivated by the desire to provide the child with a parent of the other sex. The attitude towards gestational surrogacy of the interviewees having opted for coparenting revealed the importance of this question, as reflected in the words of Laurent:

> Was the idea of having women involved in parenting important to us? I think so, even if I'm totally for gestational surrogacy, with all the right conditions. And I also think that a couple of men can raise a child perfectly well. But I think we liked the idea of having mums around.

Gender difference within the parental arrangement is important to him. As stressed by Martine Gross (2012), the presence of a maternal figure helps to reduce the transgression of social norms by defusing potential criticisms of the lack of skills on the part of men to raise children alone. The importance granted to the presence of a mother can be seen in the words of Philippe, who also talks about the importance of telling the child about its "origins":

> It's true that when I thought about having children, I didn't want to deprive the children of a mother or access to their origins. That's why I ruled out adoption, because to me it seemed… Gestational surrogacy also isn't the answer for me because… for me, it is important to know where you come from. Who your mum was, who your dad was, your grandparents, their history, and so on. And it's true that I thought I would be depriving the children of that […] When talking about adoption, sometimes I'd say I was a little against it, because it clearly cuts your roots. For me it's like a tree, it needs roots, it needs… […] This is why in structures with two dads and two mums, at least the biological parent is there, and so the history is there.

For Philippe, the issue is not just about providing the child with an accessible origins story. It is also about ensuring the presence of the biological parent(s) within the parental configuration to confirm the child's part in a family lineage. Justifications for the choice of coparenting thus reflect a certain stance on the part of the interviewees in respect to perceptions of the family, parenting and the interest of the children. In a certain manner, their configuration is about taking prevailing social norms on board as well as their own values and moral judgments.

The coparenting configuration also raises specific questions in that parenting is disconnected from conjugality and reproduction. As such, the choice of coparents is vital when choosing this model and motivated, according to the interviewees, by emotional and social proximity. For Alexandre, "it is not possible that they be

[8] Parenting work is defined as "the countless educational, domestic and healthcare actions and interiorized mental loads that life with a child requires, as well as the implicit contract of the parent, who ensures this socialization 'work'" (Descoutures 2010).

unknown". He has known his couple of women friends for a long time and stresses that he shares their activist values and political convictions. Philippe has also been friends with the mother of his children for a long time, as have Laurent and his male partner with their couple of women friends. In these situations, conception was via home insemination, as assisted reproductive technology is reserved to infertile heterosexual couples. With home insemination, the biological father gives his sperm to the mother, who proceeds herself with insemination. Humour is often used to defuse embarrassment about these "practical exercises", as Alexandre refers to them.

Recognition of the place and status granted to each parent is an important factor in coparenting. Managing multiple parents and/or the disconnect between conjugality and parenting requires that negotiations be conducted to determine each person's place. Alexandre and his couple of women friends drew up a coparenting charter in an attempt to plan for any possible problems. While the document has no legal value, it "at least makes people ask themselves questions". The charter includes items on the child's last name and first name, the place and status of each parent, the custody arrangements, and the management of any crises. The document was drafted as part of an intentionally reflective approach, which preceded the realization of the parenting project. The interviewees often present an enchanted image of their family configuration, serving to prevent the problems inherent among couples from having an impact on the relationship with the children, as Philippe:

> There is no love between the parents, so there is no rivalry. You won't hold it against the other person if they don't love you enough. So the children are not an issue [...] it's a very calm family, with no conflict between the parents. The children are not an issue.

But it can be difficult for interviewees to express the problems they have encountered during a semi-structured interview. They may appear as a challenge to the social legitimacy that the interviewees are attempting to gain. However, some of the individuals hinted at some of the obstacles they have faced: "the difficult thing [in initiating the project] was to do with each couple and making decisions between four people, which is always rather delicate. It really is a difficult construction, you have to be inventive" (Laurent). Possible identification models are scarce in multiparenting, which may lead to difficulties in terms of coordination between the parents involved.

In addition, the lack of legal status relative to the child remains a difficult aspect for parents whose filiation has not been recognized. Registration in the civil status records and the transmission of the surname appear to play a vital role in recognizing oneself as a parent and being identified as such by friends and family. Laurent, the biological and legally recognized father of the child, admits that there is "a certain amount of frustration relative to the law" concerning the legal status of his partner and that of the partner of the biological mother and legal mother of the child within the multiparent arrangement. The four of them organized a "parenting ceremony" in which they pronounced their commitment as parents in front of a few witnesses, the aim being to make up for the legal shortfall and give the coparents a symbolic legitimacy, which they felt they lacked. The position of Laurent's partner in the family set-up also caused some frustration relative to his own parents: "for my mother in particular, it was hard to accept that he wasn't the biological father". The commitment of grandparents to their grandchildren largely hinges on parental status (Herbrand 2014). Laurent said that his partner's parents "were less involved", that they were "a little bit the fifth wheel on the wagon". The choice of the child's last name and first name is often a matter of statutory "tinkering" for the coparents, including for Alexandre:

> In terms of the recognition of the child, legally speaking, he has a mother, Patricia, and a father, myself. And so he has my family name, added to by Patricia's family name. His second middle name is the family name of Régine, the second mother. So the three names appear in the civil records, even if his family name is really mine and that of Patricia.

Legal registration here appears to be a way of consolidating Régine's status as a mother. In Laurent's family configuration, the child also has the family name of its two biological parents, but the two other coparents chose the first and second middle names of the child, as a way of legitimizing their roles as parents.

The decision to coparent is relatively transgressive with regard to family norms. It requires the development of a form of relational inventiveness outside the model of the two-parent heterosexual family, with the emphasis placed on daily commitment to the child. The lack of legal recognition of coparents can be compared with that of parents-in-law in blended families[9] and highlights the insufficient consideration of these situations on the part of the law.

5.2.2 *ART and Sperm Donation*

The legal framework for assisted reproductive technology (ART) in France is set out in the Bioethics Laws of 1994 and 2004, some of the provisions of which were revised in 2011. The use of ART is legal for heterosexual couples who are infertile or unable to have a child without risk. However, it is legally possible for single women or female couples to access ART outside France, notably in nearby countries such as Belgium, Spain and the Netherlands. Five female couples in the survey population used ART: Lucie and her partner (interview 2), Liliane and Odile (interview 3), Danièle and Catherine (interview 6), Magalie and her ex-partner (interview 11), and Laure and Murielle (interview 12).

Talking about how they became mothers, the interviewees repeatedly bring up the issue of the absence of a father at the start of their project. This often led them to initially consider coparenting with a man or a male couple or a donor from their circle of friends. In the end, however, they opted for ART owing to concerns over multiparenting (Laure and Murielle), fears that the mother without legal recognition would not find her role as a parent in such an arrangement (Magalie) or unsuccessful meetings with coparenting candidates (Danièle and Catherine). Becoming a parent is a long and trying process. Catherine and Danièle chose ART in the Netherlands,

[9] For more information on these issues, the reader may refer to the work of Florence Weber (2013) and Jacques Marquet (2010).

their son being able to request access to his origins at the age of 16. After seven unsuccessful attempts at artificial insemination, they decided to try in vitro fertilization (IVF). In all, they made 12 trips to the Netherlands. Magalie and her ex-partner opted for home insemination with sperm donated by a friend. Fertilization occurred on the ninth ovulation cycle for the first child, but the conception of the second proved much more complicated. It took 3 years and 30 inseminations, some of them at home, some of them in a clinic in Belgium, before Magalie became pregnant. Laure and Murielle went through an LGBTQI+ parents organization to find a man who would accept to be a donor while remaining anonymous and having no involvement in the life of the child. They also chose home insemination, acknowledging that they had taken a risk, as they could have been dealing with a donor seeking to cause them prejudice. It should be said that their approach, as with that of Magalie, could have resulted in criminal penalties, sperm donation in France being strictly supervised. When talking about initiating their project to become parents, the interviewees stressed the importance of gaining the approval of their friends and families. Some of them also benefitted from the assistance of a general practitioner or gynecologist, who supported them in their project in France.

The place and status of the mothers involves issues similar to those seen in coparenting. While the legalization of adoption for same-sex married couples in 2013 enables the partner of the biological mother to become the second legal mother of the child, it does not respond to all existing situations. Catherine and Danièle are not planning to get married. Consequently, Danièle, who gave birth to their son, is the only person with recognized rights and parental duties concerning their child. On a day-to-day basis, Catherine's care for their son is thus subject to the varying degrees of zealousness of the relevant institutions or individuals with whom they are in contact (crèches, schools, doctors, etc.). "It's always a grey area. We make things as we go." Danièle drafted a will designating Catherine as guardian in the event of her death, but the final decision in that event would be made by the family council, which does not guarantee that Catherine would be able to continue raising their son.

Making ART legal for all women in France, regardless of their conjugal status or sexual orientation, would make it easier for lesbians to conceive a child. As things stand, it remains more complicated for the non-biological mother to obtain parental status than for a heterosexual couple. If the couple are not married, the non-biological mother may not recognize the child. If they are married, no equivalent of the presumption of paternity exists; the non-biological mother is required to file for adoption.

5.2.3 Gestational Surrogacy

Gestational surrogacy consists in a woman transferring her parental rights and duties to a child that she has carried and to whom she has given birth to one or more people, who may be referred to as "intended parents". Gestational surrogacy has been illegal in France since the Bioethics Laws of 1994. If practiced in French territory, the intended parents, the gestational carrier and any intermediaries may face criminal penalties. Gestational surrogacy practiced outside France is possible, in countries where it is legal or not prohibited, but transferring birth certificates issued in foreign countries to the French civil status records may prove difficult. While the filiation with the child's biological father is now recognized – the result of several judgements condemning France by the European Court of Human Rights – grey areas remain in establishing the filiation of the partner of the intended parent and that of a single woman or female couple.

Gestational surrogacy has a particularly high entry cost, leading to financial, as well as social and legal, constraints. Among the interviewees, two male couples opted for gestational surrogacy, in the United States: Patrick and Michel (interview 7), and Bernard and Charles (interview 9). The reasons for choosing gestational surrogacy are often informed by a rejection of coparenting, as illustrated by the case of Patrick and Michel:

> Michel: "[…] Yes, also because [gestational surrogacy] was our only possibility… Since with coparenting, you have to find…
> Patrick: It's complicated, it's sharing… It's shared…
> Michel: It's shared custody…
> Patrick: Like a divorced couple…
> Michel: And the experiences we heard about, when it worked it was great, but when there was the slightest problem, it went badly…".

The parallel they draw between coparenting and the family situation of a divorced couple shows their desire to be involved full time with the child and their refusal to "share" the child with a third person or another couple. Opting for a surrogate mother creates a distance with the figure of the mother both from a biological standpoint (the surrogate mother has no blood ties with the child) and a social standpoint (there is no day-to-day mother as there is in coparenting). People also choose gestational surrogacy because they reject adoption, in which there is no genetic connection with the child. "We ruled out adoption because it was already complicated and when we discussed it we wanted to have a genetic link" (Michel). Another interviewee commented, "So it really is our child because there is a genetic link between the child and us." To the interviewee's mind, the "truth" in filiation is based on establishing a genetic link, which is not the case with adoption, the fear with the latter being that paternity may be called into question.

Couples having chosen gestational surrogacy tend to defuse on an unprompted basis criticisms about the lack of a mother and the commodification of the female body, which reveals the importance of the social disapproval to which this form of conception exposes them. To reduce the transgression of being a father without a mother, Michel places his couple on the same level as an infertile heterosexual couple seeking to have a child:

> A lot of couples today also have problems having children… […] Fortunately, our way of having a child, apart from the surrogate mother, and the medical aspect, is common today. Yes, common, for any couple with fertility problems, which leads to the same system as us.

This is a way of evacuating the specificity of sexual orientation, relegated to the rank of secondary variable in the considerations of the parental couple. Summoning the figure of the infertile couple thus serves to conceal sexual stigma (they are men) and homosexual stigma (they form a same-sex couple). As with a heterosexual couple unable to have a child, they have a legitimate right to use medically assisted reproduction.

In these two situations, the choice of a biological parent in the couple corresponds in reality to the desire to not choose. The aim is to place the partners on an equal footing relative to the child. Bernard and Charles each gave their sperm for the artificial insemination process and do not want to know who is the actual biological father. "For us, we are two fathers, strictly equal. Neither one of us is quote unquote 'more father' than the other." For their part, Patrick and Michel tried to have "cross twins" (a single biological mother and two biological fathers) but only one of the ovocytes proved viable. They are keeping the matter of who is the biological father "to themselves", as if expressing that information would delegitimize the father status of the one who is not the biological father of the child.

The two couples having chosen gestational surrogacy are obliged to go through the legal system to establish the filiation of their child. In the United States, the procedure consists in the handing down of a ruling permitting the issuance of a birth certificate and US passport for the child. But obtaining French nationality involves a number of difficulties. To obtain a French passport from the prefecture, the applicant must possess a French nationality certificate, delivered by the competent court. Patrick and Michel did not apply for this certificate, as the court on which they depend is known for its severity in the issuing of such documents to couples having chosen gestational surrogacy. Consequently, their daughter only has US nationality and is considered to be parentless in the eyes of French law. Patrick and Michel did a DNA test to demonstrate biological filiation in the event of any legal problem, but they refuse to initiate a procedure that could potentially expose their family. And so they continue to wait for a change in the law. Their daughter's lack of French nationality is experienced as a problem in daily life. "I find it quite disturbing, quite difficult, and a source of anxiety, waiting day after day for an email, a response, information. You can't be at peace as long as you haven't received the paperwork. So it's disturbing for the family environment" (Charles). The least administrative procedure may be a source of difficulties. While Charles and Bernard succeeded in obtaining a French nationality certificate and having the French nationality of their child recognized, only the biological parent is officially recognized as the child's father. They have had problems with Charles' supplementary healthcare insurance company, which carried out an investigation into their family situation, calling for a paternity test and bank statement details.

5.2.4 Adoption

While adoption is legal and appears to be better accepted socially than gestational surrogacy, it remains an extremely difficult process. Only one of our interviewees had adopted: Jacques (interview 8), 47, in a couple for 18 years with his male partner. They began their adoption project in 2006 and finally completed the process 7 years later, having faced a series of obstacles. Jacques initiated the procedure as a single man as adoption was yet to be legalized for homosexual men at the time. Jacques also had stronger assurances of stability in terms of finances and family support. Consequently, while Jacques was legally recognized as the father of Emile, the same was not true for his partner, who has the status of godfather. Adoption has since been legalized for married same-sex couples, but it remains illegal for same-sex couples with civil-partnership, consensual-union or common-law status. In addition, any mention of same-sex parents in a file makes it practically impossible to adopt a child outside France, the majority of the countries of birth of children up for adoption preferring heterosexual couples according to the French adoption agency. In France, the number of children up for adoption is low relative to demand. Our survey lacks information on the adoption procedures made since adoption became legal for same-sex couples and on the difficulties involved in that process, but Jacques' interview sheds light on some of the problems that may be encountered.

Jacques sees adoption as a less transgressive way of becoming a parent than coparenting ("Two parents is fine, four is a lot") or gestational surrogacy, which for him involves ethical issues ("It's the idea of putting a price on the child [that is a problem for him]. It isn't about paying a woman but the fact that the approach is a commercial one. It's like ordering something, as you would on Amazon, and I'm not very comfortable with that"). For Jacques, adoption is a "humanitarian" act that gives a family to a child lacking the latter, running counter to a repeated criticism of same-sex parenting whereby "the rights of a child" are opposed to "the right to have a child". The reasons for choosing adoption also reveal a distancing of the biological connection, which places the two parents on a platform of equality relative to the child. "[The question of the biological aspect] is posed, but let's say that [adoption] put us on an equal footing, neither of us having a stronger bond than the other." Jacques also sees adoption as an arrangement that makes it easier to explain to the child his or her origins.

> When looking to the future, telling ourselves that when we explain the situation to our son, well, it will be clear. There is no… Two dads cannot have a boy, cannot have a child, clearly. Hence adoption, because I think it was easier to justify, easier than saying, 'Well, we asked a lady' and so on.

Adoption remains a long and difficult process. The first phase, which for Jacques lasted about a year, consists in obtaining an approval procedure from the social services, which carries out an investigation to verify that the applicant fulfils the requisite conditions for adoption in family, educational and affective terms. Jacques concealed his sexual orientation, as any mention of homosexuality often renders adoption unlikely. Some of the other interviewees ruled out adoption for this very reason, refusing to hide their homosexuality, which often required a lengthy process of acceptance. For Jacques, the possibility that his "abilities to be a good father" be recognized in an "objective" manner by the specialists issuing approval ultimately stood as a legitimization of his parenthood. The second phase consists of research and the ruling of the adoption judge. Jacques, who decided to adopt in Russia, entered into contact with several NGOs, local organizations and law firms. But as none of these initiatives proved conclusive, he pursued his research with the French adoption agency. His status as a single male was a source of numerous difficulties as it failed to correspond with adoption practices in Russia. Jacques had to demonstrate considerable tenacity and leverage his "social capital" to overcome the administrative hurdles in his path. After a 6-year effort, he succeeded in adopting Emile, 5 years old. He was obliged to commit to providing follow-up reports to the French government for a 3-year period as part of a condition concerning Russia specifically.

Each same-sex parenting configuration thus involves a specific form of "tinkering" on the basis of legal and social norms. The resulting arrangements – the number and sex of the parents, as well as the place and status granted to them – are also reflected in different ways of experiencing parenthood on a daily basis, be it in the organization of domestic life as part of different family configurations or in the relationship cultivated with institutions responsible for infant care.

5.3 Same-Sex Parenting in a Daily Basis

5.3.1 The Influence of Gender on the Organization of Family Life

The roles of parents have traditionally been based on a differential concept of the sexes, with mothers and fathers investing in their children in a distinct and unequal manner. While recent decades have seen the dissemination of egalitarian and emancipatory "guidelines" among families, gender relationships continue to have a powerful influence on parental roles (Cardi 2015). Extensive work has shown that gender equality in the family continues to exist in the realm of intentions and aspirations rather than in concrete achievements, women still being responsible for the greatest part of domestic and parental duties (Brugeilles and Sebille 2013). With the "new father" model conveyed by the media yet to become a true reality, we examined the way tasks are organized and divided in different coparenting family configurations and in same-sex couples raising a child together.

Coparenting arrangements appear to offer the best conditions for a more equal sharing of parental roles (Nix and Eckhoff Andersen 2019). The gendered hierarchical role influencing the division of domestic tasks is adapted according to the number and sex of the parents, but also according to differences in occupational or age terms. In the case of Alexandre (interview 4), coparenting with a couple of lesbian friends, the parents implemented a shared custody arrangement. Alexandre has the child one weekend in two and for half of the holidays. For Alexandre, this unequal custody arrangement is due to considerable occupational constraints. Though less involved than the mothers in the child's daily life, he does not demand a more substantial engagement with the child. The configuration here corresponds to the gendered hierarchical model in which the mothers take care of the large majority of domestic and parental tasks. The gendered differentiation of the parental roles appears to be based on differences in terms of conjugal status (Alexandre is single, his female friends in a couple) as well as occupational constraints. For Laurent and his male partner (interview 5), coparenting with a couple of lesbian friends, the shared custody arrangement is equal, with each couple having custody of the child on an alternating weekly basis. While the couples have agreed on a certain number of child-raising points, each couple retains its own approach when the child is in their custody. As demonstrated in the child's diet: "We talked about it. The girls are into organic food and we aren't, so we said we'd do our best but that each couple should feed he child as it sees fit [when the child is in our custody]." Philippe's coparenting arrangement with his friend Caroline (interview 10) presents other issues, as they are both single and decided to move in together with their two daughters. Philippe expresses a certain amount of bitterness with what he sees as a difference in investment between the mother and himself. Because he is able to work from home, most of the parental tasks fall on his shoulders. He talks about the "father-like role" of Caroline, who comes home late from work and is less invested in daily tasks with the children.

> The mother arranges things so she comes home late, playing at… [smiles] Often in heterosexual couples, it is the father who makes sure he comes home once the children have been bathed, fed, in their pajamas and in bed, so that they can give them a little kiss and read them a story. That's what the mother does.

He also stresses the career advantages that this arrangement provides. "It's true that the fact that we're together gives her the chance to enjoy time with the girls, despite her work […] The way I see it, as a heterosexual woman, the situation enables her to have a career and children." The difference in the parents' responsibilities and professional availability stands as a marker of the sharing of parental activities. By emphasizing that Caroline is a "heterosexual woman", Philippe is stressing the reconfiguration of gendered parental roles in their family arrangement.

In family configurations in which the child is raised by a same-sex couple, parental roles are not distinguished according to a naturalized gender norm and may be renegotiated. Most of the interviewees said that they were on an equal footing in terms of parental roles, distancing themselves from the heterosexual model through egalitarian guidelines for the two parents. Michel: "We work in a fairly equal manner, with both of us involved. We don't divide tasks between the mother and father saying that this or that is the mother's role"; Patrick: "There's more sharing than in a straight couple" (interview 7). The lack of sexual difference in a couple appears to lead to a fairer division of tasks between partners. But comments about the physical organization of families reveal the existence of a division of labour that, without repeating the social roles of father and mother, gives rise to differentiated domestic investments. Bernard and Charles (interview 9) are raising Axel, aged 8 months and conceived through gestational surrogacy, and Bernard's daughters, aged 16 and 18, from a previous heterosexual union and of whom he has shared custody. Bernard takes care of most of the domestic and parental tasks in the couple. His work makes it easier for him to manage his time than Charles, who often comes home late in the evening, so he handles "domestic logistics in the broad sense". The difference in investment in terms of time appears to be accompanied by a form of gender bipolarization in the couple, as Charles says: "And as a gay couple, all the same there's a… Tell me if I'm off the mark, Bernard, but there's a complementarity in the tasks, a little like in a heterosexual couple in the end. There's one who is more maternal than the other, and one who is…" Charles said that he was sorry he could not be more present with their son. "It's my regret, because I'm 55, and I thought I'd have more time for me and to take care of Axel more […] But I realize that the time Bernard spends with Axel makes his relationship with Axel more special than mine." This arrangement appears to bear out the assumptions of a certain amount of work on same-sex conjugality showing that the latter leads to a reformulation rather than the disappearance of the traditional gendered model (Carrington 1999; Descoutures 2010).

The ways in which same-sex parenting is organized on a daily basis among the various family configurations thus demonstrate the power of gender (Lowy 2006) over parental roles, from which is it is hard from parents to escape. Yet the social relationships of gender are sometimes replaced by other differences in status – notably in terms of age or occupational responsibilities – that affect the division of tasks between parents.

5.3.2 *Relationships with Infant Care Institutions*

Parents are obliged to deal with the institutions and individuals to which they delegate part of the care of their children. Few interviewees talked about problems with their relationships with these institutions or individuals. However, Magalie (interview 11) said that a headmistress had asked her for a document authorizing her partner to pick her daughter up from school, "as if she were my neighbour". Meanwhile, a doctor of Laure and Murielle (interview 12) has problems accepting the presence of the latter when they both attend appointments with their daughter. "I was completely clear. And I had a hard time accepting it in front of my general practitioner […] Things are much better now." The words of the interviewees suggest that homophobia is not absent but takes on diverted forms through phenomena of avoidance and distancing. Bernard and Charles (interview 9), who are on a municipal list to find a nanny, said: "Some people have clearly accepted while others have refused because we are a gay couple. We'll never know."

The information collected on experiences with infant care institutions also highlights two distinct strategies[10] used to present same-sex parenting. Some of the interviewees talk about the specific nature of the family configuration but without lingering on it. Speaking about his first interview with a crèche director, Alexandre (interview 4) said "it came up in the conversation just like that." In the same situation, Patrick and Michel (interview 7) started by telling the director about their family configuration. Same-sex parenting is talked about simply but without being highlighted in particular. "We don't hide it but we don't shout about it either." This initial strategy is used to trivialize the issue, the interviewees employing it to show that they are "regular" parents seeking the right to indifference. A further strategy, based on concealment (Artigas Burr 2017), may be identified with other interviewees who do not talk about their same-sex parenting to the institutions with which they are obliged to come into contact. Philippe and Caroline (interview 10) look in every respect like an "ordinary" heterosexual couple and play on the heterosexual identity attributed to them spontaneously.

> From the outside, no-one can see the difference with the couple of neighbours […] With the teachers, it doesn't… Because I'm not going to say that [Caroline] is not my wife, we are in a civil partnership after all, and we have children together, so what… Short of going into details that are none of their business, what do you want me to say to them? Or I say nothing… When I'm talking, I never say 'my wife', obviously, I say the 'mother of my daughters' or something like that, which could be the vocabulary of a divorced father, but I never position myself as a homosexual, just as a father. For me, this has no impact. I'm no different as a father because I'm gay.

For Philippe, homosexuality is disconnected from his role as a father and instead is an intimate issue. Similarly, the same-sex parenting arrangement of Jacques (interview 8) also has an invisible aspect, as he alone is recognized as the adoptive father. While his partner has authorized status with the school, and is notably able to pick him up at the end of the day, only Jacques is considered as the father in the eyes of the institution. "The only thing I sketched out, because in the end you have to, is that there wasn't a mum at home. That's it. No explanation. I adopted him as a single man, I was a single father." Unlike the first strategy, the second does not seek to trivialize same-sex parenting. While the principle of differentiating between same-sex parenting and heterosexual parenting is also rejected, it is accomplished in this case through an alignment with dominant family norms, Philippe and Caroline giving the appearance of a heterosexual couple and Jacques that of a single father. The first strategy is about working on norms "from the inside" by trying to change perceptions of same-sex parenting; the second is about circumventing them through tactical compliance with infant care institutions.

---

[10] The term "strategy" should not be reduced to that of "strategism". It does not correspond to a pure calculation or a pure intentionality on the part of the interviewees, but instead encourages thinking on their room for manoeuvre in the way they manage the visibility of same-sex parenting in their contacts with infant care institutions.

5.4 A Troubled Family Order?

While the survey work focuses on same-sex-parent families, it nevertheless sheds light on the social regulations that govern families and parenting in a broader sense. Same-sex parenting stands as constitutes a true anthropological laboratory for gaining greater insight into non-thoughts relative to these categories, covered by a form of "natural" evidence, as it is socially naturalized. In the words of Pierre Bourdieu (1996), it is one of those "extraordinary and almost experimental variations" offered by the social world, "which, even though they are not as fully controlled and controllable as experiments designed expressly as such, may encourage and facilitate the analytical dismantling of certain elements of social reality that were previously confused and, hence, unperceived." By separating what appeared to be inseparable – reproduction, filiation, conjugality and parenting – same-sex-parent families challenge the "given" status of the two-parent heterosexual family held up as the dominant norm. The various same-sex parenting configurations all represent forms of "normative tinkering" based on these disconnects. In a space governed by heteronormative legal and social constraints, this tinkering comprises different relational arrangements involving one or several parents, in a couple or not, of the same sex or otherwise, and calling on various reproduction methods. The day-to-day organizational systems of these families also highlight forms of negotiation relative to gender approaches that structure the gendered division of parenting roles. Same-sex-parent families thus invite us to call the dominant family model into question by deconstructing its "naturalness" and by shedding light on its constituent power relationships, which are subject to political negotiation.

Profiles of the Interviewees

For reasons of anonymity, the first names have been changed.

<u>Interview 1</u>**: ISABELLE**, 40, and **LOUISE**, 43, psychotherapists, have been in a couple for 4 years and live in the suburbs of Rennes. They are raising the children from Isabelle's first marriage. They were in contact with a Christian LGBTQI+ organization for a while but did not become particularly involved. They plan to form a civil partnership in the near future, mainly in order to simplify administrative procedures. They disagree on marriage, with Isabelle mostly for and Louise against.

<u>Interview 2</u>**: LUCIE**, 33, a school teacher, and Claire, 23, have been together for 7 years and live in a rural area in the Ile-et-Vilaine department. They are raising the children from Lucie's first marriage as well as their daughter, to whom they gave birth through AID. They formed a civil partnership after being together for 2 years, mostly for the economic benefits, and were married in 2013, which notably enabled them to share the parentage of their daughter through adoption. They are members of an LGBTQI+ parents organization.

<u>Interview 3</u>: **LILIANE**, 52, a high-school Italian teacher, and **ODILE**, 56, a market transaction execution officer, have been in a couple for 20 years. They have raised the children from Odile's first marriage and their own daughter, to whom they gave birth through AID in 2002. They were married in 2014, primarily to share the parentage of their daughter through adoption.

<u>Interview 4</u>: **ALEXANDRE**, 26, single, is the father of Arthur, 3, as part of a coparenting arrangement with a couple of lesbian friends, Patricia and Régine, 33 and 50. Alexandre is a sign language interpreter. He works in Paris but lives in Tours.

<u>Interview 5</u>: **LAURENT**, 36, a university professor, is married with Vincent, 40. They have lived together for 5 years. They have a 1-year-old son, Simon, as part of a coparenting arrangement with a couple of lesbian friends, Marine and Sophie. The two couples live close to each other in Paris. Laurent and Marine are the biological and legally recognized parents of Simon.

<u>Interview 6</u>: **DANIELE**, 42, and **CATHERINE**, 57, have been in a couple for 12 years and live in a rural area of the Vendée department. They gave birth to Alix, 3, through artificial insemination in the Netherlands with the possibility of knowing the donor's identity. Danièle is the biological and legally recognized mother of Alix. Catherine has a 27-year-old daughter, Charlotte, from a previous same-sex union, conceived through IVF with an anonymous donor.

<u>Interview 7</u>: **MICHEL**, 41, and **PATRICK**, 46, are married and have lived together for 14 years. They became the fathers of Daphné, 2, through gestational surrogacy in the United States. Patrick is the director of a dependent senior home and Michel is a manager at the French postal operator, La Poste. They live in Nantes. MAGALIE, a friend, is Daphné's godmother.

<u>Interview 8</u>: **JACQUES**, 47, an actor and singer, is the father of Emile, 7, who he adopted in Russia 2 years ago. He became a parent with the support of his partner, with whom he has lived for 18 years, and who is the godfather of the child. They live in Paris.

<u>Interview 9</u>: **BERNARD**, 47, and **CHARLES**, 55, are married and have lived together since 2005 in the suburbs of Paris. They became the fathers of Axel, 8 months, through gestational surrogacy in the United States. Charles also has a 21-year-old son from a previous same-sex relationship through gestational surrogacy in the United Kingdom. Bernard has two daughters, aged 16 and 18, from his previous marriage. He lived with his ex-wife for 15 years before their separation in 2001. Charles is a financial executive and Bernard a sixth-form teacher.

<u>Interview 10</u>: **PHILIPPE**, 43, single, has two daughters, aged 6 and 8, as part of a coparenting arrangement with Caroline, 43, heterosexual and single. The four of them live together in Paris. Philippe and Caroline are both teachers.

<u>Interview 11</u>: **MAGALIE**, 34, a school supervisor, recently moved in with Sylvie, her new partner. They live in a rural area near Rennes. Magalie lived for nearly 10 years with Rosalie, her ex-partner, with whom she had two daughters, today aged 6 and 11, through home insemination with sperm donated by a friend, Dorian. Magalie and Rosalie separated 3 years ago and now have shared custody of the children. However, Rosalie has no legal status relative to the girls.

Interview 12: LAURE, 41, an infant teacher, and **MURIELLE**, a specialized teacher, have been in a couple for 8 years and live in Caen. They have a daughter, Léa, 3, through home insemination with the sperm of an anonymous donor whom they met on the website of an LGBTQI+ parents organization. They were married last year and have completed the administrative procedures for Murielle to adopt Léa.

Interview 13: YVES, 44, a university lecturer, has two sons, aged 13 and 16, from his relationship with his ex-partner, with whom he lived for 10 years. He has had a stable relationship with Richard, 45, for 2 years, but the two do not live together. They both reside in Paris.

Interview 14: EMMANUEL, 37, and **FRANCOIS**, 27, have been in a relationship for one and a half years. Emmanuel has two children, aged 7 and 9, from a previous heterosexual marriage. He has shared custody of the children every other week. He lived with his ex-wife for 13 years, before their separation in 2012. Emmanuel is a graphic designer and François is a salesperson for a large group. They live at each other's homes on an alternating weekly basis, Emmanuel living in the suburbs of Paris and François in Paris itself.

References

Artigas Burr, F. (2017). *Femme, lesbienne, mère: Reconfigurations identitaires dans l'expérience de la parenté et de la parentalité, thèse de sociologie*. Paris: EHESS.

Bajos, N., & Beltzer, N. (2008). Les sexualités homo-bisexuelles: d'une acceptation de principe aux vulnérabilités sociales et préventives. In N. Bajos & M. Bozon (Eds.), *Enquête sur la sexualité en France: pratiques, genre et santé* (pp. 260–262). Paris: La découverte.

Bourdieu, P. (1996). Des familles sans nom. *Actes de la recherche en sciences sociales, 113*(La famille dans tous ses états), 3–5.

Brugeilles, C., & Sebille, P. (2013). Le partage des tâches parentales: les pères, acteurs secondaires. *Informations sociales, 176*, 24–30.

Buisson, G., & Lapinte, A. (2013). Le couple dans tous ses états. *Insee Première, 1435*.

Cadoret, A. (2002). *Des parents comme les autres. Homosexualité et parenté*. Paris: Odile Jacob.

Cardi, C. (2015). Les habits neufs du familialisme. *Mouvements, 82*, 11–19.

Carrington, C. (1999). *No place like home: Relationships and family life among lesbians and gay men*. Chicago: University of Chicago Press.

Descoutures, V. (2010). *Les mères lesbiennes*. Paris: PUF.

Digoix, M., Franchi, M., Pichardo Galán, J.-I., Selmi, G., de Stéfano Barbero, M., Thibeaud, M., Vela, J.- A.-M. (2016). Sexual orientation, family and kinship in France, Iceland, Italy and Spain. (FamiliesAndSocieties working papers series 54)

Digoix, M., Franchi, M., Pichardo Galán, J.-I., Selmi, G., de Stéfano Barbero, M., Thibeaud, M., & Vela, J.- A.-M. (2017). Laws, sexual orientation and intimate lives in France, Iceland, Italy and Spain: A synthetic view from a sociological survey. In K. Waaldijk (Ed.), *More and more together: Legal family formats for same-sex and different-sex couples in European countries* (FamiliesAndSocieties working papers series 75) (pp. 136–150).

Digoix, M., Franchi, M., Pichardo Galán, J.-I., Selmi, G., de Stéfano Barbero, M., Thibeaud, M., & Vela, J.- A.-M. (2018). *European rainbow families in the making: practices, norms and the law?* (Documents de travail 242). Paris: Ined.

Dulong, D. (2012). *Sociologie des institutions politiques*. Paris: La Découverte.

Festy, P. (2006). Le recensement des familles homoparentales. In A. Cadoret, M. Gross, C. Mecary, & B. Perreau (Eds.), *Homoparentalités. Approches scientifiques et politiques* (pp. 109–116). Paris: PUF.
Gratton, E. (2008). *L'homoparentalité au masculin: le désir d'enfant contre l'ordre social*. Paris: PUF.
Gross, M. (2007). Quand et comment l'homoparentalité est-elle devenue un objet « légitime » de recherche en sciences humaines et sociales ? *Socio-logos. Revue de l'association français de sociologie*, (2). http://journals.openedition.org/socio-logos/803. Accessed Sept 2019.
Gross, M. (2012). *Choisir la parentalité gay*. Paris: Erès.
Herbrand, C. (2014). Les rendre grands-parents. L'enjeu des relations intergénérationnelles au sein des coparentalités gaies et lesbiennes en Belgique. In J. Courduries & A. Fine (Eds.), *Homosexualité et parenté* (pp. 175–188). Paris: Armand Colin.
Lagroye, J., & Offerlé, M. (2011). Introduction générale: Pour une sociologie des institutions. In *Sociologie de l'institution*. Paris: Belin.
Lowy, I. (2006). *L'emprise du genre. Masculinité, féminité, inégalité*. Paris: La dispute.
Marquet, J. (2010). Couple parental – couple conjugal, multiparenté – multiparentalité. *Recherches Sociologiques et Anthropologiques, 41*(2), 51–74.
Nix, E., & Eckhoff Andersen, M. (2019). *What causes the child penalty? Evidence from same sex couples and policy reforms* (Discussion papers 902). Statistics Norway, Research Department.
Perreau, B. (2003). L'égalité inavouable. Homosexualité et adoption en France: une politique publique jurisprudentielle. *Nouvelles Questions Féministes, 22*(3), 32–46.
Perreau, B. (2012). *Penser l'adoption: la gouvernance pastorale du genre*. Paris: Presses universitaires de France.
Rault, W. (2009). La difficile mesure de l'homoparentalité. Fiche pédagogique. https://www.ined.fr/fr/tout-savoir-population/memos-demo/focus/homoparentalite/ Accessed Sept 2019.
Rault, W. (2017). Secteurs d'activités et professions des gays et des lesbiennes en couple: des positions moins genrées. *Population, 72*(3), 399–434.
Thibeaud, M. (2015). *Père et gay. Trouble dans l'ordre familial* (Mémoire de Master 2). Université Paris-Dauphine, sous la direction de Achin C. (unpublished).
Weber, F. (2013). *Penser la parenté aujourd'hui. La force du quotidien*. Paris: Éditions Rue d'Ulm.

Chapter 6
LGBT Desires in Family Land: Parenting in Iceland, from Social Acceptance to Social Pressure

Marie Digoix

Abstract More than 20 years ago, Iceland opened civil union to same-sex couples with its confirmed partnership law (*staðfest samvist*, 1996). Since then, the country has attained a high level of equality between same-sex and different-sex couples in the domain of family law, and the law has strong provisions against discrimination toward LGBT people. The increasing visibility and acceptance of LGBT people is raising questions about the social process of integration. LGBT people are confronted with heterosexual norms, a confrontation that is difficult to bypass. In this context, some may find that they are losing their identity. Iceland is a familialist society, and a key entry into the social acceptance of homosexuality has been through marriage and parenting. There is a clear gender gap in family-making. Lesbians have access to ART whereas adoption is scarcely available and surrogacy still illegal, reducing access to parenthood for gay men. However, in Iceland's small LGBT community, parenting desire has increasingly become a reality for both females and males. Based on a survey consisting of 30 interviews, the paper studies how parenthood meets a wide range of personal desires, but also how it has become a normative pressure.

Keywords Same-sex parenthood · Iceland · Family policies · Heteronormativity · Assisted reproduction techniques · LGBT rights

6.1 Introduction

In 1994, a committee convened by the Icelandic parliament to report on the situation of homosexuals in society submitted its findings to the government (Forsætisráðuneytið 1994). This report put a spotlight on the legal inequalities

M. Digoix (✉)
French Institute for Demographic Studies (INED), Paris, France
e-mail: mad@ined.fr

M. Digoix (ed.), *Same-Sex Families and Legal Recognition in Europe*,
European Studies of Population 24, https://doi.org/10.1007/978-3-030-37054-1_6

facing homosexuals. Thus began the march toward equality, with particular attention given to family law. Over the following 16 years, the law was progressively adjusted to grant homosexual couples the same rights as heterosexual couples. From a strictly legal perspective, this equality was achieved in 2010 with the adoption of a single marriage law for same- and different-sex couples (*Ein hjúskaparlög* 2010).

The present study extends a previous socio-historical study on the relationship of LGBT individuals in Iceland to this new legislation, from the first law authorizing same-sex unions in 1996 onward (Digoix 2013b). This research explores how LGBT populations have perceived and experienced recent changes in laws and society, through a series of interviews in 2005, 2009, and 2015 exploring the private lives of LGBT individuals at different stages of life – youth, coming out to self and to others, first sexual relations, unions, parenthood, separations – after three key legal transitions.

This chapter draws on the interview-based survey of 30 LGBT individuals in Iceland conducted within the comparative project *FamiliesAndSocieties*[1] in 2015, almost a decade after the country's principal laws on homosexual parenthood, and nearly two decades after the first law on same-sex unions.

The present analysis is built on their responses in these interviews. Iceland is often described as a social laboratory, made possible by the country's small size, its centralization around the capital city, and its social regime strongly focused on family and children. This aspect is highlighted by its insularity.

The survey sought, first of all, to determine whether the law had an influence, in either direction, on questions of parenthood, or family-making: in the desire for children or its absence, but also in the difficulty or impossibility of having children, from their conception to their reception in society. The aim is thus to describe the world in which individuals make their choices, and how they experience them.

In a system of legal filiation which, in the name of equality, extended the existing heterosexual model, how have homosexuals approached this confrontation with an established social norm? Given the particularity of homosexual couples, the principal targets of these laws – the impossibility of autonomous biological conception – are they able to conform to this norm? Or should they instead invent new models, do they wish to, and are they able to? What place can the homosexual family take in the world of the family in a context of widespread family recomposition, with "plural" heterosexual families? What are the points of convergence between these "new" families? Gender difference and societal microcosms will be examined.

In light of the previous research, one can expect that the youngest cohorts would have an easier time approaching the issues of coming out, daily life, and the desire for children. The study explores their relationship with legislative change over time toward the recognition of homosexuality. Previous cohorts had come to parenthood in a different context, either through other forms of relationships (heterosexual) or

[1] Funding under grant agreement no. 320116: the FamiliesAndSocieties Project, within the European Union's 7th Framework Programme (FP7/2007–2013).

by circumventing the law (e.g., use of Assisted Reproduction Technology (ART) abroad). In 2015, it was also possible to look for any differences between generations in the logic of conception and the fulfilment of desires for children.

The principal question in the analysis of the respondents' discourse on desires for children and becoming parents is whether and how these major legal changes were integrated into their personal approach to this area of life and on the impact that this may have had on the homosexual collectivity, which, within Iceland's small population, has historically been fairly tight-knit. Beginning in 2010, the homosexual community entered a pivotal period, facing questions around the transition from activist struggle to heteronormative life, where parenthood may represent the final step of integration. Again looking at differences between cohorts, the hypothesis that the advances, not only in family law, but also in the increased visibility of homosexuals, may have had an influence on societal integration in the form of assimilation, is studied. This raises questions on the future of a model of life that had previously been constituted on the basis of circumventing norms, following the various changes toward legal equality (Pollak 1985; Schiltz 1998). The little Icelandic community offers multiple answers.

Methodology and Sample Characteristics

Since the 1996 law allowing the civil registration of same-sex couples, INED has carried out three interview-based surveys in Iceland around the reception of such laws, how individuals from these groups perceive them, and how they make use of them. This research topic has been adapted over the years, and the resulting data offer resources for understanding the effects of legal changes over time in the country. The first survey took place in 2005, 9 years after the adoption of the first law; the second in 2009, 3 years after major changes toward equal rights between same-sex and different-sex couples, notably in access to parenthood and registration of cohabitation in the national register.

The corpus on which the present study is based was gathered during a survey in 2015, after the adoption in 2010 of a gender-neutral marriage law. The study was designed as part of a European project, *FamiliesAndSocieties*, aimed at comparing perceptions and behaviours in different legal contexts. The other countries in the survey were Spain, France, and Italy (Digoix et al. 2018). The semi-structured interviews were performed using a common interview grid to ensure comparability across the four countries. They centred mainly on quality of life within the legal framework available to the respondents (family life, marriage, parenthood, homophobia in society and at work).

The sample was constituted in such a way as to obtain the greatest possible diversity within the relevant population. The respondents' sociodemographic and geographical characteristics were chosen in collaboration with the Spanish, French, and Italian teams for comparative purposes.

The interviews were conducted by Íris Ellenberger and Svandís Sigurðardóttir in Icelandic, with the exception of two respondents who were not native speakers (in these cases English was used). The respondents were recruited through personal acquaintances and the snowball method. Iceland is a country with a small population, where homosexual circles are relatively small and well-organized in the capital. While the interviewers are known within this circle, they did not interview people with whom they had close relations.

Thirty LGBT persons were interviewed. They ranged in age from 23 to 53 years at the time of the survey. The youngest had always lived in a society where same-sex couples had the right to form a legal union, while the oldest had experienced the full course of changes in attitudes toward homosexuality.

The respondents were single, married or remarried, divorced from same- or different-sex partners, widowed, living with a partner or separately. Most lived in or around the capital (like two thirds of the country's population), but many originally came from other parts of the country. Six still live in the countryside.

Nineteen of the respondents had, were trying to have, or were considering having children. Configurations differed between cases where respondents already had children, were in the process of becoming parents, or were planning to do so. Five of the respondents had children born in a previous heterosexual relationship.

Five female respondents had had medically assisted procreation within the Icelandic healthcare system.

Three had had children as part of a shared plan for parenthood with friends, through artisanal home insemination. A pair of coparents were interviewed separately.

Finally, one of the respondents lived in a household with his partner's child, whose godfather he was.

The respondents' names, occupations, and places of residence have been changed for purposes of anonymity.

6.2 Homosexuality and Society

> 'I think that society needs to practice acknowledging people.' IS14 Stefan
>
> 'Sometimes legal changes have been made but the society is a little longer to change you know' IS21 Elín

6.2.1 Laws in Theoretical Context: From Differentialism to Universalism

In Iceland, the history of societal and legal questions around homosexuality is relatively recent and compressed into a short period (Kristinsson 2003). In the twentieth century Iceland was a "new" country, which had obtained its full independence from the Kingdom of Denmark only in 1944. A small island country, its social democracy follows more or less the model of its Nordic neighbours (Denmark, Norway, and Sweden) but is culturally and economically connected to these countries through an intergovernmental organization, the Nordic Council. Its own adaptation of the aforementioned model is quite flexible, but remains within the limits set by the condition of equality of persons within this shared political space.

While homosexuality was decriminalized in 1940 with the adoption of a new criminal code (*Hegningarlög nr. 19/1940*) in a time when the country was still under Danish influence, it was not until 1992 that the age of consent (14 years) was made equal for same-sex and different-sex partners (*Lög nr. 40/1992*). Moreover, the Criminal Code has prohibited discrimination on the basis of sexual orientation since an amendment passed in December 1996 (*Lög um breyting á almennum hegningarlögum nr. 19/1940*). But it is with its law on civil union that Iceland made a major advance, shifting the legal approach to homosexuality in the key domain of the family. This law, inspired by the Danish law on registered partnerships (*Lov om registreret partnerskab af 7. juni 1989*) was adopted/adapted by the other Nordic Council countries following a recommendation of the Council in 1984 suggesting a process of reflection on the social conditions facing homosexuals (*Nordiska rådets rekommendation* 1984). A particularity of this federation of historically linked states is that they mutually honour many social and family rights and entitlements, enabling citizens to circulate freely among them (Eydal 2005). Parenthood was slightly present in Icelandic law beginning with the initial law of 1996 on confirmed partnership (the latest law among the four countries: *Lög um staðfesta samvist nr. 87/1996* – abrogated in 2010 with the opening of marriage to same-sex couples as a gender neutral law), which grants individuals in such partnerships parental authority over their partner's children. This Icelandic specificity reflects a particular focus on children, which is also present to some extent in other Scandinavian countries, but which is more marked in Iceland.

The partnership law was amended first in 2000 in order to allow the "second parent adoption" by individuals in a confirmed partnership of their partner's child (Art. 6, *Lög um staðfesta samvist nr. 87/1996* (abrogated in 2010), amendment nr. 52/2000, in force since 26 May 2000), and then again in 2006. An even greater step was taken with the law of 2 June 2006 modifying the legal status of homosexuals (*Lög nr. 65/2006 um breytingu á lagaákvæðum er varða réttarstöðu samkynhneigðra (sambúð, ættleiðingar, tæknifrjóvgun)*), aimed at establishing equality for same-sex and different-sex couples. It contained amendments to 18 laws regarding the status of couples in a confirmed partnership or registered cohabitation. In the latter case, under the law on shared residence, the couple takes on a set of rights and obligations upon registration in the national register (*Lög nr. 21/1990 um Lögheimili*) (the declaration of residence is obligatory). The Adoption Act (*Lög um ættleiðingar nr.130/1999*, as amended by law nr. 65/2006) authorizes joint adoption after 3 years of living together in a confirmed partnership, or 5 years of life as a couple declared on the national register. For cohabiting same-sex couples, this disposition is concomitant with the authorization to register. This condition of registration, either in registered cohabitation (*óvígð sambúð*) or in a confirmed partnership (*staðfest samvist*), applies only in laws involving parenthood or filiation through joint adoption, and in the laws on access to Assisted Reproduction Techniques (ART) for female same-sex couples, on children, and on parental leave. (See Table 6.1 for detailed legal dispositions).

Table 6.1 Adoption of laws concerning parenthood for same-sex couples, by conjugal status

	Marriage (2010)	Registered partnership (1996)	Cohabitation (2006)
Assisted insemination Is it legally possible in this type of relationship to become pregnant through medically assisted insemination using sperm from a donor?	2010	2006	2006
IVF Is it legally possible in this type of relationship to become pregnant through in vitro fertilisation (IVF) using donated egg or sperm?	2010	2006	2006
Surrogacy Is it legally possible for both partners in this type of relationship to become the legal parents of a child through the help of a surrogate mother in the country?	–	–	–
Legal parenthood When one partner gives birth, will (or can) the other partner then also become legal parent of the child, without having to go through adoption?(for example automatically, or by way of recognition/ acknowledgement.)	2010 (only in case of ART)	2006 (only in case of ART)	2006 (only in case of ART)
Parental authority Is joint parental authority/ responsibility possible for the couple, while only one of the partners is the legal parent of the child?	2010	1996	2006?
Parental leave for both parents When both partners are the legal parents of a child, does each partner then have a statutory right to paid or unpaid parental leave?	2010	2000	2006

(continued)

Table 6.1 (continued)

	Marriage (2010)	Registered partnership (1996)	Cohabitation (2006)
Second-parent adoption When only one partner is the legal parent of a child, does the other partner then have the possibility of becoming the child's second parent by way of adoption?	2010	2000 (not if children had been adopted from another country)	2006
Joint adoption Can partners jointly adopt a child?	2010	2006 (Conditional on 3 years of living together)	2006 (Conditional on 5 years of living together, but cohabitation was only allowed in 2006)
Individual adoption Can one partner in this type of relationship individually adopt a child?	As a general rule married partners can only engage in adoption together	Before 2006 registered partners were not eligible for joint adoption so they were technically not bound by art. 2 of the Adoption Act. One partner could apply for adoption as an individual but a single person can only be granted permission to adopt under special circumstances, if the person is considered particularly fit to care for a child.	Before same-sex cohabitation was recognized in 2006 a partner in such a relationship could apply for adoption as an individual but a single person can only be granted permission to adopt under special circumstances, if the person is considered particularly fit to care for a child.

Source: H. Friðriksdóttir, "Parenting and legal family formats in Iceland". In: K. Waaldijk et al. (eds.), The LawsAndFamilies Database – Aspects of legal family formats for same-sex and different-sex couples. Paris: INED, 2017, www.LawsAndFamilies.eu

These laws on the possibility of becoming a parent in Iceland, as in the other Scandinavian countries, owe much to Sweden, which convened a parliamentary committee to report on the situation of children in homosexual families with a view to reforming its legal system (SOU 2001:10). This report, like much jurisprudence in the Scandinavian countries, concluded that it was in the child's interest to have two parents, regardless of their sex.

In 2010, Iceland adopted a gender-neutral marriage law (*Lög um breytingar á hjúskaparlögum og fleiri lögum og um brottfall laga um staðfesta samvist (ein hjúskaparlög) nr. 65/2010*) which abrogated the partnership law (existing partnerships could retain their status, or be converted into marriage simply by filling out a form). *Ein hjúskaparlög*, the 'one marriage law', placed same-sex and different-sex couples on equal footing. Both could now marry in Iceland's state church, which is mainly traditionally responsible for legally registering marriages.

However, in 2015, at the time of the survey, the law left aside questions essentially bearing on the individual, such as transsexualism (monitored by a national committee), sex reassignment for children born intersex, and surrogate pregnancy (which is particularly central to problematics of parenthood, notably for men). These still-open questions implicitly highlight the difficulty of addressing situations exclusively linked to the individual, to ethics, and to families that do not adopt existing heterosexual arrangements. Icelandic law does not innovate, and, by granting homosexuals rights equal to those of heterosexuals, has limited itself to shifting from a differentialist model to a universalist one (Digoix 2008).

6.2.2 An Insular, Egalitarian, Feminist Society

Iceland's history, its geographical situation, and its political regime are influential characteristics that have shaped its society, and that shed light on the interacting evolution of the society and its laws. First of all, Iceland is an island with a small population – 330,000 inhabitants in 2015 – whose demographic growth has been fairly rapid, from 78,000 inhabitants in 1900 to 279,000 in 2000, notably thanks to a flourishing economy. In 2008 the subprime crisis put the country in financial difficulty, slowing both economic and demographic growth. It also curbed the Icelandic welfare state, creating a small social crisis, with negative net migration over the following years (Hagstofa Íslands).

Family legislation has accompanied the societal changes of the late twentieth and early twenty-first centuries, and in this context Iceland is often at the leading edge of the movement toward an increasing well-being society. It was only in the late twentieth century that Iceland began to confront the situation of homosexuals in society, but since the state began to pass legislation in this area, the rights of homosexuals have steadily progressed. This progress follows on a long tradition of seeking equality for individuals in society, which emerged very early in Iceland, with actions for women's emancipation.

A feminist politics that began very early in the twentieth century has marked the transformations of the family ever since. Reforms had been implemented to respond to particular demographic configurations of the end of the previous century, notably economic migration to Canada (Karlsson 2000), but also challenges to the traditional roles of women in the family and in society, under the leadership of Bríet Bjarnhéðinsdóttir (Styrkársdóttir 2006). Iceland was not yet independent at the time, and family policies followed the Danish model. Women obtained the right to vote in municipal elections in 1908, in national elections with age restrictions in 1915, and finally without restriction in 1920. Finally, a 1923 legal reform granted women equal property rights within marriage as well as divorce by mutual consent (women are more likely to apply for divorce (Fine 2002)).

In practice, the most significant changes in terms of gender equality, marking the transition from legal to societal equality, surely occurred in practice after the 1960s, with the control of fertility; economic independence for women through access to the labour market; progressive clarification of the rights of children (independently of parental rights) through a specific law (the Children's Act, or *Barnalög*); and family policies and parental leave supporting fathers' participation in day-to-day child-rearing (Garðarsdóttir 2008). Gíslason (2008) emphasizes that equality in the allocation of parental leave leads to a more egalitarian perception of parenthood: taking care of young children is no longer considered a feminine occupation. "De-feminizing" parenthood is a means to achieve equality.

The integration of feminist policies in Icelandic society can be illustrated by a few significant, even pioneering steps. In 1980, Vigdís Finnbogadóttir was the first woman elected president in a western democracy. She completed four terms, remaining head of state for 16 years. Another emblematic illustration is the naming of Jóhanna Sigurðardóttir as Prime Minister of the coalition government in 2009, after the 2008 subprime crisis, which brought the Icelandic state to the brink of bankruptcy. Jóhanna Sigurðardóttir was the first openly homosexual head of government. When elected she was in a confirmed partnership; she symbolically converted her partnership with Jónína Leósdóttir into marriage in 2010 with the change in the law (Leósdóttir 2013). A little less centrally, but no less significantly, in the same period Agnes M. Sigurðardóttir became the first female Bishop of Iceland, leader of the state church, the Church of Iceland, in 2012.

6.2.3 A Familialist Society

From the very first reflections on the partnership law, activists (who were sometimes involved in or linked to academic research) highlighted the question of parenthood and the lack of legal provisions concerning children. As mentioned above, Iceland was the only Scandinavian country to include parental authority in its initial partnership law (followed by the adoption of the partner's child in 2000). However, this aspect of the law was already singled out as insufficient in 1996; indeed, more than the fundamental advances in this pioneering law, it was its lacunae around parenthood that were emphasized when it was adopted by the parliament (Friðriksdóttir 1996). This particularly pronounced interest in children and parenthood reflects the tight-knit, family-centred nature of Icelandic society (Rich 1978). Iceland, even more than other Scandinavian countries, has always had a high rate of births outside marriage, which is explained in particular by the tradition of socially recognizing births during the engagement period in the modern era (Björnsson 1971). Indeed, the opening of a family whose legal boundaries are already distended, even vague, may explain why adaptive compromises with existing norms tend to be well accepted by society.

Additionally, in Iceland children are granted particular protection through two laws: the Children's Act (*Barnalög nr.76/2003*) which defines children's rights (and the obligations of their parents), and the Child Protection Act (*Barnaverndarlög nr. 80/2002*) which sets out the obligations of the state and its child protection services toward children. There is also a Youth Act (*Æskulýðslög nr. 70/2007*), which regulates and promotes activities for young people aged 6–25 years.

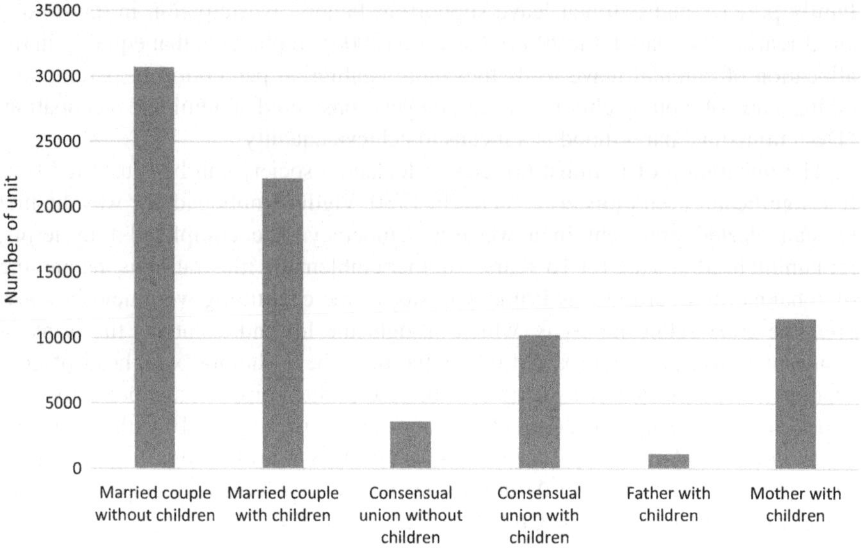

Fig. 6.1 Nuclear families by type of family (by unit), 2015
Population 1 January. A nuclear family refers to couples (married and in a consensual union) and children below the age of 18, single men and women with children below the age of 18. (Persons above the age of 18 who live with their parents are not included in nuclear families)
Source: Hagstofa Íslands: https://hagstofa.is/

Anna Einarsdóttir (2016) shows that same-sex marriage or union facilitates the acceptance of homosexuality within the family unit. She emphasizes the particularity of Iceland as an island country, more familially oriented than other countries of the north, which tend more toward individualism and the decline of tradition. This does not mean, however, that Iceland has remained in a stagnant tradition, firmly anchored in an unchanging past. Much to the contrary: the country is continually pursuing its drive toward equal rights (among citizens, between women and men) and demonstrates a plurality of family types (Fig. 6.1), which could also indicate an acceptance of greater diversity.

In a society oriented toward gender equality, where one of the marked obstacles to this equality (notably on the labour market) is motherhood, public policymaking around parenthood has focused notably on parental leave and access to childcare. Iceland is one of the countries which have most emphasized the extension of parental leave to men (Eydal and Gíslason 2015). In his study on family policies, Ingólfur Gíslason (2008) noted that, in the case of men in heterosexual relationships, '*you are regarded as weird if you don't use the paternity leave.*' There is thus a pressure toward motherhood, but also a pressure toward active parenthood for men. The relationship to the child is emphasized. The "new" man is a father exercising his parenthood. This state of mind is reflected in the desire for children expressed by male interviewees – desires that may have been revealed here by the nearness of the possibility of realization. In this connection, Hrefna Friðriksdóttir (2015) argues that laws on homosexual union have contributed to improving understanding of fatherhood, insofar as they have disrupted the traditionally gendered order of heterosexual parenthood. Legislation has thus challenged traditional family forms by emphasizing fathers' relationship to their children, and their rights and responsibilities with respect to them.

6.3 The Heteronormative Family

Having a child in daily life and in interactions with society has a normalizing effect, independently of the parents' intentions and situation, whether they are heterosexual or homosexual. Even in a highly atypical coparenting scenario, Sóley noted a paradoxical aspect of her trajectory: the arrival of a child had given her access to a 'normality' that she simply observed, although she had had no intention to seek it. '*There is now a straight element in my life that people recognize*' (IS18 Sóley). Her son has two homosexual parents who live apart but are raising him together – a model of separate parenthood whose particularity is only brought out when Sóley mentions her female partner.

More generally, the way parents and families view homosexual children has changed. Whereas in the past they raised doubts concerning the future, their social integration and personal happiness, the ability to plan for a future family put this type of difference in a new, less concerning perspective. What would have been worry about non-reproduction transforms into the expectation of becoming a grandparent.

Kolbrún, 41, described this expectation more generally as a form of social pressure.

> 'People have all sorts of dreams and I am not saying that this is not my dream, but I find it wrong to force it upon you and assume that this is what you want. There is a lot of straight people who do not have kids and are not in a relationship and are happy about it. Why this emphasis? I will not go deep into it, I could talk about it for two hours.' IS27 Kolbrún

Hlynur also perceives motherhood as a social pressure. He himself has two children from heterosexual relationships. He thinks that women face strong pressure to have children, as if it were not an individual freedom, and that not having children is treated as 'abnormal'.

> 'There was like an interview [in media] with one woman, 37 years old and she often gets, what don't you have a child, really shocked, eh, some people don't want children and there's nothing wrong with that, some don't want a boyfriend and there's nothing wrong with that they just want to be free, and you should respect that.' IS30 Hlynur

In their discourse, the persons interviewed for the survey recognized this attachment to family, which, in the struggle for equal rights for homosexuals, has ultimately taken a predominant place. Þórdís, age 51, saw this shift take place. She expressed some regret that it came at the cost of a 'homosexual culture' that arose during a period when homosexuality was stigmatized and that created and depended on friendship relations in place of distended family relations – albeit somewhat less in Iceland than elsewhere – as very well described in the research of Jeffrey Weeks and Kate Weston (Weeks 2001; Weston 1997). Among members of older generations who previously struggled to affirm their difference, a non-negligible amount of fear around normalization has developed in the aftermath of laws authorizing same-sex unions and recognizing same-sex parenthood. This is what the Danish sociologist Henning Bech, in his key work of the late 1990s, *When Men Meet*, described as the disappearance of a way of life and the birth of a new homosexual (Bech 1997).

> 'Yes, I think these are family rights sort of, the right to form a family, to get married and such. These are very important rights but you would of course like to see more emphasis on diversity, rights as individuals, for instance individuals who live alone. There is a very strong focus on the family here in Iceland. Everyone has to participate in this family package, this heterosexual family package, lesbians and gay men as well. And we have participated and it marks our culture. It is disappearing. There is no culture. There is no visible culture like before when we didn't have these rights.' IS04 Þórdís

As these rights were obtained in the name of equality for all citizens, they were constituted based on the dominant heteronormative model. While Iceland's family life is pluralistic, with notably a high value placed on cohabitation, high rates of births outside marriage, low marriage rates, and reconstituted families, homosexual culture was nonetheless constituted in opposition to it. The oldest respondents in the sample expressed many thoughts about life 'before'.

> 'I think that now all these lesbians who are having children and such, I think they are just entering into an established mould. Have kids and get married and stuff. And you wonder, if they enter this mould, are they still lesbians? Sure, they are still lesbians but they are mothers, and then kind of heterosexual mothers. Are they taking on such roles? Is their family life the same as with heterosexuals? You know, is there something called queer family life… …"how do we use these rights? Are we just conforming to this mould? And then we aren't visible.' IS04 Þórdís

Such considerations on changes in life projects since the adoption of the recent laws were often expressed by those who, although they had struggled to obtain equal rights, also had memories of a different socialization – as though the law, in assimilating homosexuals, had changed them.

It is as if the law had had the effect not simply of normalizing private, albeit familial events, but of causing the disappearance of other arrangements or structures that had come into being when homosexual practices were illegal and stigmatized. The power of the law may not be as great in a society as dynamic as Iceland's, but the situation remains far from the reinvention of ways of life recommended by the twentieth-century theorists such as Foucault (1981) and Bourdieu (1997), and the friendship network has not come to take precedence over the family network.

When speaking of desires for children and realization of plans for parenthood, the respondents continued to strongly emphasize biological family. They described decreasing levels of conflict with family around coming out, and no case of a break with family was observed, although certain reservations and behavioural anomalies persisted, particularly with extended family.

6.3.1 *The Normalization of Coming Out: Heteronormative Coming Out?*

Marriage – or cohabitation, a particularly valued model in Icelandic society, to such an extent that a specific law grants cohabiting couples virtually the same rights as married ones (*Lög nr. 21/1990 um Lögheimili*) – and above all parenthood can create social bonds and family emulation. In practice, marriage and parenthood facilitate coming out by inflecting how the "outside world" perceives homosexuality. When homosexuality is revealed through a long-term partner or shared parenthood of a child, sexuality as such no longer needs to be emphasized. It is easier for a man to come out by referring to a 'husband' or a woman to a 'wife' in an ordinary conversation, revealing their homosexuality without explicitly stating it. The same applies to the exercise of parenthood where, once the first situational revelation of the clear homosexuality of the parents has passed, attention is focused on the child and their well-being. The society's familialism produces a major tension in the parent-child relationship that is exacerbated at the moment of coming out. A previous study (Digoix 2013a) showed that coming out is facilitated for individuals who have a long-term partner and who are able to have children, as parents expect grandchildren, and before 2006, homosexuals were not in a position to satisfy this expectation with legal support. This characteristic appeared again in the 2015 survey, particularly among the oldest respondents, despite the fact that in much of their experience homosexual issues were not visible, and same-sex couples could not have children together.

Sunna, 41, described her parents' reaction to her first child as follows: *'I just think mum was relieved... she has four children so she will get enough grandchildren you know it was just like, I think it just something there that you know I get to have a child, think that was the idea, I am the only girl, maybe that mattered...'* IS26 Sunna.

In some way, then, the birth of a child creates a connection to normality.

Ingibjörg is younger than Sunna (27 at the time of the survey), and has thus been able to eliminate the extreme tension around family and children. When she came out to her mother, the latter emphasized the self-evidence of the desire for children. At the time, although the law on ART was not yet in force, lesbians were able to go to Denmark, where they were legally allowed to use ART.

> 'The only thing she basically was worried about was that I couldn't have kids at that time, because it wasn't allowed here. But she was just, "I will send you to Denmark, no worries"...
>
> It would probably be more of a shock for her if I would tell her I, I wouldn't want to have kids...' IS20 Ingibjörg

According to this discourse, then, family response is focused not so much on the fact of homosexuality, as in the previous generation, but on the ability to conform to the dominant norm, structured around the reproductive cycle – all the more so in a familialist society like that of Iceland.

6.3.2 *The Desire for Children and Its Fulfilment: Contrasting Realities*

Whether it reflects a spontaneous desire or social pressure, access to parenthood emerged as a more important issue in the 2015 survey than in the previous ones, notably because access to legal rights had lifted certain barriers.

Although the interviews were not centred on parenthood, the responses clearly reflected the topic's importance for the respondents, including among those who did not have children, and even those who did not wish to. When the sample was constructed, priority was given to obtaining a diversity of situations, but during the interviews, the respondents' perspective on parenthood almost always converged toward desires for children (or grandchildren), whether or not they had been realized.

Recent legislative advances toward societal recognition of homosexuality mean that new research is needed on how behaviour has been changing, in comparative perspective with work in the 1990s on the desire for children in a homophobic society (Mezey 2013). The internalization of homophobia and the fear of coming out no longer seem to be obstacles to the desire for children. In this respect, Iceland and the Nordic countries are doubtless precursors of new behaviours.

The desire for children is so societally charged that it is perceived and understood as a norm. Ingibjörg, who was 27 at the time of the survey, had already evoked it as essential when she came out to herself. She did so shortly before the right to ART was legally opened to lesbian women. At the time she still associated homosexuality to the inability to procreate.

> 'I mean also the first time that I realised I was a lesbian then um, the first thing I thought was like "Oh my god you can't have kids", because I then I didn't know, didn't know any better, so that, it has always been, I would always have found out how to do it.' IS20 Ingibjörg

Elín, 27, realized very early on that she wanted to have a child. Then she met her partner. They had intended to have children first and marry after. Having a child was a priority, although they were still young. But as they had difficulty conceiving a child, they decided to prepare for their marriage in order to relieve some of the pressure on themselves. Their initial choice to have a child before marriage is not an anomaly in the context of Icelandic family norms: as mentioned above, the country has a high rate of births outside marriage, and couples often marry at the time of the baptism of their first child (Björnsson 1971; Eydal and Ólafsson 2002).

> 'I am um one of those women who feels just that my calling in life is to be a mother I just somehow I just woke up one day, I was like 22 years old and I just I have to be a mother it just somehow I don't really know what it is so you know I have look into all options… So um we have been trying now for more than a year but um it isn't going very well so um it is a total it is a total priority and we prioritized it a few years ago we decided we were going to have a child and get married and decided to have the child first because we somehow felt it was just more pressing not that we are running out of time it's just something that is more important to us…' IS21 Élin

A very strong desire to be a father was found even among those who, like Haukur, have a very traditional vision of parenthood which virtually rules out the possibility of a child being raised without a mother. Haukur, 28, did not describe a particularly defined form of parenthood; his desire is a conceptual one, connected to the tradition of descendants and lineages. He explained that he would like to raise a child, not necessarily from birth, and not necessarily continuously; he spoke of the impossibility of adoption, but also of his wish to be a 'godfather', sharing through coparenting…

> 'I think having children is an important part of adulthood, but it does not need to grow up in your home. For me, it is important for the future to have a family, grandchildren and such.' IS17 Haukur

Although she emphatically highlighted the importance of the law in organizing the material aspects of parenthood, out of concern for the child and the parent without legal status, Kolbrún thought that her desire for a child would have driven her to flout the law.

> '…The laws are bonus, but not… It is not a demand that if they do not exist then I would just zzzzzip and not do it. I mean, women did this. Women have done this for decades.' IS27 Kolbrún

She thus recalled the existence of homosexual parenthood before the establishment of laws allowing it, resulting not only from married or cohabiting heterosexual relationships, but also from the use of ART abroad. In a seminal book based on fieldwork conducted when these laws were under discussion, Traustadóttir and Kristinsson (2003) collected the views of actors in such parental situations.

Both the law and having a partner allow this desire to be fulfilled in a more rational fashion. Although at the time of the survey Erla and her wife were seeking to have a child together, each had been planning to have children before they became partners. Having a partner facilitated the realization of these desires, with access to ART, whereas they had previously thought of resorting to a friend.

> 'Yes, at some point, when we were both single, we had talked to our friends about having children with them. I with a single friend of mine and she with a single friend of hers. Before we got together. Somehow relationships didn't seem to be working out for us so we found other ways to have a family. But when we became a couple then we became a family and the other options just dropped out of the picture.' IS12 Erla

6.4 Reinventing the Family

6.4.1 Legal Support

The official recognition of homosexual parenthood through legal dispositions revealed diversified modes of procreation: these reflect, first, situations created by the temporal unfolding of the law, and then the opening of an increasingly complete range of choices, allowing for many more parental configurations. Simplifying somewhat, it began before the law was passed, in the context of heterosexual relationships or artisanal insemination for lesbians; and continued after 1996 with new legal mechanisms permitting legal authority over the partner's child, the adoption of the partner's child in 2000, and finally in 2016, ART and full adoption.

Regardless of how homosexuals become parents, their parenthood is always the result of a plan, which may be elaborate, or more minimal. Anton emphasized that things are not 'so simple', and that the law offers only support.

> 'If you want to have a child together and particularly, I mean, gay and lesbian couples have to go the extra mile. I mean, straight couples, it's boy meets girl on a Friday night and nine months later they are parents whether they want to be or not. I mean, and gay and lesbian couples, that's an effort. You have to find a route to basically have child through either surrogacy or through adoption or, I don't know, any programs that are available out there. You have to go through a long process. It's not organic. I'm almost saying it's not natural, but it's not organic in a sense of the ability to reproduce." IS13 Anton

There is a fairly pronounced difference between generations. The perspectives on parenthood of interviewees from the older age group are clearly connected to the legal situation in the country when they entered their twenties. This split could be observed among those with children from a heterosexual relationship as well as those who had not had children, either because they did not foresee being in a heterosexual relationship (ephemeral or long-term), or because the absence of a law meant familial insecurity to them, in terms of the child's rights or the adult's personal rights with respect to the child.

Many pointed out that in case of conflict during separation or simply problems in daily life, the biological relationship is favoured over the social. This puts the legally unrecognized parent in a position of inferiority, a vulnerability that weighs particularly heavily in case of separation. Þórdís, 51, described the feelings of insecurity around the desires for children that she did not realize in a time when the law was hostile to homosexual parenthood.

> '…I also thought about having a child with one of our gay friends. But it was just like, we never went through with it because everything was so insecure… it also shows that these rights, when we obtain them, like here in Iceland, first in '96 and then in 2005, or whenever it was [in fact 2006], it has a different meaning for different generations in this society. For those of us who are of a different generation than those who are younger, our quality of life has been impaired when it comes to issues like children. There is a certain regret there. You could have had children but you weren't given the opportunity and you see that some of the women who belong to the older generation are marked by this lack of rights as well.' IS04 Þórdís

Kolbrún also emphasized the importance of the law and its ability to provide security with regard to the child, who legally has two parents – again, in the context of a normative vision of parenthood.

> '…I think the idea of two parents of the same sex is directly connected to the laws. Because before that time, say that I would have been in a relationship with a woman who had had a child, the old-fashioned way still without a dad. And when we break up, I would have no insurance that… And therefore I think that women were having children on their own and being like "This is my child and you are welcome in our lives as long as we stay a couple…" …Yes I think those laws really mattered. I think the person that benefited the most was the

> child. The child now has two parents. Not one mom and occasional stepmoms… I find it comforting that the legislation is there so everything is clear from day one. Instead of saying "Oh, we will fix this somehow afterwards, I will adopt the child." But what if you break up a month later? It is extremely important to know exactly where you stand. From the very start. I think most people would want that. This is such a huge event. It is like buying a property and there exists no laws regarding real estate business.' IS27 Kolbrún

Elín sees these laws mainly as a simplification. Because the laws exist, her plans for parenthood do not extend beyond the conception of the child. Just as marriage offers legal security to the spouses, the law guarantees it for the parents.

> 'It of course wouldn't be possible if this law wasn't in place so you know I would think it was really bad if um we couldn't both be mothers from the start or you know had to adopt you know the other mother would have to adopt or something like that so of course the simpler the system the more someone can be bothered doing this.' IS21 Elín

Access to ART

The legalization of homosexual parenting has disrupted social norms historically anchored in the law. This change made it possible to clearly distinguish filiation and parenthood (Fine 2013). While lesbian motherhood predates the law, the legalization of access to medically assisted procreation for female same-sex couples – first in closely linked Scandinavian countries (Denmark, Sweden) and then in Iceland – had a major impact on the lives of lesbians. With it they could plan to be parents without needing to provide for the presence of a man/father. For some, this had the effect of loosening ties to the homosexual community, and even of bringing them closer to heterosexual couples having technical difficulties procreating, as early as the planning phase. Information on infertility (technical or physical) is transmitted through websites and Facebook groups (and, previously, forums), which are not linked to the participants' sexuality.

Medical acts for this purpose are legal only if they are performed in a clinic accredited by the Ministry of Health. At the time of the survey there was only one such clinic, then operating under the name Art Medica. It has since been bought by a Swedish company and now operates under the name Livio.

The service offers users the possibility of a known or an unknown donor. Under Icelandic law, children have the right to learn the name of a known donor on reaching the age of majority. Conversations around these questions are the first to arise in lesbians' construction of their plans for parenthood.

In this context, one complex topic is the choice of a donor. Contrary to Sweden, which does not allow unknown donors, on grounds of children's right to know their origins, Iceland has offered this option since 2006. In Sweden, the requirement that the donor's identity be known allows the authorities to verify the child's genetic origin. Double gametes donation, of sperm and egg (to allow a woman's female partner to bear her embryo) has only been permitted since 2019 in Sweden (Leibetseder 2018).

Icelandic women make full use of Cryos, the Danish sperm bank, the main European provider in this sector (https://dk.cryosinternational.com/).

Little by little, most lesbian couples have come to choose the services of Art Medica/Livio as the simplest way to have children. It allows them to plan to become parents together, situating themselves together in the realm of the biological couple, choosing who will bear what child and whether the sperm donor will be known or anonymous.

6.4.2 Not One, But Many Lesbian-Parented Families

Before access to ART was legally extended to lesbian couples, it reproduced the heterosexual system of filiation through a legal fiction. In the case of a heterosexual couple using ART, sperm can be drawn from the male in the couple, or, in case of infertility, from a donor. In the latter case, while a third person was in fact involved in the birth, as the sperm donor was typically anonymous, it was as though he did not exist. Couples could even hide the fact that they had used ART, with filiation attributed to the two members of the couple. In contrast, the origin of the child of a lesbian couple is always biologically questioned. In lesbian medically assisted procreation, everyone knows that a sperm donor is involved. Questions around the origin of this sperm are thus often core concerns for lesbian couples. This may also happen for heterosexual couples, with the biological dimension re-emerging after having been legally suppressed: if the possibility of anonymity for donors were to be removed for lesbian couples in the name of children's right to know their origins, this would have to be done for heterosexual couples as well. Children of lesbian couples challenge the legal presumption of 'paternity'. In the context of ART, if the process takes place within the Icelandic healthcare system, the law stipulates that the member of the couple who is not bearing the child must give consent (Art. 3a, *Lög um tæknifrjóvgun og notkun kynfrumna og fósturvísa manna til stofnfrumurannsókna, nr. 55/1996*), regardless of gender. This person is then automatically considered the child's parent. Lesbian access to ART thus challenges the absolute naturalism of heterosexual ART, while establishing or affirming a legal version of lesbian parenthood. As emphasized by Daniel Borrillo, '*procreation could now be conceived as a freedom that merits specific legal protection as a manifestation of private life.*' (Borrillo 2018).

6.4.2.1 A Challenge for Lesbians: A New Model

The legalization of homosexual filiation brought a new visibility to family configurations that would come to be models. Affirming the equality of homosexuality with heterosexuality, in daily life and in the family context, is fundamental for future generations of homosexuals, notably in facilitating the process of coming out. Equality before the law does not necessarily imply sameness. In the years following the legalization of parenthood, the tension between normalization and assimilation came to the fore. Some saw this period of transition as an occasion to open up conceptions of the family beyond the heterosexual nuclear model, although these too have shown a strong tendency toward diversification, notably with family recomposition after separations.

Reinventing the family also means changing, not only the meaning of the parental couple, but also its content. The legalization of ART offered female same-sex couples the means to reflect on the meaning of their parenthood, and to work toward new norms. The latter have been diversifying, although the work of construction happens within the intimate sphere. Lesbian plans for parenthood arise through a series of choices negotiated between partners. These include choosing who will bear the child, who will provide the egg, who will be the sperm donor (sperm bank, friend, stranger, etc.), and the method of insemination. These choices relate both to the biological and the societal. And yet the choice of a known or anonymous donor does not necessarily remain confined to the private sphere. Once again, it raises questions about the couple's personal relationship to the biological, but can also provoke the societal gaze to which, de facto, lesbian parental couples are exposed.

From a legal perspective, having an unknown donor totally prevents children from knowing who provided the sperm needed for their birth. The irreversibility of this choice is at the heart of a debate that sometimes extends far beyond the couple. Having a known donor leaves children free to choose, whereas an unknown donor affirms both legal filiation and the female couple's exclusive status as the child's parents. And yet – whether or not it is expressed – the child's origin is a question to which the couple must constantly respond, as in the case of single mothers or fathers.

Lesbian motherhood offers the possibility of doing without the figure of the father in planning family life. But this remains a precursor at best, as society expects a biological father to exist, if not to be present. Respondents in our sample who made the choice not to involve a male parent in any way explained that others often found this choice more troubling than they did.

Family and friends are not absent from this debate. It is also often discussed in the LGBT circles, both among lesbians and among gay men, particularly as this question raises that of gay fatherhood, which is legally possible but limited in practice. The respondents systematically spoke of the contribution of the sperm donor, known or unknown, whether or not it was directly relevant to them.

In the sample analysed here, men also took part in the discussion around the existence of a father. Among those who expressed a desire for children during the interviews in 2015, the topic of ways of becoming a father brought out the desire to be a coparent (to share parenting with a person or a couple outside your relationship and/or household).

6.4.2.2 The Lesbian Nuclear Model

A new challenge for lesbian women is to experience their motherhood without letting the judgments of others affect their choices, and to take full advantage of what the law offers them. With the choice of an unknown donor, the two members of the couple are the sole and exclusive parents of the children.

Sigrún, for example, while not denying the involvement of a 'biological father' in the conception of her two children, explained that the children had no 'dad'.

> 'Yes, we talked about it and we both wanted to have him unknown. We have had to debate that because people of course don't agree. People have different views on the issue. But we chose to have him unknown because these are just our children and some sperm donor in Denmark, or wherever he is, would never be our children's father… These are our boys and we will always be their moms and there is no dad in the picture. Even though there is this biological father then it is just some information on paper you can't do anything more with.' IS10 Sigrún

The respondents offered several reasons for their choice of an unknown donor. For Lilja, it was a matter of centering the birth of her child within the couple. She totally rejected the presence of a father, biological or social. She did not bear the child, but she conceived parenthood as a duality, because "*as the "other mother", I would just find it difficult*" while rejecting the figure of a biological father, she also did not want a "social" father drawn from a circle of friends.

> 'I just want to have a child with my partner and maybe it is also difficult to know immediately when you have the baby that you will have to share it every other week with a person who doesn't belong to the relationship. Maybe this is a kind of selfishness, I don't know. But I just can't see it as a realistic option.' IS05 Lilja

In discussing the choice of a donor, known or unknown, Lilja nonetheless found it difficult not to think of the figure of the progenitor. She saw this as a point of vulnerability for her as a lesbian – one that she thought she had already left behind.

> 'There is an emotion which arises when you are choosing donor sperm. This may be the first time in my life that I feel my sexual orientation inhibits me in doing something. You know, wanting to do something on your own and just not being able to. Needing to get some man to… and that is just a weak spot. And I don't know why. I just found it really difficult and you know, should you try and match him with your appearance or not and everything like that.' IS05 Lilja.

Because she is not the biological mother, she also raised the issue of her relationship to the child's physical appearance, imagining herself in a day-to-day context where heteronormative society looks for the parent's features in the child.

Erla also mentioned this question of the gaze of others. Her story shows that while the negotiation takes place within the couple, they must also face their family and friends.

> 'You know that 50% of the child's genetic material wasn't mine but belonged to someone we didn't know at all. People wanted to ask. Who is he? Where does he come from? Do you know something about him? You know, do you know how the child you are having will look? You know, all these things that were just in the air but people were afraid to ask about them.' IS12 Erla

Kolbrún, who at the time of the survey was undergoing ART, also chose an unknown donor, after deciding against coparenting. She explained that she wanted to parent exclusively with her partner. She thought that this might be considered selfish, and that the presence of a third parent could be beneficial for the child, but she expressed fears about such multiple relationships.

'I used to think that it would be normal and fine to get some gay friend to be the donor. That was then, and after I paid more thought to it, then I came to the conclusion that it is not fair towards the other parent. You are a non-biological parent, how can you be sure that you are anything to the child unless you are there for at least five years? And you cannot guarantee that your partner will still like you after three years and then you are just no good. The child cannot remember you and what are you going to do?

...There is no solution to this, this is just life. But yes. After a lot of consideration I find it extremely important that this is an option and this is an option that I would choose.

S: Unknown donor?

K: Yes, like anonymous. But yes, this is a selfish point of view, because maybe it would be best for the child to have three parents. But since you are investing all this time and energy and everything, you want to have some minor chances of playing some role in the child's life.' IS27 Kolbrún

This sensation of selfishness relates to several possible scenarios. The first is ART's facilitation of parenthood without the involvement of a man. Haukur clearly expressed this as he reflected on his limited opportunities to become a father. This subject is clearly at the heart of debates around male parenthood in homosexual circles.

'I also find it, you get a little annoyed with lesbian couples. We have had heated discussions about this, among other things. You feel like they should stand by you. And I experience this as a little selfish, knowing.... I have a close relative, a lesbian and she and her wife went through artificial insemination in Denmark and they have, as so many other lesbian couples that I know, not wanted any known donors. That the kid can never find out anything about its father. We have had this hot discussion once in a gay pride party where there were mostly women there who had kids and the discussion was: There is no father. But for sure there is a father!' IS17 Haukur

6.4.2.3 The Persistence of the Biological Tie

Like Lilja and Sigrún, Auður chose ART in order to avoid involving a third adult in her family sphere. Contrary to them, however, she and her partner chose a known donor. They thus did not choose to definitively eliminate the reference to the biological in their family by blocking the child's access to its origins, although they did not wish to involve a father. They felt that their child should have access to the donor's identity if the child so desired.

'We both wanted to experience being pregnant and we just somehow wanted to have the child without there being a third party involved. Of course we have the donor but just that it isn't someone we know. But we decided to use, you must know [unclear], to use a known donor because even though we don't have to know who it is then we didn't want to take the possibility away from him [the child] if he would want to know one day. But we just figured that we wanted to have a stranger because if I don't know who it is and I look at the child, then I only see my girlfriend in him. I don't see anyone else. Like "Ah, he has Peter's nose" or something. I would feel like I was the third wheel.' IS09 Auður

This choice was reinforced by the couple's desire to have a second child from the same donor, with Auður as the biological mother. By choosing to use the same donor for both children, Auður was also creating a common "biological father" for the two, to make them biological half-siblings.

> 'I would like to become pregnant later on. We both wanted to experience being pregnant so even when we went to Art medica then we were just "Do you want to begin? Should I begin?" We were almost deciding it in the office. Just, okay, she began, just because she is one year older than I. That was the only deciding factor. And we will try and use the same donor when I have a child. So we are very 50/50 in everything we do.' IS09 Auður

Another situation where lesbian couples have maintained an attachment to biological filiation is the use of IVF with double donation. In Iceland, the law allows concomitant sperm and egg donation. This offers lesbians the possibility of one of the mothers bearing the other's embryo, and thus of shared "biological" involvement in filiation. This can be understood as a desire to recreate two realities drawn from heterosexuality, expressed in this case through the mother – understood as necessarily biological – and the father, whose paternity is either presumed (in the case of a husband) or recognized (for other couples). In the case of egg donation within the couple, both women consider themselves de facto biological mothers, conferring a 'natural' status that is otherwise seen as absent from lesbian parenthood. This has no legal effect under Icelandic law, which establishes filiation simply through the recognition of parenthood within legally recognized couples, but it is a choice that some couples make in order to naturalize their family. Élin made this choice.

> 'We have gone through IVF so we take an egg from [her partner] and fertilise it so she is of course the biological mother but I am of course like I always say jokingly you know that I am the surrogate mother except of course just like I get to then keep the baby but people of course have all kinds of like you know doesn't she think it's sad not carrying the child or say to me don't you think it's sad that the baby won't look like you and you and you know we don't care at all about that you know but um I think it's amazing to be able to do it the way we are doing it.' IS21 Élin

Élin's discourse features a mixture of the justification of equality with a denial of the importance of the views of others. This debate around maternity brings out the social primacy of the biological in the form of the child's resemblance to the parents. It highlights what the law allows and what society sees.

As we saw above, Lilja did not choose this way of family-making, but she finds it difficult because everything is referred back to the biological.

> 'I think it's just this fear of not connection [with the child]. Fear which is maybe completely irrational and disappears immediately when you have a child in your arms… and also the fear of hearing "Oh, she is just like her mother." That the child looks biologically like one of the mothers… it is insanity to consider yourself parent if it is not your biological child.' IS05 Lilja

The interviews performed thus show that the lesbian respondents fully invested in ART in all of their richness (Insemination and IVF), drawing on the complete range of possibilities they offer. A single desire, to become the parents of a child, took form as different realities.

6.4.3 Challenges to the Legal Framework

6.4.3.1 The Three-Adult Family

Coparenting is increasingly common, despite the fact that it still conflicts with the law, which recognizes only two parents for a given child. This configuration means a backward step for the children in social terms – a discrepancy in recognition between their legal parents and their social parents. This is the choice that was most often mentioned by male respondents speaking about the desire for children, notably because of the difficulty of adoption. It is also a model that could be adopted when ART was not available, and thus has a relatively long history. It is, if not accepted, at least known.

Sóley (IS18), who at the time of the survey was in an informal couple with a woman, conceived a child with a male friend, Bjarki (IS07). The two close friends developed the plan when Sóley was single; she met her partner only after the insemination had taken place. After several failed attempts at ART with Art Medica, she ultimately became pregnant through personal insemination (which took place outside the medical system, through the use of a syringe and her friend's sperm collected in artisanal fashion), and gave birth to a son.

Personal insemination allowed her male friend to recognize the child without the need for adoption, as in the case of a non-cohabiting heterosexual couple jointly declaring the birth on the national register. This is exactly what they wanted. Indeed, the desire for a child originated with the father, Bjarki, who wanted to coparent, participating in raising the child. Sóley's partner, however, has no legal rights with respect to the child. When the father has recognized the child, the mother's partner can only have rights if the father gives them up. Furthermore, the two women are not bound together by law, not even through a registered cohabitation. The three are raising the child together under these unsatisfactory conditions.

The example of Sóley and Bjarki is atypical of homosexual families which are not protected by the law, in that the two friends had made their plans to become parents in a situation of mutual trust, and the third person was added during the process. They did not sign any contract, or even establish any documentation to compensate for the absence of legal protections for their family.

> 'We have received a lot of criticism, or not criticism, but like questions and…, and doubts from people, we, from both sides. "Hey, hey people don't you have a contract? Didn't you sign anything?", you know, and stuff like that.' IS18 Sóley

Sóley met her partner in the final months of the process, who then became involved, accompanying Sóley through the different steps, notably medical; but only two people were involved in making the original plan. Sóley's partner spent much of the first months after the child's birth abroad; this period was thus mainly a shared experience for Sóley and Bjarki as a pair; the latter took paternity leave. This almost conventional model of coparenting, one woman and one man, is less subversive socially than it is legally, and led others to express contempt for their situation. Sóley also perceived that this similarity with the heterosexual model had an effect on her daily life. She is often perceived as the mother of Bjarki's child, and the two as a heterosexual couple.

In another model of coparenting, Sveinn has two children with a female heterosexual friend. They also conceived the children using a syringe, at home, when they had reached their thirties; both were driven by a very strong desire for children. Both of their children were conceived in this way, even though the younger child was born after the law expanding access to ART had been passed:

> 'We didn't think about it. We were surprised that it had gone through. I think we didn't even check. Also because if we had taken advantage of the laws it would have cost us half a million. But instead we bought a syringe for 330 crowns.' IS08 Sveinn

The mother of Sveinn's children does not have a partner, but he is in a confirmed partnership with a man. He is the biological parent of both children, as the desire for children was more his than his partner's. His conjugal status did not affect or influence his choice to be a parent: '*If I hadn't been in a relationship then I would have had kids at a similar time. I would just be a single father.*' In practice, his husband has no rights with respect to the children. This choice does not currently pose any problem for them in daily life, but he thought it was difficult for his partner's parents.

> 'Because somewhere is this need to procreate and it is creating a legal uncertainties for a lot of gay couples and it is destroying relationships around us. And I have felt that it is an issue in my home. It can be difficult to deal with, for instance for the grandmothers and grandfathers who are not related by blood. It took them a longer time to connect because people are afraid of starting to love something and then it is taken away from them.' IS08 Sveinn

He offered a normative account of his choices around parenthood, explaining that he thinks it is good for children to have a mother and a father. In framing his own parenthood, he sees the feminine, maternal figure as very important for children. He nonetheless presented the situation by saying: '*I'm married to a man, … and we have two children with a woman.*'

Contrary to Sóley and Bjarki, who made no plans concerning the organization of daily life, Sveinn and the mother of the children wrote down the material aspects of their planned parental situation together.

> 'We were preoccupied with writing everything down, to have everything down on paper, even before the child was conceived, so we would have a written agreement about, you know, right of access, finances and everything. We would have shared custody and just everything 50/50 except the children would have their domicile at her house.' IS08 Sveinn

His only worry in relationship to the law concerns his husband's rights with respect to the children. After the initial worries, they were reassured by the initial experiences with the child in public, where they found him to be identified as a child like any other, with an extended family.

> 'We both thought, since we both know how it is to grow up being different, are we bringing a child into a world where it won't be left alone because it has gay parents? But we stopped thinking about it very quickly. It just came and went in an afternoon. Especially when the kids were in kindergarten. Everyone has two homes and three fathers. It has never been an issue. We had role models. Our friends went down this path with a lesbian couple 16 years ago or something. We spoke to them a little bit.' IS08 Sveinn

His words recall that coparenting existed before the changes in family law, but also highlight the importance of models and their visibility.

Novelty Within Tradition in Four-Adult Parenting
Hrafnkell (IS23) was married and planning to have a child with his husband. Their preference was for coparenting with a female couple. This choice was motivated by a conception which he explicitly recognized as relatively traditional, with both masculine and feminine figures as parents of the child: *'I think all children benefit from having maybe also a little like, some male role models, and female of course.'* On the other hand, he saw having four parents as a significant protection for the child. He described himself as being in a stable relationship; he had been with his husband for 16 years, and, ideally, he hoped to find another similar couple. Two men and two women: this configuration does not challenge the reality of today's recomposed families, whether heterosexual or homosexual, where couples form, dissolve, and reform around each adult's respective children.

6.4.3.2 Transgender Parenthood

There have as yet been few studies on transgender parenting (Fortier 2015; Marchand 2017; Stotzer et al. 2014), and those few have often approached it from a psychological, clinical, or even legal angle. It raises questions of its own particular order, just as broad as those around homosexual parenting. The present chapter will not survey these questions, as only one of the respondents was in this situation. However, it is worth briefly considering a few points that recall certain problematics around homosexual parenthood discussed above.

The legal framework around transgender identity is not settled, and was still less so at the time of the survey (in particular concerning the control of the state – which defined transsexualism as a psychiatric illness – over different steps in the transition). Like the children of homosexuals born of heterosexual relationships when homosexuality was stigmatized, children born to transsexual parents, or who become transsexual themselves, continue to face the judgments of others in daily life. For some, the transition of the male or female biological parent to the other sex calls into question the terms "mother" and "father". Having a woman as a father or a man as a mother is currently a new situation – one that is poorly understood. This does not facilitate the processes of coming out and transition.

Águst had children within heterosexual relationships, before coming out and beginning a gender transition. The very existence of children in the household – from different fathers who were largely or entirely absent – led Águst to delay the transition, out of the fear that social services would take them away.

Águst is legally registered under his birth gender and the official documents of his children, which leads to difficult situations in daily life.

> '...this is something that I want to take out. Not all kids have a mother and not all kids have a father and some kids have two mothers and... So I think this should be changed to parent,

> or legal guardian. I have even spoken about this at the county magistrate's office. She totally agreed with me. I don't know what it takes to change this.' IS29 Águst

Águst sees this situation, which is a matter of ongoing debate, as a problematic one.

Because of Iceland's adaptability to individual cases, and the fact that only one informer was interviewed, no generalization can be drawn from Águst's experience. However, given the restricted number of structures – indeed, perhaps only a single one – with some relation to the services that interact in cases of transsexualism, Águst's situation likely reflects the state in which society has reacted to transsexual identity. While the law establishes filiation, it does not construct parenthood. In France, for example, a married transgender woman who kept her male reproductive organs came to be referred to as the 'biological parent' on the birth certificate of her child (Dervieux 2018). This was a compromise allowing the child to be considered to have been born to two mothers. This refusal to consider that two mothers can give birth to a child does not arise in Iceland, where the recognition of maternity applies to both members of married lesbian couples in the ART process for same-sex female couples within the legal healthcare system but it seems not to have been considered in the case of two fathers.

6.4.4 Male Parenthood in Question

The interviews with male respondents who had not had children in a heterosexual relationship raised other questions. The opening of ART to female same-sex couples offered lesbian women a point of entry into, and even a default option for, desired parenthood. Gay men, however, continue to find themselves in often complex, difficult, and sometimes ethically challenging situations (the same, moreover, as those facing women with difficulty procreating) with regard to access to the child.

> 'How can we have children? Here is a clear difference between gay and lesbian couples. They can have as many as they want without any hindering or anything. I think that the current discussion is like "Yes you have all rights, you can have children if you want." Yes, it is one thing to be allowed and another to be able to. There has been the right to adopt for years, but not a single gay couple has managed. So Iceland does not have to risk those [international] adoption contracts it has. I think this is a process we have to think about. Even if we do not want to have children right now, we have to take this discussion; this is a five-year process or something.' IS17 Haukur

The men who were interviewed often spoke of coparenting – for example with a single woman, or a lesbian couple. However, since lesbians gained legal access to ART, this has proven quite complicated. Haukur complained of a lack of organization to promote male parenthood.

> *'I think this is missing, a club or something. Should I post an ad to* Fréttablaðið *[Icelandic newspaper]: "A gay couple wishes to donate sperm to a nice woman on the condition that the child will know its father"? Where do I post this? Where do you bring this up in a conversation?'* IS17 Haukur

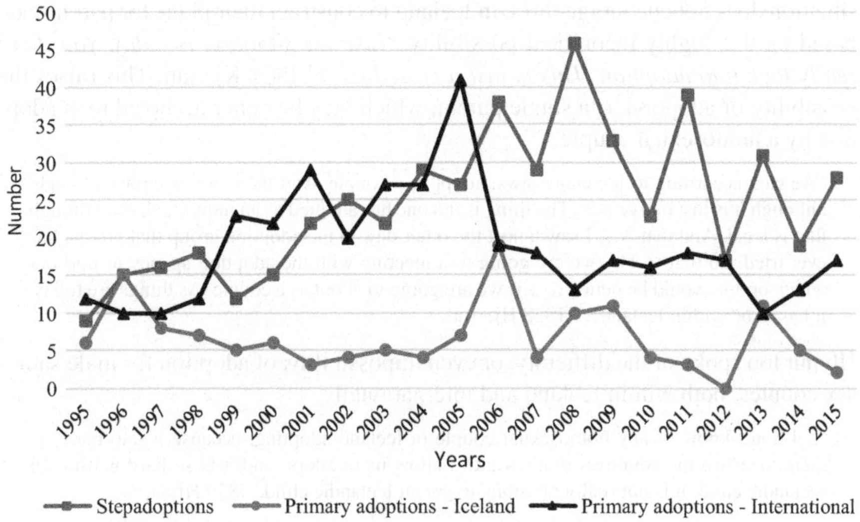

Fig. 6.2 Adoptions by type of adoption (1995–2015)
Source: Hagstofa Íslands https://www.hagstofa.is/, retrieved April 2019 Stepadoption refers to an adoption of partner's child (or previously adopted child of partner). Primary adoption refers to an adoption of a child other than the child (or previously adopted child) of the partner

6.4.4.1 Elective Filiation: Adoption

'If I have kids, then it is adoption.' IS16 Andri

Both women and men spoke about adoption as a means of becoming a parent, but the difficulty of adopting pushes women to choose other solutions first. References to adoption came mainly from men.

Adoption confronts the Icelandic state with an issue that is not entirely under its control. There are few children to adopt in Iceland, as in most countries with a welfare state. Icelanders thus resort to international adoption, which itself is in decline (Mignot 2015), and which as a result is increasingly selective about the countries and individuals who are granted access. Adopting countries depend on the stance taken by the children's country of origin on homosexuality and same-sex couples.

In Iceland, both adoption overall and international adoption in particular have been in decline for the last decade (Fig. 6.2).

In Iceland there is only one organization with the accreditation to organize the legal process of adoption, *Íslensk ættleiðing* (Icelandic Adoption). Iceland has few agreements with countries where there are children for international adoption, and the conditions of some do not allow adoption by homosexuals, regardless of whether they have a partner[2]. In 2015 it was allowed for children from only one country, Colombia, for children who are older or who have particular characteristics. This

[2] http://www.isadopt.is/is/lond, accessed April 2019.

situation does not encourage those in Iceland to construct their plans for parenthood based on this highly theoretical possibility. '*Like the situation is today, you don't really look into adoption. This is just a closed door.*' IS01 Kjartan. This raises the possibility of adoption as a single parent, which may be better accepted than adoption by a homosexual couple.

> 'We can, according to Icelandic laws, adopt as a couple. And there are examples of such, although it is just one or two. The thing is, no one has adopted as an individual, even though that is legal. And that is… I saw a post the other day, in the adoption group that no one has ever tried. So that is why we are going to a meeting with the adoption agency to find out which option would be better… …if we are going to adopt as a couple. As things are today, it has to be within Iceland…' IS28 Hjörtur

Hlynur too spoke of the difficulty, or even impossibility, of adoption for male same-sex couples, both within Iceland and internationally.

> '…I don't know of any homosexual couple in Iceland adopting, because it's so hard for them, because the countries don't want to allow us to adopt, and it is so hard getting an Icelandic child, it is not really possible, to get an Icelandic child.' IS30 Hlynur

While the law permitting adoption for same-sex couples was passed in 2006, it was not until 2013 that the first male homosexual couple adopted a child (Valgerðardóttir 2013). The child was a girl born to an Icelandic mother living abroad and an unknown father, putting this case in a separate category, which is difficult to generalize.

6.4.4.2 Men Demand That Surrogacy Be Both Legal and Ethical

Despite the obstacles facing them in becoming parents, none of the men interviewed seemed willing to resort to surrogacy in the existing legal situation. Their position here concerned not only the law, but above all ethics. Most of the respondents saw the recent laws as a form of support for parenthood, but not a prerequisite for the decision to become a parent, whereas with respect to surrogacy, opinions diverged. For the respondents, a law was needed to ensure that the practice would not be abusive for the surrogate mother.

Egill ruled out this possibility completely: '*I don't think it is that important to pass my genes along in order to put another person through carrying a child and then have it taken away from her. You know, I just think that would be too selfish.*' IS11 Egill. Sveinn was not as categorical, but remained cautious: '*I think that surrogacy should be all right where it is ethically OK. Where you are not abusing people.*' IS08 Sveinn.

Stefan spoke very frankly of surrogacy in India, which he associated to poverty and the exploitation of women, a topic that is discussed internationally (Rozée Gomez and Unisa 2014). '*I couldn't take part in systemic injustices tied to surrogacy. I can argue about it or participate in discussions about it but to go and find an Indian woman and destroy her life or something. No, that wouldn't happen.*' IS14 Stefan.

Similarly, Hrafnkell (IS23), who is seeking a way to have a child, thought that more work should be done to create a law regulating altruistic surrogacy, but who said he '*wouldn't want to take that route*' because he did not wish to take advantage of a woman in a situation he did not properly understand, referring to surrogacy in India.

Respondents thus emphasized ethical questions, despite the fact that this form of parenthood is legal, and thus regulated, including for non-citizens, in a number of nearby countries – either on an altruistic basis (in Great Britain for example) or a commercial one (United States of America) – and that it is very common among American and European gays (Berkowitz 2013). In Iceland the debate is highly charged: it confronts, on the one hand, a situation where men with a strong desire to be parents are not able to do so with, on the other, a highly feminist society oriented toward social progress but also toward taking great care with the use of the female body. '*There have to be really strict laws and supervision and... so um, it's at least something you can't rush into.*' IS24 Vigdís.

At the time of the survey, the Parliament had plans to discuss a framework for altruistic surrogacy, but this parliamentary process was then indefinitely adjourned.

6.5 Normalization, Integration, or Assimilation?

> 'I'm not sure it has anything to do with being a lesbian, or just being an Icelandic woman, I think it has more to do with that. That, we, in Iceland, we are so consumed with having children. And we are very consumed about having a man and having children. Or being in a relationship and having children.' IS18 Sóley

Progressively, legal struggles to gain acceptance for homosexuality have led homosexuals into a tendency to conform to heterosexual social norms, and in particular those around the family. This is an international trend which originated in the process to obtain equal rights, notably the right to have a family. Contrary to marriage equality, which the respondents described more as a symbolic right than as a need, they described rights around parenthood as vital to their lives. Contrary to what might have been expected, few expressed an aspiration to keep their distances from these norms. The principal exceptions were the oldest individuals in the sample and those in the most marginal position with respect to the dominant trends. One example is Aþena, who, possibly due to a disability that meant she was not in the easiest situation to assume the characteristics of a "normal" population, expressed a somewhat skeptical position:

> 'We have to stop forcing homosexual individuals into this heterosexual norm. You know, it is ok to be homosexual because you have a wife and a child and everything is normal. When I came out that was the focus at the National Queer Organization. We are normal people and something like that. It poses a bit of a problem. We can be homosexual as long as we are normal.' IS06 Aþena

Aþena also subversively transformed the desire to be a mother, which others see as a normalization, by provocatively emphasizing the role of her disability in any future parenthood. Nonetheless, the responses seem to show that the most reflexive of the respondents, from Aþena to Ólöf, experienced their own desire for motherhood as a confession.

Kolbrún thought that the attention to laws around marriage and parenthood had diverted the queer movement not only from an ideal of equality for all – including for those who do not wish to marry and have children – but also from struggles toward true integration, rather than normalization. Moreover, more or less in direct opposition to the first LGBT demands, the emphasis on parenthood and the right to have a family has led to pressure to fulfill this goal. In a familialist society, it seems that this choice was not contested, but according to Kolbrún, it marginalized those who do not identify with these aspirations, and who feel they have been robbed of a culture that was once their own.

> "[This politics was thought up] by some spin doctors, some women from the Social Democratic Alliance [*Samfylkingin*] 15 years ago and this is politics that was thought up by straight people. Beautiful thought, no evil motives… But what it does is that it marginalizes all the others within the queer community. And it was not until recently that people have started to… like Samtökin 78 to take up the trans issue, which I think is great. But to take this minority which some are thinking about and making it into the central issue. I sometimes feel stupid, because I do not have a child yet. I sometimes see the Facebook discussions of those women that I was hanging out with 15 or 20 years ago and it is just like the sewing circle in [name of a city]. And I think to myself, we have lost something. Is this what we wanted in the first place? I am not saying… I know a lot of cool mommies, but there is something, we have lost something for a higher reward. It is time that we start to look inwards and stop caring about what other people think.' IS27 Kolbrún

Researchers have recently begun to study the increasing numbers of women in European societies who voluntarily do not have children (Beaujouan et al. 2017). In this context it seems paradoxical that some women experience the greater freedom that should result from the law in Iceland instead as a form of pressure, and even an obligation, to conform to the current norm. Studies on women choosing not to have children have revealed a certain subversiveness on their part, a desire to emancipate themselves from the reproductive function urged on them by the state, turning instead toward greater individual fulfilment and even economic comfort. Icelandic lesbians, however, seem to be moving in the opposite direction. This desire for parenthood, articulated by both male and female respondents, may be an effect of the law that will subside with time, decreasing as it has among heterosexual women. And indeed, the most recent trends[3] show a decline in birth rates and progressively increasing age at first birth, which remains low among Icelandic women in comparison to the rest of Europe (Garðarsdóttir 2008), possibly indicating that this traditionally familialist society has taken a new turn.

It is also possible that this period of transformation, with the particularly favourable climate that surrounds the birth of a child, has seduced younger cohorts who (may still?) have found coming out to be difficult, by suppressing the idea of difference between heterosexual and homosexual parenthood in social mechanisms and collective awareness. The rejection of homosexuality and difference often results from a fear of the unknown, which is lessened in a small society with strong family ties (Digoix 2013a). Supportive legislation is important for multiple reasons. New

[3] https://www.icelandreview.com/society/in-focus-dropping-fertility/, 2019 based on Hagstofa Íslands, 2019

family laws have conferred on homosexuality a certain visibility as a sexual behaviour like another, and enabled the establishment of models. They favour the acceptance of homosexuality, facilitating the process of coming out: parents find they can see the future of their children as "normal", insofar as Icelandic society revolves around the very strong spirit of the family line. Parents expect their children to have children, and homosexuals' parents too. Over time, lesbians had come to take it for granted that having children would be difficult or even impossible. But a period of legal change has made it possible for homosexuals to reinvest in this familialist society. Homosexuals, both women and men, have desires for children just as heterosexuals do, whether or not they are clearly expressed or fulfilled. These desires are sometimes vague, and not clearly stated as a personal or social desire. The oldest respondents, who had experienced circumstances where there was less opportunity to conform to the norm, were more conscious of this than the others. However, this ideal of parenthood can be frustrated by nature, given the difficulty of having a child, sometimes for women, but mainly for men. It remains to be seen how male parenthood will be constructed in the coming years. Many questions revolve around surrogacy: For most of the respondents, surrogacy can only be acceptable if it is legally regulated. Some raised the possibility of family surrogacy (with a child borne by a sister, for example) as a possibility, a compassionate gift. Discussion of the law has been delayed, while international circuits have changed and developed in more ethical directions.

Contrary to the totally assimilationist interpretation of Icelandic LGBT desires for parenthood, the work of planning for parenthood reflects a reappropriation of gay and lesbian specificity. This work is all more original in the case of lesbians, with the possibilities opened up by ART, and notably IVF techniques, including the double donation of gametes. It is also present, mostly (still) through extra-legal arrangements, in coparenting scenarios involving multiple possible combinations of components, in terms of parents and also of reproductive techniques. In this context, parenthood can involve the construction of pairs, sets of three, or double pairs; bring together heterosexuals and homosexuals, or homosexuals alone; people who are in a intimate relationship or are not; who live together or apart; with partners involved or not. Here, heterosexuals and homosexuals complement one another, tracing the outlines of a new egalitarian society.

Notwithstanding the notion that this attraction to parenthood may be transitory, the interviewed residents of Iceland, whether Icelandic or not, female or male, do not seem to have felt held back in their desire for children, contrary to what has been found in empirical studies on desires for children in other countries (Gato et al. 2017). In Iceland, the negative characteristics which hold back gays and lesbians elsewhere are either absent or not sufficiently strong. Their personal motivations often reproduce the heterosexual model, the analogy on which Icelandic homosexuals drew in demanding full equal rights. Their experiences at workplace remain positive, legal and social determinants are not barriers, and they are able to count on the support of friends and family, as well as social structures surrounding parents, notably schools (Digoix et al. 2018). Here, parenthood – not only the actuality of being a parent, but even the desire to become one – overrides, or at the very least surpasses, personal specificity. For society, individuals are parents first, before they are lesbian or gay. This process may be seen as assimilation or as integration, but it has the advantage of making coming out – which remains difficult, even if the difficulty of the experience is decreasing with time – less destabilizing. It will be interesting to observe developments over the next decade in order to discover further improvements in the quality of life of homosexuals.

Profiles of the Interviewees

For reasons of anonymity, the names of the respondents have been changed. Place of residence is mentioned only where it was not Reykjavík and its suburbs.

IS01 Kjartan, 33, childless and in a non-registered cohabiting relationship, grew up outside the capital region. He and his partner had already discussed how they planned to have a child. Their preferred option was coparenting: they were very aware of the difficulty of adopting and mistrustful of surrogacy, particularly if it was not legalized. He was counting on the law to help him to become a father.

IS02 Ólöf, 50, childless, in a registered cohabiting relationship. Her position on lesbian parenthood was ambiguous: on the one hand, she defended it in the name of equal rights, while on the other hand, she described it as the decline of queer culture. She would have liked to have had a child at some point in her life, but her partner did not want children. She did not want to embark on becoming a parent alone, as she was from a generation where '*it was complicated, but doable*.' She liked the idea of coparenting, and thought of it as a way to help men.

IS03 Katla, 40, single and childless. She did not have a partner and thought that this had 'restricted' her personally in considering having a child, whereas this was not a problem for heterosexual single mothers or fathers. She liked the idea of adoption, of helping a child, but knew that it is rare in Iceland.

IS04 Þórdís, 51, childless, was divorced from a sham marriage with a gay man used to stay in the country where she previously lived with her partner. At the time of the survey she lived with her partner and was raising her partner's child. Although the partnership was not registered, she had parental authority. Her feelings were slightly mixed, between pleasure at the legal advances in favour of homosexuals and the conformism into which the gay community had fallen in its desires for children.

IS05 Lilja, 27, in a registered cohabiting relationship. She and her partner had begun the process of medically assisted reproduction. She had a strong desire for a child and '*would have had a child, even if it weren't possible in Iceland*.' She had used a forum to learn about ART methods and share information and experiences. She found Art Medica impersonal, but was satisfied with how she and her partner had been treated. If ART did not work she hoped to adopt, although she knew it was difficult. She did not wish to involve a third party.

IS06 Aþena, 23, single and childless. Aþena was a student and an activist. She enjoyed being provocative. She felt doubly stigmatized, as a queer woman and as disabled. Her thoughts revolved largely around her disability, how she could manage it in society and its role in her future plans. She wished to have children, with or without a partner.

IS07 Bjarki, 38, single, coparent of a child with Sóley (IS18). He liked the idea of raising his child with the mother, a very good friend. He is from outside the capital region. Coming out had been difficult for him. He thought that there were too many ethical problems with surrogacy.

IS08 Sveinn, 41, married, coparent of two children with a heterosexual single woman. They conceived the children on their own, at home. He had divorced from a man and remarried. His husband had no rights with respect to the children. Sveinn, his husband and the children's mother shared the task of rearing the children, planning everything together. Their life revolved around the children.

IS09 Auður, 29, in a cohabiting relationship. She had had a child via ART with a known donor, because she and her partner wanted the child to have the option of learning about the donor. She wanted to get married for the sake of material security. All of her friends were heterosexual, and she felt very well integrated in society.

IS10 Sigrún, 33, married, two children via ART. She married for material security. Her parents and those of her partner were relieved to have grandchildren.

IS11 Egill, 28, single and childless. Egill had never been in a stable relationship. In his view, marriage and registered cohabitation are the same thing, and it is important to be in one of the two before having a child. He said that it was not easy for men to become parents, and that the law had changed little in this regard. He wanted the state to establish contracts with countries that allow homosexuals to adopt.

IS12 Erla, 29, in a registered cohabiting relationship. At the time of the survey, she was expecting a child borne by her partner. They chose ART through Art Medica. The legislation on this was very important for her, as it made the situation with respect to the child and her partner clear: with Art Medica, they had signed a contract, and they were mothers of the child from the beginning of the procedure. Genetics was not important to her, and she did not wish to resort to double donation of egg and sperm.

IS13 Anton, 50, born abroad, divorced from a woman, with two children from different heterosexual relationships, and a grandfather. Living outside the capital region. He had had difficulty owning up to his homosexuality and coming out. He had worked in occupations where homosexuality is stigmatized. His children had reacted well to his recent coming out. He considered himself a gay man but a 'straight parent', as until then he had presented himself as a heterosexual to his children.

IS14 Stefan, 49, divorced from a man and a woman, grandfather. He had two children from a heterosexual relationship when he was quite young, and had played the role of father for two others. When he came out to himself, he sank into alcoholism. He saw marriage as good for the recognition of homosexuals, but remained attached to heteronormative reality. He was formally opposed to surrogacy.

IS15 Halldór, 23, single and childless. His dream since his earliest youth was to marry and have children. He was very attached to the idea of family, structured by marriage. He said he would like to resort to surrogacy if it were legal, but in Iceland. He had female friends who had volunteered to bear the child.

IS16 Andri, 34, married and childless. The couple had married without a precise plan for having children, but with a desire to do so and the idea that a couple had to be married for 5 years to adopt. He saw adoption as the solution he would choose in order to 'save' a child, but he knew that this was difficult because few countries allow gay couples to adopt. He thought that relations with the mother in a coparenting situation would be complicated if she were a friend. He thought that men should fight for access to parenthood.

IS17 Haukur, 28, childless. He is from a little village and lived outside the capital. He did not live with his partner, and although they were preparing to marry, he wanted to do 'something else' other than the heterosexual norm. Speaking of the social pressure of having a wife and children, he said that being gay had, in a way, kept him at a distance from that pressure. He thought that the law was not sufficient, as it allowed homosexuals to have children, but doing so was nearly impossible for men. He spoke of adoption. He also said he would like to give his sperm to a female couple and be a father, for his personal fulfilment and to help out, without necessarily coparenting as defined by rules for joint custody.

IS18 Sóley, 41, had a child with Bjarki (IS07). She grew up outside the Reykjavík area. She did not live with her partner. She did not have a very clear-cut position concerning her legal situation, was not thinking of marriage, and did not have a contract with Bjarki, although he was her child's legal father and they had shared custody. She did not feel she had faced prejudice against her coparenting situation, but said they had been criticized for not enshrining it in a legal agreement.

IS19 Ásgeir, 22, single, childless, living outside the capital region. Spoke of a desire for a child during the interview. A child with his own DNA. He related marriage to family, but for him, having a partner was not necessary. He wanted to have a good relationship with the child's mother. If surrogacy were legal, he would want to choose it.

IS20 Ingibjörg, 27, in a non-cohabiting relationship, childless. Said she would marry only to have access to the associated rights. She wanted to have children and thought she would have succeeded even without changes in the law. She was thinking of ART because adopting is a very long and complicated process, and she wanted to have the child within the legal system, without a father.

IS21 Elín, 27, engaged. She was preparing for marriage because she had had problems conceiving a child, although doing so was a priority. She had chosen to have a child by means of IVF with double donation of sperm and her partner's egg, so that both would be biologically connected to the child. She found Art Medica very competent.

IS22 Carl, 45, divorced from a woman. He is not Icelandic but had been living in the country for more than 10 years. He had married a woman in his country of origin because he wanted a child, but had divorced very soon afterward. He was still reluctant to speak about his homosexuality to those around him. His family was not very accepting of his homosexuality, but his parents wanted a grandchild. He had a very marked desire to be a father. He wanted to have and raise a child.

IS23 Hrafnkell, 37, married for nearly 10 years, childless but planned to have a child in the very near future. He preferred coparenting as there were examples around him where it worked very well. He complained of the difficulty of finding a reliable network for establishing a coparenting situation. He supported altruistic surrogacy.

IS24 Vigdís, 51, single, two children from a heterosexual union, grandmother. She came out at age 35. Had chosen to revive a group for children and parents to better manage her parental situation. She had not wanted children in her heterosexual relationship: the first happened by chance, the second to accompany the first.

IS25 Ísak, 27, single, childless. Ísak lived outside the capital region. He said that legal mechanisms such as marriage facilitate the decision to have children, although this was more turned toward women than men for the time being. He saw surrogacy as acceptable only if it took place under ethical conditions. He had thought a little about coparenting, and had followed the debates on surrogacy, but did yet not feel ready.

IS26 Sunna, 41, divorced from a woman, had a child with that woman and a stepdaughter. Her son was born within that relationship. Formalizing her union in a confirmed partnership was not important for her, but at the time when her son was born, having a wife was a condition for access to ART.

IS27 Kolbrún, 41, divorced from a woman, in a registered cohabiting relationship, living outside the capital region. She did not have children but was trying to do so using ART. She explained that this is difficult outside the capital region because the only clinic, Art Medica, is in Reykjavík. She chose an anonymous donor because she was thinking of the non biological mother. She felt under pressure to have children, and thought this was a shame.

IS28 Hjörtur, 27, in a relationship, living in outside the capital region. Before coming out to himself, he saw himself having children and sometimes a wife. He was planning to have a child, and before registering with his partner, he was planning to make an appointment with the adoption agency to see if his chances of adopting as single would be better. Thought it was a shame that Iceland was so lacking in links to countries that allow adoption by homosexual couples. He was against surrogacy, above all in commercial form.

IS29 Águst, 32, divorced from a man before his transition. Had three children in heterosexual relationships before coming out and then thinking of transitioning. Waited to be certain he would be able to keep his children before beginning the transition. Wanted another child. Thought that surrogacy could be a beautiful gesture if it were undertaken altruistically and ethically, but would not use this method. Preferred ART with a sperm donor.

IS30 Hlynur, 53, divorced from a woman and widower of a man. Two children from his heterosexual relationship. His wife had reacted very badly to his coming out, and refused to allow him to be with his youngest son for some time. The divorce was very difficult because of his homosexuality. He was hoping to have grandchildren.

References

Icelandic Laws

Barnalög nr. 76/2003
Barnaverndarlög nr. 80/2002
Hegningarlög nr. 19/1940
Hjúskaparlög nr. 31/1993
Lög nr. 21/1990 um Lögheimili
Lög nr. 40/1992 um breyting á almennum hegningarlögum nr. 19/1940
Lög nr. 55/1996 um tæknifrjóvgun og notkun kynfrumna og fósturvísa manna til stofnfrumurannsókna
Lög nr. 87/1996 um staðfesta samvist (abrogated in 2010)
Lög nr. 65/2006 um breytingu á lagaákvæðum er varða réttarstöðu samkynhneigðra (sambúð, ættleiðingar, tæknifrjóvgun)
Lög nr. 130/1999 um ættleiðingar
Lög nr. 65/2010 um breytingar á hjúskaparlögum og fleiri lögum og um brottfall laga um staðfesta samvist (ein hjúskaparlög)
Æskulýðslög nr. 70/2007

Danish Law

Lov om registreret partnerskab af 7. juni 1989

Nordic Council Recommendation

Nordiska rådets rekommendation om homosexuellas sociala situation i samhället nr.17/1984/j

Beaujouan, E., Sobotka, T., Brzozowska, Z., & Zeman, K. (2017). La proportion de femmes sans enfant a-t-elle atteint un pic en Europe ? *Population & Sociétés, 540.*

Bech, H. (1997). *When men meet: Homosexuality and modernity*. Cambridge: Polity Press.

Berkowitz, D. (2013). Gay men and surrogacy. In A. E. Goldberg & K. R. Allen (Eds.), *LGBT-parent families: Innovations in research and implications for practice* (pp. 71–85). New York: Springer.

Betænking nr. 1127. (1988). *Homoseksuelles vilkår, afgivet af kommissionen til belysning af homoseksuelles situation i samfundet*. København: Det juridiske laboratorium ved Københavns Universitet.

Björnsson, B. (1971). *The Lutheran doctrine of marriage in modern Icelandic society*. Oslo: Universitetsforlaget.

Borrillo, D. (2018). *La famille par contrat: la construction politique de l'alliance et de la parenté*. Paris: PUF.

Bourdieu, P. (1997). Quelques questions sur la question gay et lesbienne. *Liber, 33*, 7–8.

Cryos. (2019). https://dk.cryosinternational.com/. Accessed 17 Apr 2019.

Dervieux, V.-O. (2018). Du transsexualisme à la transparentalité. *Dalloz Actualité, 14 mai 2019*. https://www.dalloz-actualite.fr/flash/du-transsexualisme-transparentalite#.XW45U2d5GsE. Accessed May 2019.

Descoutures, V. (2010). *Les mères lesbiennes*. Paris: Le Monde.
Digoix, M. (2008). Le concept nordique d'égalité entre différenciation et universalisme. In V. Descoutures, M. Digoix, E. Fassin, & W. Rault (Eds.), *Mariages et homosexualités dans le monde* (pp. 18–33). Paris: Autrement.
Digoix, M. (2013a). *Coming out et ordre normatif en Islande*. Paris: Ined, Documents de travail 198.
Digoix, M. (2013b). Mariage pour tous: Expériences scandinaves. *P@ges Europe, 28 janvier 2013, La Documentation française © DILA*.
Digoix, M., Franchi, M., Pichardo Galán, J.-I., Selmi, G., de Stéfano Barbero, M., Thibeaud, M., & Vela, J.- A.-M. (2018). *European rainbow families in the making: Practices, norms and the law?* Paris: Ined, Documents de travail 242.
"Dropping fertility". (2019). Iceland review, February 19. https://www.icelandreview.com/society/in-focus-dropping-fertility/. Accessed August 2019.
Einarsdóttir, A. (2016). Family matters: Women who « marry »women in Iceland. *Journal of Sociology, 52*(2), 173–189.
Eydal, G. B. (2005). *Family policy in Iceland 1944–1984*. Göteborg University: Department of sociology.
Eydal, G. B., & Gíslason, I. (2015). Caring fathers and parental leave in prosperous times and times of crisis: The case of Iceland. In G. B. Eydal & T. Rostgaard (Eds.), *Fatherhood in the Nordic welfare states* (pp. 325–345). Bristol: Policy Press.
Eydal, G. B., & Ólafsson, S. (2002). *Demographic trends in Iceland*. First report for the project Welfare Policy and Employment in the Context of Family Change. Mimeo.
Fine, A. (2002). Qu'est-ce qu'un parent ? Pluriparentalité, genre et système de filiation dans les sociétés occidentales. *Spirale, 21*(1), 19–43.
Fine, A. (2013). Avoir deux pères ou deux mères. In I. Théry (Ed.), *Mariage de même sexe et filiation* (pp. 115–128). Paris: Editions de l'école des hautes études en sciences sociales.
Forsætisráðuneytið. (1994). *Skýrsla nefndar um málefni samkynhneigðra*. Reykjavík: Höfundur.
Fortier, C. (2015). Transparentalité: vécus sensibles de parents et d'enfants (France, Québec), *Enfances Familles Générations*, 23, http://journals.openedition.org/efg/385. Accessed 28 May 2019.
Foucault, M. (1981). De l'amitié comme mode de vie (entretien avec de Ceccaty, R., Danet, J. & Le Bitoux, J.). *Gai Pied, 25*, 38–39.
Friðriksdóttir, H. (1996). *The Nordic gay and lesbian "marriage": No children allowed*. Cambridge: Harvard Law School.
Friðriksdóttir, H. (2015). Nordic family law: New framework-new fatherhoods. In G. B. Eydal & T. Rostgaard (Eds.), *Fatherhood in the Nordic welfare states* (pp. 53–78). Bristol: Policy Press.
Friðriksdóttir, H. (2017). Parenting and legal family formats in Iceland. In K. Waaldijk et al. (Eds.), *The LawsAndFamilies database – Aspects of legal family formats for same-sex and different-sex couples*. Paris: INED. www.LawsAndFamilies.eu, LawsAndFamilies-IS-Section3.pdf.
Garðarsdóttir, Ó. (2008). Fertility trends in Iceland in a Nordic perspective. In G. B. Eydal & I. Gíslason (Eds.), *Equal rights to earn and care* (pp. 45–63). Reykjavík: Félagsvísindastofnun Háskóla Íslands.
Gato, J., Santos, S., & Fontaine, A. M. (2017). To have or not to have children? That is the question. Factors influencing parental decisions among lesbians and gay men. *Sexuality Research & Social Policy, 14*, 310–323.
Gíslason, I. (2008). You are regarded as weird if you don't use the paternity leave. In B. Eydal & I. Gíslason (Eds.), *Equal rights to earn and care* (pp. 87–110). Reykjavík: Félagsvísindastofnun Háskóla Íslands.
Íslensk ættleiðing. (2019). *Samstarfslönd íslenskrar ættleiðingar*. http://www.isadopt.is/is/lond. Accessed Apr 2019.
Karlsson, G. (2000). *The history of Iceland*. Minneapolis: University of Minnesota Press.
Kristinsson, Þ. (2003). Samkynhneigð og löggjöf á Íslandi. Stutt ágrip. In R. Traustadóttir & Þ. Kristinsson (Eds.), *Samkynhneigðir og fjölskyldulíf* (pp. 259–262). Háskólaútgáfan: Reykjavík.

Leibetseder, D. (2018). Queer and trans access to assisted reproductive technologies (ART): A comparison of three EU-states – Poland, Spain and Sweden. *Journal of International Women's Studies, 20*(1), 10–26.

Leósdóttir, J. (2013). *Við Jóhanna*. Reykjavík: Mál og menning.

Marchand, J.-B. (2017). La transparentalité, une nouvelle façon d'être parent. *Dialogue, 216*, 105–118.

Mezey, N. J. (2013). How lesbians and gay men decide to become parents or remain childfree. In A. E. Goldberg & K. R. Allen (Eds.), *LGBT-parent families: Innovations in research and implications for practice* (pp. 59–70). New York: Springer.

Mignot, J.-F. (2015). L'adoption internationale dans le monde: les raisons du déclin. *Populations et Societés, 519*.

Pollak, M. (1985). Male homosexuality- or happiness in the ghetto? In P. Aries & A. Bejin (Eds.), *Western sexuality. Practice and precept in past and present times* (pp. 40–60). Oxford: Basil Blackwell.

Rich, G. (1978). The domestic cycle in modern Iceland. *Journal of Marriage and the Family, 40*, 173–188.

Rozée Gomez, V., & Unisa, S. (2014). Surrogacy from a reproductive rights perspective: The case of India. *Autrepart, 70*(2), 185–203.

Schiltz, M.-A. (1998). Un ordinaire insolite: le couple homosexuel. *Actes de la recherche en sciences sociales, 125*, 30–43.

SOU 2001:10. (2001). *Barn i homosexuella familjer:Betänkande från kommittén i homosexuella familjer*. Stockholm: Justitiedepartementet.

Stotzer, R., Herman, J., & Hasenbush, A. (2014). *Transgender parenting: A review of existing research*. Los Angeles: The Williams institute.

Styrkársdóttir, A. (2006). *Women's suffrage in Iceland*. https://kvennasogusafn.is. Accessed May 2019.

Traustadóttir, R., & Kristinsson, Þ. (Eds.). (2003). *Samkynhneigðir og fjölskyldulíf*. Reykjavík: Háskólaútgáfan.

Valgerðardóttir, S. (2013). Fyrsta samkynhneigða parið sem ættleiðir barn. *Vísir*, 27. júní.

Weeks, J. (2001). *Same sex intimacies: Families of choice and other life experiments*. Abington: Routledge.

Weston, K. (1997). *Families we choose: Lesbians, gays, kinship*. New York: Columbia University Press.

Chapter 7
Postface. After Legal Recognition

Wilfried Rault

Abstract This postscript highlights the key features of this book, especially its combination of different approaches using legal, demographic and sociological analysis tools, and the comparative perspective that is present throughout. The approach is particularly useful, because the three disciplines that structure the book do not view same-sex families in the same way. Another strand in the book is a more direct reflection on marriage. While marriage has been the symbol of the recognition of sexual minorities in recent years, the book shows that it cannot fully embody it, and invites us to think "beyond marriage". The last part of this postscript will suggest research themes that could usefully be investigated, provided that suitable tools are used – particularly the tools of quantitative sociology, since the social and scientific visibility of same-sex parenthood does not always mean statistical visibility.

Keywords Same-sex couples · LGBT families · Europe · Marriage · Methods

Research on same-sex parenthood has been going on in Europe for some 30 years. The trend owes much to the movement for political, legal and social recognition that began in the Scandinavian countries in the late 1980s, starting with Denmark in 1989. It then spread to most countries of Western Europe, taking different forms in different countries, and is now emerging in some East European countries. Although most of the earliest provisions recognizing same-sex unions, such as registered partnerships and civil unions, included no provision for filiation and parentage, it was due to them that same-sex-parented families (called "same-sex families") were included in the political agenda and gradually became objects of study in the social sciences. But these kinds of family were not new. Lack of legal recognition and a term to call them by never prevented LGBT families from existing. They were "nameless families" in the words of Pierre Bourdieu (1996) – low-visibility families.

W. Rault (✉)
French Institute for Demographic Studies (INED), Paris, France
e-mail: Wilfried.rault@ined.fr

M. Digoix (ed.), *Same-Sex Families and Legal Recognition in Europe*,
European Studies of Population 24, https://doi.org/10.1007/978-3-030-37054-1_7

Often, they were due to lesbians and gays in same-sex relationships having had children through a previous heterosexual relationship, the only legitimate form of private life at the time. Sometimes they came from other kinds of arrangement. Homosexuality being strongly stigmatized, even sometimes repressed, these individual configurations had to keep to the shadows. That made political mobilization difficult.

That changed in a big way in Western Europe in the late twentieth and early twenty-first centuries with the legal recognition of same-sex unions, which led to the social and sociological construction of "same-sex parenthood" as a category. A central factor in this trend was the fact that the new legal devices were often inspired by the institution of marriage which, a few decades ago, still associated family (and sexuality) with marriage, whose necessity was still only weakly contested. Gradually, the political demand for recognition of same-sex unions raised the question of homosexual people's families, as couples and families both became socially visible for the first time. As the legal vacuum in which same-sex couples lived was brought to light, so was the existence and legal and social situation of the families. The countries that had pioneered the recognition of same-sex unions necessarily started thinking about extending existing provisions for heterosexual couples and their families to same-sex couples. Discussion around the couple inevitably opened the way to discussion of filiation and parentage. Should the existing provisions be simply transposed to same-sex couples, knowing that these provisions were not limited to recognizing the union but were also intended for officialising filiation? Or should they be amended so that they concerned only the (same-sex) union, removing certain provisions that were assumed (erroneously) to not concern them? It was often the latter option that was taken at first, so that things had to progress in two stages: first same-sex unions were recognized, then discussion of filiation began[1]. The first step seems to have been necessary for envisaging the second. Socially necessary because it made the issue of children visible, and changing the juridical possibilities for couples also helped to change representations of the family. This two-step change (three steps where civil partnerships were introduced before same-sex marriage) was also in many cases the fruit of a political strategy, since demanding recognition of same-sex union and the same-sex family at the same time was unlikely to succeed, especially in countries where hostility was strongly expressed or where the government majority had lowered its initial intentions.

So, gradually, same-sex parenthood or homosexual parenthood became a commonplace notion and, in parallel, a topic for social science and a research subject, in sociology especially. The trend was led by a number of young researchers, who took up this new subject within a research community whose forms of resistance have made it difficult for to acknowledge their originality and relevance. LGBT research can itself be faced with a degree of heterosexism, even today.

The first researchers in Europe to address the issue of same-sex families looked at the challenges of legal recognition. They conducted original, qualitative surveys of low-visibility family configurations, describing the families, their diversity, their

[1] Iceland differed from other pioneer countries in that the law introducing registered same-sex unions in 1996 already included the possibility of exercising parental authority over the same-sex spouse's children (see Chap. 6).

contours, how they functioned day to day and how their daily lives were affected by the lack of legal recognition. These studies helped to further weaken the strict association of parenthood with heterosexuality, and the widespread representation of homosexuality as being incompatible with parenthood collapsed. But they also helped to renew research into parentage and filiation in general, a field that had already been shaken up by the increase in separations and blended families since the 1970s. In both cases, the research conducted gave expression to questions raised by the dissociation between day to day parenting, legal recognition (filiation and parentage) and biological parenthood. These issues are particularly salient, in various ways, for same-sex families. The research also questioned assumptions such as that children have two parents (can you have more than two?), and that heterosexuality is the only bedrock on which the private sphere can be built (can one have two parents of the same sex?). Finally, it raised the basic question of "What is a family?", which became a new political issue.

This book, edited by Marie Digoix, while following in the footsteps of these founding studies[2], refreshes the view of same-sex families by taking into account today's context, where the existence of such families is widely acknowledged, although this still varies considerably between countries and they are not always recognized by the law. This postscript first addresses the book's original contributions, particularly its combination of a multidisciplinary approach and European comparisons. Thirty years after the first official registration of a same-sex union, the book provides some hindsight on changes in the ways homosexuality and same-sex parenthood in Europe is addressed in law, demography and sociology. Another strand in the book is a more direct reflection on marriage. While marriage has been the symbol of the recognition of sexual minorities in recent years, the book shows that it cannot fully embody it, and invites us to think "beyond marriage". This centrality of marriage, and of legal issues more broadly, has structured research into same-sex couples and LGBT parenthood to a large extent. The current state of progress in legal rights is propitious for research in other directions. The last part of this postscript will suggest research themes that could usefully be investigated, provided that suitable tools are used – particularly the tools of quantitative sociology, since the social and scientific visibility of same-sex parenthood does not always mean statistical visibility.

7.1 More Viewpoints for Better Understanding

7.1.1 Roads to Legal Recognition

The key features of this book are its combination of different approaches using legal, demographic and sociological analysis tools, and the comparative approach that is present throughout, either direct comparison as in the first two chapters, or

[2] See Gross (2015) and Goldberg & Allen (2013) for a broad overview of research on LGBT parents.

indirect in the surveys conducted in different countries. The approach is particularly heuristic, because the three disciplines that structure the book do not view same-sex families in the same way. The legal approach looks at the *legal provisions* available in European countries, and their history from the earliest legal recognition measures (Waaldijk) up to 2019. So the book has been produced in circumstances very different to those obtaining when the first studies of same-sex families in Europe were made. Recognition of the couple has advanced in all of Western Europe, but differently in different countries, and same-sex families are also more commonly recognized, both legally and socially. An overview of the European continent shows a transformation that seems fairly uniform, especially in comparison to the world as a whole. But if we compare the legal data compiled between 2005 and 2016, as analysed by Kees Waaldijk, it is hard to speak of *a* European policy of recognizing same-sex couples and families, because national histories, though often similar (especially if we look at groups of countries, e.g. Scandinavia) also show a distinct pathway specific to each country, its social history and its political power balance.

Thirty years after the first same-sex partnership legislation was enacted, in Denmark, the situation in Europe is mixed. Legal equality had been achieved in some countries by 2017, when the process was just beginning in others. Each country's situation is the fruit of its particular history. In some places change has been very gradual, through a succession of new legal provisions, while elsewhere several flagship measures have been taken more of less at the same time, radically changing the legal situation for sexual minorities. The contrast between Great Britain and France is an example. In Great Britain, several legislative changes were concentrated around the adoption of civil partnership, some concerning gays and lesbians more broadly, not just couples and families[3]. In France, the first form of recognition for same-sex couples, the pacs, in 1999, was legally timid but nonetheless a symbolic turning point. It has been amended a number of times in the 20 years since then, often in ways that make it more like marriage. Even so, when marriage was made available to same-sex couples, although provision for making ART available to women couples was considered, it was not included in the final bill[4]. Apparent similarity between European situations masks a diversity of legislative trajectories. As Commaille and de Singly (1997) suggest with regard to family policies in Europe, the results of a comparative analysis are founded on distance of observation. A remote, overall view gives the impression of a certain unity, but when one zooms in on particular countries or groups of countries, or compares two countries, one sees national particularities rather than uniformity. A look at legislation timelines reveals both the similarities and the disparities, and also the different processes. In some countries, for example, local authorities advocated for forms of

[3] See Weeks (2011), who tells how the adoption of the Civil Partnership in the United Kingdom in 2005 was accompanied by numerous other measures concerning the LGBT population. Ignacio Pichardo-Galán highlights a more or less similar process in Spain, in 2004.

[4] For France, see e.g. the analyses by Camille Robcis (2013) and Michael Stambolis-Ruhstorfer (2018).

recognition and implemented them before national laws were introduced, or in parallel. Marina Franchi and Giulia Selmi stress the importance of such initiatives in Italy. In some other countries, local authorities have intervened only symbolically. In France, in the late 1990s, some municipal councils introduced "cohabitation contracts", which had no real legal force but were a way of expressing support for recognition of same-sex couples. In Spain, some regional authorities devised forms of civil union before same-sex marriage was introduced nationally in 2004. So diversity is evident not only in the strictly legislative trajectories but also before recognition of same-sex couples is even put on parliamentary agendas.

Similarly, a comparative observation of social movements triggered by these political and legislative changes reveals many differences between European countries, as well relative similarities in the demands. While in some situations, especially in northern Europe, the adoption of measures to recognize same-sex couples aroused no very hostile movement, in other countries there was virulent opposition (often supported or indeed instigated by certain Roman Catholic movements), though none became a dominant force in the country concerned. A possible development from Kees Waaldijk's work might be to analyse the extent to which legislative trajectories are tied to political background and the political colour of the government. Numerous differences and similarities appear in this regard. For example, while many Social Democrat/Socialist/Labour majorities have sought to bring in laws establishing LGBT rights, they have done so to differing degrees and with varied results, contradicting the idea that any "left-wing" majority would automatically want to actively promote moves towards equality for sexual minorities. In Spain and the United Kingdom, for example, these majorities were particularly keen for change, whereas in other countries, although the majority was theoretically in favour, there was a lack of consensus for putting recognition of same-sex unions on the political agenda, the measures were more timid, more gradual (in France) or proved impossible to enact (Italy). Opposition movements also differed from each other. In France, Spain and Italy they were more or less united around an extremely hostile "naturalist" rhetoric, sometimes structured in terms of combatting "gender theory" (Garbagnoli and Prearo 2018), which was a way of expressing condemnation of homosexuality without using explicitly homophobic language. Political and social opposition was less virulent in the United Kingdom, Germany and the Scandinavian countries. Parliamentary bills sometimes met with assent by political groups that had not initiated them, and were sometimes adopted by broader majorities that included more conservative parties, or some of their members. In Germany in 2017, a quarter of Christian Democratic Union MPs voted for making marriage available to same-sex couples, so ensuring a majority in favour of the bill. But although people of various political persuasions have backed policies that helped transform the family and private life in Europe, recognition of sexual minorities seems still to be a sharply divisive issue. In the short term, the political context plays an important part in the adoption or revision of laws to increase the social inclusion of LGBT people, but it is probably not the only contextual factor that counts. Other social factors seem to be involved in more diffuse but no less fundamental ways. The map of LGBT rights in Europe seems to correlate inversely with maps of gender inequalities[5]. A comparitively low level of inequalities between the sexes and the degree of individualism reflected in the law on family and private life seem to be correlated with legislative changes in favour of gays and lesbians. The countries where individualism was strongest, notably those of Northern Europe, were the earliest to give legal recognition to same-sex couples. Religious context seems to be another factor: the countries where Catholic institutions are most powerful have rarely been in the vanguard for recognizing same-sex couples and families.

7.1.2 From Law to Demographic Behaviour

The second approach is a demographic one, focusing on types of union in Europe and considering how these legal provisions are being used in practice, through a comparative study of several countries (Cortina and Festy). It provides a different way of studying the legal contexts, looking at whether or not the various forms of union are used. As often in demographic research, this approach first raises a methodological issue: what data do we have available? Do they allow us to make international comparisons? Here too, the available data mainly give an impression of diversity. Public records, civil registers, censuses and survey data reflect different statistical cultures and have different advantages and limitations as data sources. Some, such as civil registers, are by definition intended to be exhaustive, but are sometimes limited by the number of data points they record. Conversely, survey data characteristically have a wealth of variables in a number of sociological and demographic dimensions, but their use poses other problems: response rates are not always satisfactory, samples are small, there are recurrent problems in analysing the LGBT population via surveys of the general public, and there are problems of a more technical nature that may be due to errors in filling out the forms (Festy 2007). From this standpoint, the analysis of gay and lesbian populations is exemplary of the study of sources in demography, in that it requires a rigorous examination of the types of data that can be used. The approach used by Clara Cortina and Patrick Festy, irrespective of the results it produces, shows what demography can contribute to a study of sexual minorities and their unions. Their comparison of several situations brings out a number of questions. How closely are behaviours linked to national contexts? Can we speak of "European behaviour patterns"? Do they change

[5] For example, looking at the Gender-Related Development Index drawn up by the United Nations Development Programme, we find that most countries in the world with a low inequality rating have legal provisions for recognising same-sex couples (2014 data). But there are exceptions to the rule. Italy has a high rating but a low level of recognition for gay and lesbian couples and families, yet the United Kingdom, Spain and Portugal have slightly lower inequality ratings but high levels of legal recognition. It is perhaps the historical depth of policies in favour of sexual equality that are most determinant here. Anecdotally, between France, Iceland, Italy and Spain, the countries covered in this book, the order in which legal recognition has been given to same-sex couples is exactly the same as the order in which women's suffrage was achieved.

in line with legislative changes? The approach complements Kees Waaldijk's legislation mapping and shows us how legal rights and actual practice seem to connect. It makes certain comparisons possible – between same-sex couples first of all. Do gay couples and lesbian couples differ in the ways they use available forms of partnership? How are the differences to be interpreted? Comparison with opposite-sex couples too: are matrimonial behaviours converging? The data implicity suggest certain strategic approaches to the law: legal arrangements seem to be chosen more often if they bestow particular rights, especially if they are necessary steps towards parental rights, tax allowances or welfare rights. But legal reasoning is not the only factor driving people's decisions about legal union. Political and cultural contextual factors also shed light on behavioural trends.

7.1.3 The Import of the Law

The third approach in this book, using the tools of qualitative sociology, gives a better picture of people's *experience*, through interview surveys in three European countries (Digoix, Thibeaud, Franchi and Selmi). Through their recent histories of legislation, these countries give a good illustration of the diversity of pathways to recognition of same-sex couples and families, in terms of timing (with Iceland in the vanguard with the Scandinavian countries and the Netherlands, France following on and Italy coming last) but also how the changes were made. In some cases, existing provisions for heterosexual couples (partnership, civil union, marriage) have been extended to same-sex couples, while in others provisions have been created for same-sex couples independently of any history of these forms of union. This has made it easier in some situations than in others to dissociate filiation from couplehood. An overall view of the country studies allows comparison with the legal and demographic approaches of Chaps. 2 and 3. In this way some individual experiences can be seen in light of broader contexts. Where the legal framework is particularly narrow, as in Italy, individual behaviours seem to be more influenced by the constancy of the "institutional work" of the family (Bourdieu 1993): people pay special attention to anything that can be used to give meaning to the family entity in day-to-day interactions (notably interactions with institutions like local authorities, schools and health structures) and ritualized occasions (celebrating a civil union, naming spiritual parents, etc.). This approach is less needed where institutions, marriage especially, become more inclusive: legitimacy is acquired through their practice, and sometimes by staging the event. It is not even always necessary to use these provisions; their very existence has a powerful legitimizing impact. This is perhaps a paradoxical effect of a legal right. When it exists, it legitimizes situations that make it less indispensable in daily life. Thus when two people of the same sex can be legally recognized as full parents, filiation is socially acknowledged and its justification in law seems less indispensable.

From the study of different situations we can see both similarities and differences between them as regards individual trajectories, from aiming for parenthood to achieving it and then living it day to day. We see how experiences are structured by the legal and social context. Undeniably, the possibilities a country provides for filiation frames the choices its citizens make, regardless of their personal aspirations. It is up to each person to give meaning to the 'choices' they make. In situations where a multi-parent family (more than two parents) is easier to achieve than same-sex parenthood using ART or surrogacy, parents and future parents point to its advantages, such as the richness of the child's parental network. Where ART is possible, it is sometimes chosen precisely because the conjugal entity matches the parental entity, or because if it is repeated with the same donor the children will be biologically linked. Sometimes this points to "homages that heresy pays to orthodoxy" (Bourdieu 1996). The multi-parent option, which is particularly transgressive with regard to the classic conjugal/parental couple, is presented as a way of bringing "sex differences" into the child's educational framework. ART, whose transgressiveness lies in its removal of "sex differences", is preferred because it maintains the conjugal/parental couple formula.

These sociological approaches also complement the legal and demographic chapters in that they highlight the complexity of people's relationships with the law and describes the meaning it has for people on a more subjective level. Not everyone who uses the newly-created legal provisions sees them, or uses them, in the same way. The choice of a particular form of union may reflect different attitudes in different couples. Some marry or choose a civil union or registered partnership out of conviction, but many take a considered, critical view of the form they have chosen. Choosing one form over another can also be felt as a constraint because it is the only way to benefit from certain provisions or because, in the absence of a suitable provision, a half-measure is better than none. Civil unions as introduced in France and elsewhere were revealing in this regard. Some chose them precisely because they were the first form of legal recognition, even though they maintained a hierarchy of sexual identities at various levels, while others decided not to use them precisely because to do so would be to endorse a law that minoritises gays and lesbians. Similarly, those who opt for marriage do not always see it as an unambiguous choice. It is a sign of equal rights, but some still see it as a concession to the existing order, still first and foremost an institutionally staged endorsement of heterosexuality and heteronormativity. So much so that some people won't consider marriage even though it brings legal recognition of filiation. An example of this is two Icelandic women who have a little girl born through ART, and only one of whom is recognized as a parent (see Chap. 6). This new legal context, which pertains in many European countries, also generates cognitive dissonance in that it introduces injunctions and uses of the law that people are not always at ease with. This applies, for example, when marriage is the only way to get recognition of filiation. And this is not only the case for gays and lesbians. Research could usefully be done on the concessions made in any use of the law.

7.2 Marriage Overshadowing Other Concerns

Marriage is a strikingly central feature of the picture painted in *Same-sex Families and Legal Recognition in Europe*, whichever discipline is used to approach the subject. But the book also invites us to reconsider its place. It is undeniable that making marriage available to same-sex couples has seemed emblematic of the recognition of same-sex couples and families, both because it represents social inclusion of gays and lesbians, something that was unthinkable even a short while back, and because it marks a complete turnaround in the way governments and societies view homosexuality — which a few decades ago, to varying degrees according to countries' political and legal situations, were met with opprobrium[6], stigmatization and repression or indeed penalization. In the 1960s and '70s, the gay and lesbian movement was demanding the abolition of marriage, regarding it as one of the oppressive tools of a heterosexist, bourgeois patriarchal society. Distance from the norm brought with it a particularly strong critique. Since the 1970s, this has been constantly diminishing. Several changes occurred that gradually made the demand for marriage thinkable. First, its social significance changed. From the '60s and '70s, marriage was no longer a necessity and came to be seen as one among several ways to organize one's private life. Gradually it ceased to be a mandatory prerequisite for living as a couple and even for having children. People were marrying at later and later ages, usually when they were already living together and often only after the arrival of a child or children. Its institutional nature was also weakened by the increasing frequency of divorce and the fact that more people had several couple relationship in the course of their lives. It lost its status as an indispensable norm for becoming a couple and starting a family, and was used in a wider variety of ways. At the same time, the coming of AIDS put a spotlight on the legal vacuum in which same-sex partners were living. Gay and lesbian movements were demanding a protective legal framework from the 1980s, and even earlier in Northern Europe. But marriage was rarely the first form of recognition demanded, given its many unappealing connotations – heteronormative, religious, familialist, moralizing in matters of sexuality. But as these connotations faded, opening the possibility of marriage seemed a logical next step from the creation of the first forms of recognition such as registered partnerships. At that stage, criticizing marriage became more complicated, as it seemed to play into the hands of those opposed to recognition of same-sex couples and families. Same-sex marriage has been or is in process of being adopted in several European countries, but its place in the process of recognizing homosexuality and same-sex parenthood is worth investigating. First of all, we should remember a rarely mentioned fact: although marriage is often regarded as a fairly

[6] In some cases, repressive measures were repealed almost at the same time as provisions recognizing same-sex couples were brought in. In the United Kingdom, Section 28 of the 1988 Local Government Act was repealed a year before civil partnerships were introduced. Under that Act local authorities were prohibited from mentioning homosexuality, for example in schools, on the grounds that this was effectively to "promote" it.

homogeneous, universal reality, it is actually a different social and legal reality in different countries. (Even scientific studies that make international comparisons often fail to ask about the content of what is being compared). The LawsAndFamilies database (Waaldijk et al. 2017), which records the legal consequences of different forms of union in some 20 European countries, and Kees Waaldijk's analyses of it, reveal some of these aspects. Not all European marriages entail the same legal provisions. In the same way, the institutional staging of marriage follows various different rationales. While in France marriage has to involve a ritual in a town hall, conducted by a mayor or her/his representative in the presence of witnesses, the interactions involved can vary widely in their solemnity, and elsewhere a marriage can be conducted by a non-governmental institution, religious or otherwise. Its ideological content also varies widely. In some countries there is no mention of faithfulness, while in others there still is, a sign of the secular state's partial appropriation of the Catholic or more generally Christian marriage. Some scripts mention parenthood and suggest that the purpose of a marriage is to prepare for the arrival of children[7]. They can also include provisions that other forms of union do not: in some countries, only marriage entails the possibility of taking the partner's surname or adding it to one's own, whereas in other countries this is also allowed with other forms of union. Similar disparities exist with other types of union: registered unions and civil partnerships do not bestow the same rights in all countries where they exist, which is by no means everywhere in Europe. The same applies to recognition of de facto same-sex couple situations. This book suggests that prudence is called for: when we speak of marriage, we are not talking about quite the same thing in all contexts.

7.2.1 Is Marriage a Sufficient Condition for Equality?

The introduction of same-sex marriage is often considered to be the end point of the drive for equality that began in the 1990s. The chapters of this book invite us to reconsider this representation and take a more nuanced view of the idea that marriage is the alpha and omega of recognition for same-sex couples and same-sex families. In many countries, particularly the pioneering countries of Northern Europe, even without marriage the situation was already close to equality. When marriage was introduced, it represented a symbolic step because the pre-existing legal provisions already ensured almost equal legal recognition.

[7] This aspect is particularly explicit in France since the Law of 5 March 2002, with a text that must be read out at town hall weddings, regardless of the age of the couple getting married: "Parental authority is a set of rights and obligations whose purpose is the interests of the child. It is the duty of parents, until the child comes of age or achieves adult status, to protect its safety, health and morality, provide it with an education and enable it to develop, with all the respect due to his or her person". Ironically, it is in one of the European countries where births outside marriage and marriage at older ages are commonest that this text has to be read out. The State's staging of marriage has little to do with demographic reality.

Associating marriage with equality can also be misleading because the introduction of same-sex marriage has not always brought legal equality. Sometimes the form of same-sex marriage introduced lacked some of the provisions of heterosexual marriage, notably with regard to filiation. In some countries this is still the situation. But above all, the introduction of same-sex marriage does not provide for recognising the full diversity of same-sex family configurations. In some countries such as Belgium the debate over LGBT rights has resulted in a clearer dissociation between marriage and filiation; in many others marriage still binds filiation to conjugality. It may seem 'suitable' for two-parent configurations, which are quite like the heterosexual couple. But many same-sex parenthood configurations are not (or not only) based on this kind of parental couple; sometimes two couples are involved, or a couple and a single person, or several singles fulfilling parental roles. Thus in any given family unit, some individuals may have their parental role recognized where others cannot. This creates a distinction between non-statutory parents and those that are granted official parent status (Descoutures 2010). This lack of recognition causes numerous problems. To start with, unrecognized parents are in a more legally vulnerable situation than recognized parents. Secondly, in day to day interactions with schools, health services and other individuals, unrecognized parents can be denied even though they play a full part in the parenting work. They are also in a more vulnerable position for confronting post-separation life if the couple breaks up. The asymmetry in parental status between partners can also have an impact on their relationship. And finally, such lack of recognition can be deleterious for a person's self-image. Further, focusing recognition on same-sex couples has probably retarded the visibility of the various other LGBT family configurations. Even now little or nothing has been done to examine the possibilities for juridical organization of other relational arrangements on the fringes of the couple proper, although they are visible in the scientific literature.

7.2.2 Legal Equality and Hierarchy of Sexual Orientations

Another effect of the predominant place of marriage in the development of rights for non-heterosexuals, recognition of same-sex couples and same-sex families may be that it masks the persistence of a social hierarchy of sexual orientations. From country to country it is easy to see that recognition and acceptance are not played out solely in the legal sphere. They are constructed in daily life and in all social interactions. Interview-based research, especially when based on a sample that includes diverse generations, shows that in many countries coming out has become easier over time. But individual narratives show that it is still a major turning point in people's lives and is likely to be met with disapproval. There is a gap between public discourse, which now favours tolerance and acceptance, and individual experience, which still frequently involves prejudice and rejection. Although legal equality is a weapon against differential treatment of individuals and families by institutions such as schools and hospitals (which can refuse to recognize certain family configurations that are not recognised in law), it does not put an end to the normative discourse of which same-sex families are frequently the target. What is striking in the chapters based on field surveys is the tone of some individual interactions. Even when the contexts seem relatively favourable to sexual minorities, gays and lesbians, whether or not they want to be parents, are constantly faced with intrusive, disparaging remarks by third parties. Members of the kinship network, friends and less closely connected people all have their word to say and sometimes express strong views on many aspects of the survey respondents' lives. Their parenthood projects (or lack of), their parenting style, their social relations in general: both men and women are often reminded how things 'should' be seen or done. This is probably one of the effects of the individualization process that European societies (among others) have been going though in the past 50 years. The normative role of some institutions has been eroded. This is particularly true of institutions with a strong ideological impact such as religions, but also of the State which, through the law and other instruments it wields, plays a role that appears more regulatory than prescriptive, so facilitating a normative plurality. But the resulting plurality of viewpoints leaves people whose arrangements do not fit the dominant norms, such as gay and lesbian parents, particularly exposed[8]. Parenthood projects involving assisted reproductive technology with a known or anonymous donor, co-parenting involving couples and/or single people: everyone involved is faced with a normative discourse telling them how things "should be done". Even in such places as Iceland, where there has long been a consensus for legal recognition of sexual minorities and same-sex parenthood. The discourse varies between opinion, prescriptive advice, regrets, as when a lesbian couple use ART and parents deplore that their daughter won't be carrying the pregnancy. There is also intrusive normative curiosity, for example when third parties want to know more about a non-anonymous donor's gametes, physique, life story, education and profession. These attitudes, evident in all the contexts studied in this book, reflect the dominant representations around these issues. For example, it is considered better to use a known donor than an anonymous one[9].

Once the family exists, these intrusions shift their ground: how to educate the child day by day, relations with kin and with institutions. The gays and lesbians involved in these arrangements have to demonstrate, or indeed make a display of, the exemplary way they do things, as if constantly under suspicion of incompetence;

---

[8] Although this does not only apply to them. Separated parents and blended families also come up against these problems, signs of a plurality that still generates anxiety when configurations stray from the familiar norm.

[9] Such distinctions do not emerge only in day-to-day interactions, they are also embodied in the laws, the forms in which filiation is registered and the accompanying discourse. Roughly speaking, two views emerge in this connection. The first valorises knowledge of the donor and their social and biological characteristics on the grounds that the child will know his or her origins, the genitor being seen as a fully-fledged social player in the procreation. This seems to have predominated in Europe in the late 2010s. The other view is more in favour of breaking away from the very idea that the donated gametes have any 'origin' other than biological, and also makes more of a break with the heterosexual and heterosexist model of procreation.

'non-standard' parents seem still to be regarded as odd. Sexual minorities are not the only ones to suffer such intrusive behaviour; one-parent families also seem to be particularly affected. Perhaps it is because their recognition has not been fully achieved. Same-sex marriage has not made homosexuality an insignificant matter. Other forms of public action are sometimes introduced to foster a genuine acceptance of minority sexual orientations. Examples are forms of systematic inclusion of gays and lesbians, more inclusive media representations, more closely targeted initiatives, especially in schools, where discussion spaces are designed for teaching respect for diversity among students and their sexual affinities. This kind of initiative exists, for example, in the United Kingdom, with information kits for school students about different sexual orientations, gender roles and identities, conjugal configurations and forms of family. But such initiatives, whether at the planning stage or operational, are often met with opposition, especially in countries where legislative progress is gradual and still very partial, like France and Italy. Maintaining heterosexuality as the norm is still at issue.

7.2.3 Beyond Marriage

The central focus on marriage in the movement to achieve recognition of same-sex couples and families has also drawn attention away from some of the changes going on. The movement has not only shifted the boundaries of marriage and the family by including some previously excluded configurations, it has also broadened the normative spectrum by amending some provisions or creating new legal forms. One example is the dissociation of marriage from filiation in some countries. Similarly, opposite-sex couples can sometimes opt for forms of partnership that did not exist a few decades ago. In Belgium, the introduction of legal cohabitation before marriage was opened to same-sex couples created a new kind of partnership that was not tied to conjugality but could fulfil a different kind of demand for organizing the relationship between two people who might have no intention of marrying, including pairs without a love relationship or sentiment. In France, the *Pacte civil de solidarité* (pacs) was created in the first place to meet same-sex couples' demand for recognition without creating a provision specifically aimed at them. It proved a big success among opposite-sex couples, so that today there are almost as many such civil unions in France as there are marriages: in 2017, between persons of opposite sex, 187,000 civil unions and 227,000 marriages were registered. There are several likely reasons for this rise (Rault 2019). For some couples, a pacs is different from marriage but does not prevent them from marrying in the future, while for others, it is an alternative form of union which has none of the connotations we mentioned earlier. It is also easier to do in one's own way whereas, despite recent changes, the couple's kin groups often interfere considerably in a wedding. For some, the easy procedures for starting and dissolving a pacs make it more compatible with the fact that many people today go through several couple relationships and love relationships in their lives.

This type of alternative contract has been in the news in the UK in 2019. The UK had created a Civil Partnership for same-sex couples before it made marriage available to them; now that both are available to same-sex couples, opposite-sex couples looking for an alternative to marriage are demanding access to the Civil Partnership. These new provisions undeniably reflect a widening of legal options that stems indirectly from the creation of provisions for sexual minorities[10]. This trend presents two limitations, however: not all European countries are a part of it, and the new provisions are still built around the couple as the core unit (and usually the cohabiting couple), rarely considering other family configurations. Various arrangements more in tune with LGBT relationship cultures and that could also appeal to other fringes of the population could be explored more. The possibility of organizing interpersonal bonds in such a way as to include friends, former partners or others who are neither kin nor related by marriage, or of envisaging private life independently of the monogamous conjugal framework, remains to be constructed.

The centrality of marriage and of the couple as the unit to be recognized raises the question of their injunctive and normalizing potential. This is addressed in several of the book's chapters. If the law loses its role in issuing authorizations and prohibitions, marriage and access to parental rights are ambiguous signs of progress. It may seem that they represent the socially desirable way for sexual minorities to organize their private lives; it may construct a model of sexual legitimacy and restrict the "sociality of the body" to what is considered acceptable (Butler 2004). One of the ambivalences of the advent of gay and lesbian rights is precisely that it focused on obtaining rights regarding the couple and the family, often aligning their demands with the rights enjoyed by different-sex couples. This has been the case in the great majority of European countries. In the surveys reported here, conducted in France, Iceland, Italy and Spain, respondents were often well aware of this. One Icelandic woman mentioned by Marie Digoix reports that it could be reassuring for her family to have "a straight element in [her] life", while another respondent mentioned that her pregnancy was a "liberation" for her mother. To what extent might parenthood, like marriage, work to erase homosexuality? Interviews like these show also that the familialist ideology, defined by a symbolic dominance of the family unit over the individual, has been reconfigured, and that it is perfectly compatible with contemporary individualism. It is perpetuated not so much by institutions or by government policies explicitly dictating social behaviour – as they did a few decades ago with marriage and family policy – as by social norms and injunctions reflected in people's day-to-day interactions. We might also ask how far the European trend in favor of gays and lesbian rights has contributed to construct distinctions between

[10] There are also less obvious examples of the way the heteronormative nature of marriage has been affected by opening it to same-sex couples. In France, before May 2013, the law on transmission of the family name, which allowed parents to transmit both their names to their children, stated that if the parents disagreed about the order of the two names, the father's name was to be placed first. Making marriage available to same-sex couples and allowing filiation for both same-sex partners made this provision null and void: in the event of parental conflict, the names are now put in alphabetical order (Article 311–21 of the Civil Code). Similarly, the articles stating that parental authority belongs to the father and mother has been amended to refer to "parents" (Article 371–1 of the Civil Code) – and it does not specify how many parents.

'legitimate' homosexual or bisexual relationship configurations and the rest – i.e. between those more or less based on heterosexual institutions (legal recognition of the (cohabitating) couple and/or the prospect of procreation) and configurations that are structured more around sexual and/or friendship networks or even other kinds of interpersonal ties.

7.3 Improving Social Science Research Tools

The political centrality of the recognition of same-sex unions (notably through marriage) and of same-sex families is also reflected in the way social science research into homosexuality has developed. Whereas most such research used to focus on sexual behaviour, notably in the context of AIDS, when the recognition of same-sex couples and families became a political and media issue in the 1990s and 2000s, a lot of research was done on that issue. Many addressed the mismatch between the legal framework and actual family situations: could two parents of the same sex be legally recognized in the same way? When three or four people are joint parents, how do they construct and establish their parenthood from day to day? How does a non-statutory parent, to use Virginie Descoutures's term, find their place in a same-sex family? Another frequently chosen angle, which could be combined with an approach focused on legal recognition, was to study the actual forms of same-sex family configurations and the reproduction methods used. How do people decide whether to build a family by co-parenthood or donor insemination? Why opt for a known donor or an anonymous one? When two women each have a child by this means, do they choose the same sperm donor? Why? With two women partners, when one donates the egg and the other carries the pregnancy, what does this choice reveal?

The many studies taking such approaches have revealed the normative systems at work in such choices. They have been particularly fruitful for gender studies. For example, they have shown how reproduction, and also domestic and parenting tasks, are organized between same-sex partners, the usual gender-based division of labour in the home being inoperable. Several studies have questioned the legal asymmetry between parents, day-to-day parental roles and transmission, asking what impact same-sex parenthood has on gender and how gender is (still) liable to structure the formation and daily lives of same-sex families. In sociology, the choice of research subjects has been consistent with the methodological possibilities: qualitative surveys have been preferred precisely because they can be used to study realities that are statistically invisible or are rendered invisible by the statistical methods in use[11]. In this last section, we consider the possibilities for constructing new research subjects and developing the necessary tools, with the focus on quantitative approaches, which have been little used so far.

[11] For example, in the exhaustive census used in France until 1999, when a same-sex couple was revealed in the questionnaire's housing sheet, they were recoded as two friends sharing a dwelling (see Digoix et al. 2004)

Why develop new quantitative tools? New data could be used to formulate new research questions in different terms to qualitative approaches or procedures based on convenient samples[12] and to take a more macro-sociological approach. Below we give a few examples.

7.3.1 *Identifying the Impact of Context on the Declaration of Lifestyle and Identity*

The chapters of this book show that in Western Europe over the past few decades, the increasing visibility of homosexuality and same-sex families has occurred in close step with changes in the legal and social context. One advantage of developing more quantitative instruments is that they could be used to discover how far this context encourages the declaration (or existence?) of homosexuality, same-sex coupledom and same-sex families. In some countries where it is possible to use these approaches they have shown a clear increase in declarations of such situations. As regards same-sex couples, which it can be complicated to enumerate accurately[13], there are now studies that shed light on the strong increase in numbers of same-sex couples cohabiting where the situation is favourable. The approach requires the use of sources whose data gathering methods are fairly similar. Clara Cortina noted a major increase in numbers of same-sex couples in Spain between 2001 and 2011 (Cortina 2016). In Germany, Andrea Lengerer and Jeanette Bohr (2019), using census data, have also revealed a sharp increase: same-sex couples amounted to 0.3%

[12] Innovative ad hoc procedures using samples of volunteers are methodologically problematic in terms of representativeness but have nonetheless enabled researchers to do some original work (see e.g. Gross and Courduries 2015). Such surveys often use relays (such as Internet sites, social networks and associations); this structures the samples differently to surveys based on the general public. This means that some thought must be given to the effects these forms of recruitment have on the results. Procedures of this type have enabled researchers to investigate several new issues, though always with prudence, given the limitations of their methods. They offer many possibilities, including creating detailed categories that are particularly relevant to the situations observed but would be difficult to use in a broader survey. For example, it might be important for the study to know whether a child arrived by previous heterosexual union, adoption, insemination with a known or unknown donor, surrogacy, joint parenthood with a single homosexual or heterosexual person, or joint parenthood with a couple, etc. They also make it possible to record details of the legal status of the adults in the family (legally recognized parent, parent by adoption with or without annulment of the biological parents' rights, etc.), to introduce a range of parental roles or to ask about the desire for children.

[13] When data are gathered by self-administered questionnaire, as in censuses, a mistake in filling in the form can turn an opposite-sex couple into a same-sex couple. This can compromise data quality. The concern to correct this kind of error has given rise to a considerable amount of experimentation. A combination of several methods can be used to reduce uncertainty, such as checking the sex of the respondent from other data (associated surveys, first name etc.) or introducing explicit questions as to whether the respondent is living in a same-sex couple (for France, see Banens and Le Penven 2016; Algava and Hallépée 2018).

of all couples in 2000 and 0.6% in 2013. In France, that percentage rose from 0.6% in 2011 to 0.9% in 2018 (Buisson and Lapinte 2013; Algava and Penant 2019). The same trend is found in the US and Canada[14], and also when one looks at other indicators of homosexuality, self-identification or sexual practices[15].

On the other hand, although there are some data on family configurations, lack of adequate indicators makes it difficult to assess the situation in 2020. It is almost impossible to determine how far the transformation of the law analysed in Kees Waaldijk's chapter has been accompanied by an increase in LGBT families. One side-effect of the contemporary shift to legal recognition is that, because the law has focused on recognition of the couple, mainly through marriage, the same-sex family with cohabiting parents has become more statistically visible, while other configurations are less easily covered by the indicators used in major surveys. To address this, research approaches should separate parenthood from its association with marriage and look beyond the framework of the single shared home. There are opposite-sex couples that do not fit these two criteria, and the trend may be stronger among same-sex couples. Given that questionnaires are still shaped by the marriage/cohabitation framework, this may make some forms of family more visible than others[16].

A new approach to family ties in questionnaires would not only enable people to declare children born or living in same-sex configurations. It would also give respondents more ways to describe their family relationship network and speak of people who have acted as parents or held parental status. As things are, statistical survey questionnaires rarely explore the network of ascendants, and questions about parents are not always included. When there are such questions, they are often posed in terms of "father" and "mother", limiting the scope to a heterosexual couple and only sometimes asking whether they are still together. One innovation would be to enable respondents to report more types of parental figures and relations who have been involved in their life course, from their own point of view.

[14] The number of same-sex couples increased by 61% between 2006 and 2016 in Canada and by 61% between 2009 and 2017 in the United States.

[15] In France, surveys on sexuality and marriage (and also surveys on violence) show a rise between 1992 and 2013 in the numbers declaring previous same-sex partners (Rault and Lambert 2019). The trend is particularly marked for women. In Italy, where there has been no major survey on sexual behaviours, they are studied through approaches targeting narrower populations. An example is the Sexual and Emotion Life of Youth survey of university students (Castiglioni 2019). This surveys, run in 2000 and 2017, showed major changes in sexual behaviour over the period, especially as regards homosexual practices and identity.

[16] Major surveys of the general public that identify non-cohabiting marriages and same-sex partnerships show that living apart together is markedly more frequent among same-sex couples. In France, the 2011 Families and Housing survey showed that non-cohabitation was four times as frequent among same-sex couples as among opposite-sex couples (see Rault and Lambert 2019).

7.3.2 Investigating the Influence of Social Background

Quantitative tools would also enable research to explore the impact of social background on same-sex parenthood. The importance of background often emerges indirectly in interview surveys, especially in the way material constraints affect the founding of a family. For example, in countries where artificial reproductive technology is not allowed for women in same-sex couples or lesbians without a partner, use of ART inevitably raises the issue of material resources as well as those of health, social norms etc. Undertaking ART involves regular visits to a clinic in another country and can be very costly; surrogacy even more so. The research focus on legal and relational aspects has initially resulted in sidelining the material aspects and social background issues more generally, but these dimensions are often mentioned. There are also methodological reasons why it is complicated to address the material aspect: people who volunteer to take part in an interview survey are often from a narrow range of backgrounds. They are often highly educated[17], and connected with political organizations or advocacy groups, even when they have not been recruited through their connection with an organization. So it may be that research sidelines some profiles and configurations that qualitative surveys are less likely to cover sociologically. And yet there are many questions about these families' social situations that are worth investigating. Does fulfilling a parenthood project depend on social and material resources? To what extent do social origins play a part in these projects?

The question is not only about the material possibilities for undertaking a parenthood project. From most statistical work on homosexuality, whether focused on same-sex couples, persons who say they are non-heterosexual or persons who have sexual relations with others of the same sex, it emerges that homosexuality indicators are often linked to social factors: high educational qualifications, to a lesser extent privileged social origins, greater likelihood of belonging to certain middle or upper classes, and younger average age. Do these distinctive factors, apparently connected with a minority sexual orientation, hold for same-sex parenthood? Are same-sex family configurations characterized by particular kinds of resources? The advances in social visibility and recognition highlighted in this book might go hand in hand with a relative democratization in access to parenthood as it becomes less dependent on a certain level of social resources. These questions can only be addressed by using suitable statistical tools.

The construction of new instruments should be encouraged because they would make it possible to address many more questions and make more comparisons. Spatial issues could also be explored: are there disparities in the distribution of

[17] This is also found in large statistical surveys that have indicators usable for studying part of the gay and lesbian population. Whether the indicators are to do with identity, sexuality (having same-sex partners) or conjugality (having a same-sex spouse), which reflect very different realities, the profiles of the people concerned always show high educational qualifications and, more often than the rest of the population, urban residence.

same-sex families, as there are for same-sex couples? It would also be useful to take generational approaches; the chapters in this book have shown that the different generations approach parenthood projects in different ways. Country comparisons and especially comparison with non-European situations – North and South America, Asia etc. – would help reveal features that are specific to Europe or part of Europe. An epistemological examination of comparison methods and the categorizations used would be essential for this kind of approach. Indicators of same-sex parenthood, filiation, sexuality, gender identities and transitioning are by no means routinely transposable to all situations and the meaning of the phenomena they refer to is always context-dependent.

References

Algava, E.& Hallépée, S. (2018). *Estimer les effectifs de couples de personnes de même sexe au recensement : expérimentation d'une solution de validation du sexe par le prénom*. Document de travail F1807, Insee, direction des statistiques démographiques et sociales.

Algava, E., & Penant, S. (2019). In 2018, 266,000 persons live in a same-sex couple. *Insee Première, 1774*.

Banens, M., & Le Penven, E. (2016). Sex miscoding in the census and its effects on the enumeration of same-sex couples. *Population, English edition, 71*(1), 131–144.

Bourdieu, P. (1993). À propos de la famille comme catégorie réalisée. *Actes de la Recherche en Sciences Sociales, 100*, 32–36.

Bourdieu, P. (1996). Des familles sans nom. *Actes de la Recherche en Sciences Sociales, 113*, 3–5.

Buisson, G., & Lapinte, A. (2013). The many varieties of unions: Non-cohabiting partnerships, same-sex couples, civil unions… and more. *Insee Première*, 1435.

Butler, J. (2004). *Undoing Gender*. London: Routledge.

Castiglioni, M. (2019). *Introduction to the workshop « Quantitative researchon non-heterosexual populations: Measuring homo-bisexualattraction, behavior, orientation, living arrangements, and opinion on homo-bisexuality in a population perspective »*. Milano: Universita Bocconi.

Commaille, J., & de Singly, F. (Eds.). (1997). *The European family. The family question in the European community*. Kluwer Academic Publishers.

Cortina, C. (2016). Demographics of same-sex couples in Spain. *Revista Española de Investigaciones Sociológicas, 153*, 3–22.

Descoutures, V. (2010). *Mères lesbiennes*. Paris: PUF-Le Monde.

Digoix, M., Festy, P., & Garnier, B. (2004). What if same-sex couples exist after all ? In M. Digoix & P. Festy (Eds.), *Same-sex couples, same-sex partnerships and homosexual marriages. A focus on cross national differentials* (Documents de travail 124) (pp. 193–210). Paris: Ined.

Festy, P. (2007). Enumerating same-sex couples in censuses and population registers. *Demographic Research, 17*(article 12), 339–368.

Garbagnoli, S. & Prearo. M. (2018). *La crociata «anti-gender». Dal Vaticano alle manif pour tous*, Kaplan.

Goldberg, A. E. (2013). In K. R. Allen (Ed.), *LGBT-parent families. Innovations in research and implications for practice*. New York: Springer.

Gross, M. (2015). Gay, lesbian, and trans families through the lens of social science: A revolution or a pluralisation of forms of parenthood? Enfances Familles Générations *[Online], 23*, http://journals.openedition.org/efg/893

Gross, M., & Courduries, J. (2015). La construction conjugale dans les familles homoparentales : Une organisation financière communautaire ou indépendante ? *Politiques Sociales et Familiales, 120*, 45–60.

Lengerer, A., & Bohr, J. (2019). Gibt es eine Zunahme gleichgeschlechtlicher Partnerschafter in Deutschland ? Theoritische Überlegungen und empirische Befunde. *Zeitschrift für Soziologie, 48*(2), 136–157.

Rault, W. (2019). Is the civil solidarity pact the future of marriage? The several meanings of the French civil union. *International Journal of Law, Policy and the Family, 33*(2), 139–159.

Rault, W., & Lambert, C. (2019). Homosexuality and bisexuality: Contributions of the EPIC survey. *Population, 74*(1), 167–186. https://doi.org/10.3917/popu.1901.0173.

Robcis, C. (2013). *The law of kinship: Anthropology, psychoanalysis, and the family in twentieth-century France*. Ithaca: Cornell University Press.

Stambolis-Ruhstorfer, M. (2018). Producing expert capital: How opposing same-sex marriage experts dominate fields in the United States and France. *Social Movement Studies*, 1–25. https://doi.org/10.1080/14742837.2018.1482206.

Waaldijk, K., Digoix, M., Nikolina, N., Zago, G., Damonzé, D., Caporali, A., & Nait Abdellah, K. (Eds.). (2017). *The LawsAndFamilies database – Aspects of legal family formats for same-sex and different-sex couples*. Paris: Ined. http://www.LawsAndFamilies.eu

Weeks, J. (2011). A very British compromise?: Civil partnerships, liberalism by stealth and the fallacies of neo-liberalism. In J. Jones, A. Grear, R. A. Fenton, & K. Stevenson (Eds.), *Gender, sexualities and law*. London: Routledge.

Index

M. Digoix (ed.), *Same-Sex Families and Legal Recognition in Europe*, European Studies of Population 24, https://doi.org/10.1007/978-3-030-37054-1

The manufacturer's authorised representative in the EU is Springer Nature Customer Service Centre GmbH, Europaplatz 3, 69115 Heidelberg, Germany. If you have any concerns regarding our products, please contact ProductSafety@springernature.com

Printed and bound by CPI Group (UK) Ltd, Croydon, CR0 4YY
30/09/2026
02225470-0018